THE CLASSIC
CAR
ADVENTURE

THE CLASSIC CAR ADVENTURE

DRIVING THROUGH HISTORY ON THE ROAD TO NOSTALGIA

LANCE COLE

PEN & SWORD
TRANSPORT

Also by this author (non-fiction)

Secrets of the Spitfire
Secret Wings of World War II
VC10: BOAC, Boeing and a Jet Age Battle
Vickers VC10
Saab Cars The Complete Story
Saab 99 and 900
Citroën The Complete Story
Long Haul
Heavies
The New Illustrated Encyclopaedia of the Automobile

First published in Great Britain in 2017 by
Pen & Sword Transport
an imprint of
Pen & Sword Books Ltd,
47 Church Street,
Barnsley,
South Yorkshire.
S70 2AS

A CIP record for this book is available from the British Library.

ISBN 978 1 47389 641 3

Printed and bound by Replika Press Pvt. Ltd

Pen & Sword Books Ltd incorporates the Imprints of Pen & Sword Aviation, Pen & Sword Maritime, Pen & Sword Military, Wharncliffe Local History, Pen & Sword Select, Pen & Sword Military Classics and Leo Cooper.

For a complete list of Pen & Sword titles please contact
Pen & Sword Books Limited
47 Church Street, Barnsley, South Yorkshire, S70 2AS, England
E-mail: enquiries@pen-and-sword.co.uk
Website: www.pen-and-sword.co.uk

Contents

Acknowledgements		7
Dedication		8
Introduction		9
1	Plastique Fantastique	23
2	Lancia Lamentation	31
3	Rear-Engined Entities	42
4	Madame Itier's Bugatti and a Carrossier Conundrum	50
5	Malcolm Who?	55
6	Sydney Allard's Towering Achievements	72
7	Riley to Rootes	81
8	The Porsche Passion	94
9	Old Saabs and Old Sods	99
10	Neckarsulm's Neophyte	112
11	Michelotti: A Triumph of Design	123
12	Fiat's 'Fake' Ferrari	128
13	Citroën GS	134
14	Mazda Cosmo	140
15	Leyland's Antipodean Efforts	144
16	Volvo-Itis	148
17	Rover's Revenge	152
18	Unsung Heroes	157
19	Innes Ireland	168
20	The Last Chance Saloon	181
Notes		203
Bibliography		207
Index		211

Acknowledgements

This book is a collation of classic car moments taken from the three decades of motoring writing and driving that I have been fortunate enough to experience since winning the 1983 Sir William Lyons Guild of Motoring Writers Award – the key to the door for which I remain so grateful. Along the way I have received help from many people and would like to thank them for assisting me in my annoying youth and in my more recent maturity – as I enter old git territory. I owe a debt to a host of classic car, car design, and motoring writing people who it has been my privilege to encounter or know. They know who they are. Thanks also to *The Daily Telegraph*, *The Independent*, *The Automobile*, *The South China Morning Post*, *Autocar*, *Classic Cars*, Hemmings *Sports and Exotic Car*, *Classic Car Weekly*, *Saabs United*, Haymarket, the Crowood Press, Pen and Sword Books, and the other publications that have commissioned and printed my words and pictures over the years. Original versions of some of the words herein were previously published by: The *Daily Telegraph Motoring*, the *Independent*, the *Automobile, Classic Cars*, Crowood Press, and Pen and Sword. A younger (pre-*Octane* fame) David Lillywhite gave me my opportunity at *Classic Cars* magazine many years ago, and I thank him. Paul Hudson made space for classic cars and my words about them at the *Daily Telegraph*. Sean O'Grady did likewise at the *Independent*. Richard Gunn and James Walshe both noted motoring writers have been of encouragement and help with some of the conversation in this book, as has Mark McCourt at America's *Sports and Exotic Car*. I offer appreciation to my classic car friends at the Allard Owners Club, Porsche GB and Porsche Club GB, the Bugatti Trust, the Bristol Owners Club, various Citroënistes, Robin Morley, the Saab Owners Club, Autofarm, Dick Lovett. I owe Bjorn Envall my thanks and respect. Thanks also to the Royal College of Art Vehicle Design Unit and certain tutors for allowing me access over the years. My thanks and admiration for Allard days go to Allan Allard, Mike Knapman, Blair Shenstone, Dave Loveys. My gratitude for great drives and friendship to John Hole. A salute also to Michael Read – classic car enthusiast, friend and owner of Charlotte the Chenard.

Dedication

To unsung heroes

Also for Emily and Jack, in the hope that you are seekers beyond the constraints of the conditioned mind

Introduction
Vintagent to Modern Classic

Nostalgia is better than it used to be and in the world of old cars, nostalgia is an engaging and addictive passion. Yet the term 'classic car' means different things to different people, be that an early veteran car from *circa* 1905, a pre-1930s vintage affair – a 'vintagent' car – a 1940s-1970s classic, or 1980s 'modern classic'; each strain or tribe of the old car movement has its devotees and dedicated inhabitants. Some people love cars across all these groups, others only have interest in one era or one specific marque. Whatever their differences, all share the great enthusiasm, the great affection for inanimate lumps of metal that seem to have far more personality than normal psychiatry might admit, and certainly far more character than today's new cars. The psychometry of the classic car is an intriguing story. Between these pages cars appear without hierarchy. Space precludes including every classic car, but does permit a subjective journey through the classic years of steel and glass-fibre that gave us so much in a time before today's anodyne amalgam of what we call the modern motor car. Because we can now see that from the late 1920s to the late 1970s, car design gave us much, it is possible to look back to days when cars were cars, men were allowed to be men (within the bounds of responsible behaviour) and health and safety, political correctness, and the court of public opinion did not dictate design.

Back before all this transpired, car designers and engineers could think freely and individually, rather than conforming as so many of them now have to (or are educated to do so) in a prescribed fashion of the passing moment set down by apparent preachers of perceived opinion dressed as fact. True, a lot of people died in cars, but so did they horse riding, flying, or playing rugby. Above all, earlier cars were the essence of something vital in society. That may not be so true of today's new cars.

The excitement of early cars 1905-1939 was possibly mirrored in a different context by the cars of the 1940s-1970s, but then things began to change. Perhaps we ought to say in generalisation that the contemporary classic car movement frames a love of products framed from about 1945 onwards, but in the four decades *before* that, a great era of cars ruled and we should not forget them or their owners within our perceived classic movement. According to the Federation of British Historic Vehicle Clubs current report, forty eight per cent of the British population think that historic vehicles (built prior to 1985) should be preserved for the future. Throw in the Fédération Internationale des Véhicules Anciens, add, North American, Australian, Asian, African, European, and South American classic car enthusiasms, and the true scale and value of our love of old cars is obvious. This is a global addiction and an adventure in a great story amid marque mania.

America categorises its 'classic' cars as Antique (pre-1930), Edwardian, Vintage and Pioneer, amid varying subsets and dates. Germans and other northern Europeans refer to 'Oldtimers' and 'Youngtimers'. Whatever such definitions and tags, surely all old cars can be utterly classic irrespective of the foibles of time, age and opinion. European and American car design may have taken different routes before the Second World War and after it, but this should not stop us supping at the cup of their respective delights simultaneously, should it? All over the world, old cars – whatever their era – are held in increasing esteem and, from here on in, I shall call them classic cars. They provide us with delights, disasters and, often, financial distress. It is a huge sphere and a global passion that breaks down boundaries and overcomes language and cultural barriers. Every television channel seems to have a classic car programme and even the *Daily Telegraph* has a classic cars column. New niches are emerging all the time – enthusiasm for Eastern Bloc classics is rising, as is a burgeoning modern classics story, itself layered with subcultures ranging from Japanese supercars to rotary delights and 1980s European hot hatches. Neither should we forget that in America, Germany, France, Italy, or Japan, to be an engineer or industrial designer was to be a respected professional, whereas in Britain such professions were (and remain) subject to snobbery and a lack of respect for decades. Is this one reason why British engineering was allowed to wither?

Cars are about dreams, fantasies, design or even that dreaded term, style. Yet once, in a classic car past, style referred to sculpture in steel, today it refers to a more two-dimensional, computer-drawn and fashion-fed opinion of what is stylish. And cars and their designs are the worse for it. Throw in digital throttles, electric steering racks, double-clutch computer game gearboxes and copycat styling and many new cars have become a pointless amalgam of the absurd intervention of man's arrogance. So the classic car enthusiast must therefore be a design connoisseur – consciously or subconsciously. Old cars have character in the true etymology of that word as an embossing or stamping of identity in steel –

glass-fibre is also permissible. New cars and their designs seem to have become a different interpretation of 'character'.

This is my own opinion, but I believe that the uncomfortable truth is that much of the magic of our motoring has gone, lost in a new-fangled, new world of anti-design and the synthetic experience of anti-driving in a digitally signalled authoritarianism.

Drive-by-wire is reality.

Car 'platforms' are shared across manufacturers who simply dress their own respective variations up with a bit of retro-pastiche shaping (I hesitate to call it design) and lean on their past to sell metal consumer goods that are less and less like cars and more and more like genetically modified 'virtual experience' mutations. People buy them because they are too young and, sometimes, too uneducated to have known what went before and what has been lost. After all, we are *drivers*, not 'driving experience' digital interface gurus seeking out entirely synthesised motoring. But there *are* a few new cars out there that steer, handle and go with real mechanical brilliance and not all are expensive; for example, Ford's little Fiesta (especially in three-cylinder form) steers and handles with an ability that is worth three times its price and which is often missing from cars that cost that much and more. The reason why is the legacy of Ford's SVO division and Mr Mansfield's past works that imbued once humble Fords with real dynamic ability. We also live in a world where Mercedes-Benz have got 346bhp (DIN) out of a 2 litre four-pot engine as fitted to their A Class AMG model. Three cylinder engines are also the new focus of efficiency, yet Saab perfected such devices in the 1950s!

Despite the better moments of modern motoring, we can say that it is in the driving of the 'old' cars of the analogue or clockwork eras that we can secure the true, intimate, motoring experience as something more akin to the reality that was once manifest as the motor car. That is now even more highlighted because modern cars have become fly-by-wire and dominated by the intervention of technology and apparently some sort of weird conspiracy theory to separate the act of driving from the mechanism of doing it. And 'design' seems to have become something else too – as many car designers of a certain age will confirm.

Compare a new VW Golf as GTI or R, with the original and now classic Golf Mk1 GTI and the change to our cars and to our driving is encapsulated; the original is small, lithe and a delight to drive, while the newer iteration is a good car but one that has put on far too much weight and is stifled by its trickery. We might say the same about many other cars, notably the obese and barnacled that have become the norm.

Like me, readers will look at old cars with different eyes and yearn for a 'proper' car that does not have 'health and safety' anti-slip, anti-skid, anti-roll, radar controlled anti-driving devices that intervene in an autonomous Airbus-style command 'mode' that leaves you wondering what the hell 'it' is doing now or next. We even have computerised 'I-Drive' BMWs that have to be programmed before use, and a BMW Seven Series that might stop you steering where you want to go if it disagrees with your choices! We also have a Rolls-Royce that uses GPS to pre-select your gears for you as the road unravels ahead. Is this *driving*? And is it really safety conscious to denude a driver of his or her situational awareness and physical involvement in the act? Does it not create a less-skilled, less-attentive driver? Look to civil aviation and its recent disasters in which digitally detached computer-guided pilots, unskilled in hands-on flying, having lost the computer mode plot, have been found unable to hand-fly the airliner. Several major airline crashes have resulted from this electronics-led, skills bypass. Are new cars and driving are going the same way?

There really is something tangible about the joy of owing a classic car – be it a £1,000 jalopy or a £100,000+ supercar classic. If, like me, you are as interested in a 1920s Bugatti as you are in a 1930s Lincoln-Zephyr containing the conceptual thinking of Eugene Gregoire, John Tjaarda and Edsel Ford, then you may be hooked. Alternatively, are we not also entrapped by the differing delights of the 1970s output of BMW, Saab or Triumph? What of a Ford Capri Mk1, an Alfa 164 or 75, a Dodge Charger, Jensen Interceptor, or a Honda NSX and so much more? Surely, the world of classic cars is a unique 'fix'. Whether driving on the road or competing in an event, classic cars provide joy. Amid the tribes of classic car ownership there is a new, classic car lifestyle and, perhaps regretfully for those outside its enclave, there is also a new, exclusive deluxe tribe of moneyed men and women. We also see the rise not just of VIP events, but the affairs of the concours celebrities. But should we really say that the old, oily world of classic car motoring on a budget were *bad* old days? I think not. Can't we enjoy both ends of the classic car spectrum? Surely the sales of posh – and not-so-posh – classic car magazines prove the point that there is room for all of us and our cars and what we do with them? Yet many of us are now denied entry to the world-class of veteran, vintage and classic car ownership because of cost. But in a global classic car industry worth billions on an annual economic scale (£5.5billion a year in Britain alone) maybe we should embrace high values and high class restorations – unless of course the resulting cars bear little resemblance to what they originally were? Throw away the originality and what have you got? Some say, a superficial shine.

Amid the restoration debate, there is a converse argument to a preference for originality, that in fairness, we must state; if you want to save an old car that

Definitely not, van ordinaire: classic chevrons

otherwise will die, then full restoration with new parts *is* the only way of saving it. Similarly, if an original car is so tired, so ragged, that the act of driving it bears no resemblance to its originally intended function, preserving its patina becomes probably pointless. But, does everything have to be 'saved' by being replaced with 'better than new' and epoxy coated and re-trimmed in all-over beige vynide? There is an argument about what a more balanced act of restoration and the derivations thereof could be. Should 'restoration' remove, or in part, *preserve* originality and patination, thus preserving a car's story, or should restoration mean total annihilation of originality? Like many, I would prefer a lightly tided original yet mildly refurbished car, one that kept its layers of laid down age and character. Surely this is more 'real' than some newly moulded Airfix-kit of an acrylic-coated, leatherette-lined concours show queen that contains not one jot of its soul as accrued across decades, then to be discarded at the altar of some perceived passing wisdom of what someone has preached should be the 'show standard'? As *The Automobile* magazine has defined, original 'Oily Rag' condition is a new and glorious state, one to be celebrated if at all possible. Sadly, some of California still thinks unrestored means 'Concours de Lemons' – an event where people laugh at rusty, mouldy cars on a scale of crapology, but things are changing, originals *are* gaining ground.

Surely an old car should be a family friend, and a car that you can actually drive? Such affairs, such loyalties, are what make men and women prefer their marque of choice and of ownership – unless like me, you suffer from some form of multiple classic car marque enthusiasm disorder that is sometimes populated by affairs with marques others than those closest to your heart. Is the classic car enthusiast really supposed to be monogamous when it comes to cars? Some people are...

I have always tried to have a foot in or a visiting card to, all the classic car camps and tribes and this book is intended to reflect that. The classic car world is one that is always evolving; it is not a preserved-in-aspic redoubt of the certain and their certainties; try politics or religion for that. So herein is a journey, a series of conversations – adventures as essays across the classic car landscape – from the cars of the expensive to the execrable.

As an example of how classic cars can always teach us something, for many years I thought that the Ferguson Formula Jensen FF was the world's first serious attempt at a production four-wheel drive car (as opposed to an off-road type) but then someone told me that in fact that honour went to Russia, GAZ and Moskvitch. It seems that the first mass-produced 4WD car was the 1939 GAZ 61-73 as launched under the shadow of war in 1941. Moskvitch also turned out the M72 Pobeda 4WD military car in 1955 in large numbers. Have you heard of the 1920s Leyat Helica propellor car? You have – ah, but did you know (I did not) that in the Second World War, the Russians built their own version, mounted many of them on skis and beat the Germans back from within 15km of Moscow? A Russian Helice, what joy that would be at a car show; Goodwood poseurs would surely be silenced.

An age of engines has gone too. Evocations of greatness such as the Coventry Climax, Triumph Straight Six, Pontiac GTO V8, Felix Wankel's rotaries and many more, have gone, snuffed out on a wave of emissions and economy purges. And lest we forget, it was Peugeot that created the hemispherical head cylinder design – not Chrysler! Such are the details of the classic car tutelage.

Classic cars can be such good companions – like a dog but with more noise, greater mess, and ever-increasing expense. Just as with a dog, the classic car owner often seems to spend a lot of time picking up detritus that has fallen rearwards from the stern of the vehicle and popping it in a plastic bag. It is simple, you put money in at one end and clear up at the other, and in between there is a reward; perhaps it is also just like having a child, an often unruly one at that.

Some might say that the content and structure herein are too diverse, too random or non-chronological, but *that* is the point – I wanted to write something without prescribed rankings, a book that you can dip into again and again and expand your tastes at will, or not. The idea is that this book is mobile, readable – anywhere. Classic cars are an entrancing addiction and there is so much to cite as perfection, and the classic car world is the best fun to be had. It contains its own arguments and its own fantasies about ultimate perfection – dare I be so shallow to suggest something like – oh, Gillian Anderson in a silk shirt behind the wheel of a 1970s Porsche 911 RS...

Of driving moments and of favourite journeys? I treasure them and hope you treasure yours. Not so long ago in France, inside my own classic car chase, I encountered a Wankel-rotary-engined, hydro-pneumatically suspended derivative of a Citroën 2CV. This was one of the rare Citroën Ami M35 fast-backed designs – less than 500 built. It was a bizarre yet utterly captivating and compelling amalgam of cheap French parts and advanced NSU German engineering. As such, it was both weird and wonderful. The car had a personality, but such things are of yesterday. And what of NSU's own Ro80 in a tomorrow of a then today that prefaced a new age? Ro80 remains an enigma, an addiction and a certain investment. Driving my Morris Minor van 'Magnus' was always a joy, so too were the Porsche moments that have also come and gone; tentatively 'throwing' an NSX off the hill at Laguna Seca was fun. Driving Allards has become an addiction, but I will not forget my 911 rally drive on Africa's dirt roads; fear does not even begin to describe the experience. It was while living in Africa that I discovered that Ford had made, in South Africa, the Len Bailey engineered, Ercole Spada influenced GT70 – a glass-fibre mid-engined rally car 'special' that, in 1971, pre-empted later rally car Group B developments and was set for British production with a German-built V-6, only to be cancelled and shipped off as a South African project car powered by an Escort four-cylinder BDA unit. It was also in Africa that I drove a Land Rover 5,000 miles in the outback, an experience never to be forgotten. Ah, Land Rovers and old Range Rovers, myth, magic and utter oily addiction. I can smell my Landie now.

As cars get blander, it seems that shining lights have gone out. Blue and gold have given way to flat beige and dull grey; we have been transformed from leather and metal to plasticised polymers and composite, both seemingly impervious to absorbing emotion, resistant to patination and its release of a story as the psychometry of passed moments of a history.

Today, unless we use a classic car on a daily basis as a 'daily driver', we are driving cars that are usually glossy, 'bling' affairs with obese proportions, chubby bodywork, ridiculously low-profile wheels and tyres, and moulded interiors capped in shiny strips of a masquerade of metal. Alternatively, we drive wardrobes-on-wheels called 'people-movers', or faux 4WD 'soft-roaders' and 'SUVs' that in many cases are devoid of soul and are of utterly anaemic character.

My own classic car obsession probably began as a small boy, when I would often sit behind the wheel of my grandfather's dark green Citroën DS; in fact it was a Slough-built British version of the Parisian goddess. I learned to drive in my mother's Land Rover, a Fordson Major tractor and also drove a Saab 96 and a VW Beetle around our farm on mud, ice and snow from the age twelve – which taught me car control; they were all formative and at times, scarring influences. I used to get a lift to school in an assortment of cars ranging from a wood and leather lined Austin Westminster 4-Litre R to a roaring Fiat Dino Coupé, a rather well-driven Austin Allegro and a lurching Morris Marina with its utterly woeful front suspension design that could not cope with country lanes taken at speed. A Citroën GS often carried me over the same roads and there, aged about fifteen, I learned about the difference between the stumbling Morris Marina's under-designed evocation of the old and the GS's over-designed brilliance of the new; GS rode, handled, steered so well, and felt brilliant – even to a teenager. Today, a Citroën SM remains perhaps my current dream car this side of lottery winning money. Sadly, a Jaguar XJ13, a Voisin C27 or a Bugatti Atlantic Type 57SC, all lie beyond the horizon of the fiscally rational. But wonderful as old Citroëns are, I became and remain a dedicated fan of Porsche, Saab, Jaguar, NSU, Bristol, to name just a few.

My uncle, a man named John Pride, owned and ran Toyota GB and his garage at home was full of Japanese exotica as personal imports. As a lad, I used to sit and drool over them – they were always white. The 1960s Toyota 2000GT that John showed me, remains, to my mind, an amazing achievement – they fetch $1 million dollars now. Sean Connery's Bond fantasy female interest in *You Only Live Twice* drove a special soft-top 2000GT and both it and she (Akiko Wakabayashi) were perfectly formed. Throw in a Ken Wallis-piloted gyrocopter and the classic fantasies just could not get better. Some say Albrecht Goertz shaped the 2000 GT as a design idea for Nissan that found its way to Toyota, but I was told by John Pride that Toyota's young designer Satoru Nozaki had styled the car into its late-1960s reality.

I remain an addict to driving and to car design – and even 'styling' – to use a term now so often denigrated by industrial designers. Recently, I have begun to develop feelings for old Hondas and also for old Mazdas – the rotary Cosmo, R-130C and the early RX7 as they seem to be a forgotten tranche of advanced Japanese twentieth century design thinking. Has the world forgotten the Wankel engine? Maybe we should recall that the first Wankel-powered aircraft first flew in 1969 – built by Lockheed and powered by a Curtis-Wright licence-built RC2-60 engine. Lada meanwhile built rotary engines for years behind the Soviet border.

Volkswagen's Sirocco and Corrado seem to me to be forgotten gems that can only become true classics in time. De Tomasos, Maseratis, Alfas, and Lancias continue to entrance me and many others. Mid-1970s Pontiacs, Oldsmobiles and Buicks also beckon with shades or velour and chrome-lined nostalgia. As for discovering Tatra, what a journey, what an utter joy of a car so steeped in design, in thinking and in sheer character as true Bohemian brilliance.

As this is written, I have discovered cyclecars and voiturettes with names like the Bedelia (motorised coffins!) and the Amilcar; this is a niche where the act of driving and of mechanical interaction seems so real, so raw, so different in these early cars. So I and others have discovered another new chapter of classic car friendships amid bicycle-inspired early cyclecars and voiturettes or vélocars *circa* 1900-1920. Just standing in the crowds at Prescott on a vintage day watching these devices cough, as the smell of combusted oil and petrol seeps into your hair and your clothes, as the noise of valves popping and cranks thumping, with whirring and wheezing all around you, the vintage era bug really does begin to take hold. Delightful terms such as 'skiff' are now returning to a wider audience. Oh to be a *cyclecariste*. In fact, cyclecar events have sprung up – notably a 'Festival of Slowth' – which *The Automobile* has suggested is a humorous antidote to the Festival of Speed. [Ref 1] You really are never too old to learn.

Indeed, as an example, we might say the same about the work of Gabriel Voisin whose incredible cars remain a mirage to all but those who know of him and his work. And whatever the issues some people have about moneyed enthusiasts and their aims, Voisin's cars and those of Ettore and Jean Bugatti are reflected in the passion of men like Peter Mullin and his incredible Bugatti and Voisin themed museum. It may be in California's VVIP zone, but Mullin's museum is marvellous and must be cited as ultimate classic car nirvana where an enthusiast has spent his own cash. And if the Voisin C25 does look like a Citroën 2CV that has been stretched and lowered, that should not be a surprise, given Monsieur Lefebvre's involvement in both. If you are in Los Angeles, then a visit to the Petersen Museum is also a must, Mullin having a hand in that too.

Let's get my self-indulgence over with now – the why and how I wrote this book. I entered car design training as a youth and having realised I was not going to be the next Farina, Michelotti, Sacco, or Bertone – a hard task for a twenty-one-year-old's ego – I started to write about car design. Then, thanks to winning something called the Sir William Lyons Award courtesy of Jaguar and the Guild of Motoring Writers, I took a different turning on the road of life. After that fateful moment of winning the Lyons Award, doors opened more easily and a world of new cars and classic cars (and classic aircraft) consumed me. I was transposed overnight from aspirant hopeful facing closed doors, to *Autocar's* offices, the tutelage of Ray Hutton and Michael Scarlett, and an open door at Jaguar. It was so exciting. So too was the day I rang Porsche and asked to see and photograph the 959 Gruppe B prototype 'one-off' that had just been revealed. I just rang in and, next, the door opened to an appointment. When I got there, I was allowed instant access – with Porsche's top PR man Jeremy Snook telling me I was the first British journalist to see the car and complimenting me on my approach. It was magic, an incredible early moment. I got *paid* for doing this! Somehow I ended up as motoring correspondent to the *South China Morning Post* when Hong Kong was still a place where you could arrive and make it big in a few short weeks…

I learned much from early experiences of many cars – from 1930s exotics to humble 1970s wagons. In my twenties, motoring journalism got me behind the wheel of everything from an MG Metro, a Ferrari 308, to an XJ-S and a Porsche 928 at the magical 'bahn-storming 150mph south of Munich. Old Saabs do however, remain very close to my heart, not least as Erik Carlsson and his wife were so kind to me. I wrote Erik's obituary for the *Daily Telegraph* and at his memorial service found myself sat next to Sir Stirling Moss, and Paddy Hopkirk (who cheekily parked his new Mini in the Saab-only parking lot and laughed and swore when asked to move it!), Gunnar Palm, and other luminaries. You may think

I am name-dropping, but I am not, I mention it because it was an honour and such men are my heroes; afterwards we had tea and I left with memories to treasure into my old age. I knew Innes Ireland too, and he was my first interviewee when I was a painful young hopeful. Without him, I would not be writing this, which is why this book contains words to his memory. Not everyone admired Ireland, but there was more to him than most knew.

Such men, from a different era, may have been unique. Their type does not exist today. Society, and its cars, have both changed greatly, for which you may or may not be grateful. Today, female car designers abound and several lead styling studios for big marques and teach at car design centres; decades ago, women were rare in car design. We can be glad of that change for sure.

Like many I have turned to the world of classic cars for my fix, a world full of discovery. Rarely does a week pass by when the classic car world does not yield up some new fact, some forgotten marque, a 'barn find' or a story about a designer of great talent, yet whose name has been obscured by time and the corporate tide of motor industry affairs.

Back in the memory of my youth, I read the wheeled wisdoms of Leonard Setright, Ian Fraser, Mel Nichols, and of Douglas Blain, Ronald Barker, Roger Bell, George Bishop, Tony Dron, Edward Eves, Rex Greenslade, Ray Hutton, John Miles, Michael Scarlett, Jeff Daniels, Henry Manney III, Innes Ireland, Mike McCarthy, Dennis Simanaitis, Paul Frère, and Jerry Sloniger (whose father was Sloniger in Ernest Gann's *Fate is the Hunter*). I devoured all these words as a young car nut and so too did my friends. We lived for the latest issues of *Autocar, Car, Motor, Motor Sport, Road and Track, Car and Driver* or Australia's *Wheels,* oh and latterly, Quentin Wilson's classic gems. Martyn Goddard's photographs, notably in *Car,* and in *Supercar Classics* and on LP covers also remain an inspiration. Perhaps might we argue that today it is the classic car magazines that offer us a glimpse backwards to a fondly remembered past when 'go-faster' stripes were real.

Today, I am addicted to the classic car writing of men like Martin Buckley, Phil Bell, Stephen Bayley, Reg Winstone, Jim Donnelly and Mark McCourt, to name some exponents of current wheeled classicism. Over at the beloved *Autocar,* Steve Cropley and Hilton Holloway provide me and others with a weekly excellence of observation that crosses many divides. But has some writing about *new* cars lost its zeal, its consumer focus and its ability to challenge – not least because new cars are so good and 'lemons' are so rare? You might think so, I dare not comment...

Motor sport (and *Motor Sport)* is also an essential part of the classic movement, and attending events that are packed with wonderful old cars that are risked in races and sometimes, get wrecked, only adds to the moment and the addiction.

Now, I yearn to publish *Old Jalopy* magazine with columns named, Rust, Ooze, Strut, Fettle, and Gunge. The editorial staff would wear shirts and ties under blue overalls – boiler suits labelled with names like Vickers Supermarine, Voisin, Amilcar, de Havilland, Pierce Arrow, and drink proper beer and brandy (separately, although ...). Lunch would be cheese-based. The offices would have to be at Brooklands Museum, or maybe at Bicester Heritage or in deepest France or a place in Italy named Grugliasco. The office dog would be called Saab. Days out would be taken to Prescott, Goodwood Members Day, Cholmondley Pageant, Thatcham Classics, and via the beloved and always superb Brittany Ferries, to autobrocante events in rural France. Team building would be a trip to Monterey's classic car week, the Quail event, or the Ritz Carlton at Amelia Island – flying at the front of the fuselage on Lufthansa, the airline that takes its First Class passengers from the Frankfurt lounge to the steps of the airliner in a fleet of Porsches! From the lounge to the 'Queen of the skies' 747-800 (much nicer than an A380) in a dark blue Panamera driven by a cap-wearing chauffeur. Joy, deep joy. Elitist? Of course, but would you really say no?

Perhaps *Old Jalopy* might get invited by Christies to their VVIP exclusive Tehma Golf Club classic car show during Monterey Week? Or Sir Michael Kadoorie might ask us to the 'The Quail? I can't think of another way that I, or you if you are not a millionaire or a celebrity, might get let in to these, perhaps the world's smartest classic car events. Back down the hill at Monterey's lawns, getting in to the Jet Centre for the auction is a touch easier. But money talks, as it always has.

I believe that it is the act of design and of the driving of the design that makes a classic car. The exterior and interior experiences are the core of the 'feel', alongside the mechanical interactions and details. Yet, the great era of design may have been the 1970s, or the 1930s, or any other decade except this one. Witness the Citroën Traction Avant or the DS, the Audi Quattro, or the Citroën SM or the Alfa Romeo

Jaguar grand saloon design proposal by the author

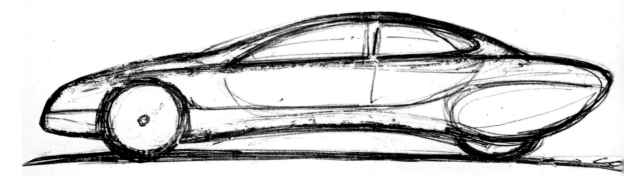

Montreal – and their little siblings the GS and the Alfasud. They would never be made now, because accountants would not allow it. We could say the same of the last of the lovely Lancias or Matra's Murena or Bagheera, and others – cars as rare and alluring as the Monteverdi 375L or, a Tatra. In fact, as new cars all begin to look and feel alike, we might wonder if 'design' is actually dead?

Perhaps like yours, my classic car tastes have become strange indeed, but am I alone in being able to see the attraction of a Voisin or a Bugatti at one end of the scale and of a Suzuki SC100 Whizzkid at the other? If you cannot see that Suzuki's diminutive, rear-engined 970cc roller skate is a true modern classic, then you may be missing something. I suggest you drive one to revel in its utter delight. Perhaps only eclipsed in terms of micro car joy by the Cappuccino, the Cervo/SC100 or 'Whizzkid' as it was termed in export markets, remains a weird yet wonderful device, yet one that sold 890,000 or so in just three years 1979-1982.

Honda's S800 offers similar emotion and pure design in its miniaturised portent of genius.

I have been lucky enough to drive interesting cars all over the world. In France, I have pottered around Provence and the Var in a Ferrari 275, a Maserati Ghibli, and in a Renault 4 too – sunroof peeled back and all lurching roll angle lean and wheezing engine as the cicadas sung and the sun shone upon the Renault's faded patina of La France profunde. A run through Brittany in a Citroën SM will never be forgotten. African, American and Australian excursions in classic cars have also been undertaken. I will never forget seeing a 1930s Le Mans-type Bentley hasten past my truck in the outback of Victoria in a storm, its driver tugging at the helm as the passenger hunched down as the car headed up into the Pyrenees range of Australian hills shaded purple and blue as a bruised sky performed its oratorio and the road beneath it became a tributary to a river.

As this is written, I have got involved with saving an 'oily rag' Chenard et Walcker 1929 saloon. It's a runner and has a Delage clock fitted to the dashboard and Delahaye hubcaps: sheer delight. And, suddenly, 1950s Panhards also seem newly fantastic and addictive. Ledwinka's Tatras have gone deep in my psyche too. CCCBT therapy is clearly needed – cognitive classic car behavioural therapy!

I wrote this book for everyone who loves the classic car conversation, the companionship of the cars and the owners within this world of enthusiasms – the uniqueness of its people and its passions. The narrative deliberately alights like a butterfly on different subject matter, rather like reading a magazine or being at a classic car show and its feast of marques and associated personality types. Herein lies the exquisite classic car and the beloved old jalopy.

Please forgive my ego, the indulgence I have taken in paying tribute to my heroes. I hope they might be yours too. This story is meant to be fun and, to take you there, at the wheel of a classic car enthusiasm. If you are a posh purist with a man to polish your cars, and you really are only bothered about making your old car look like a plastic replica, to do nothing more than shine in utter and unintended perfection, perhaps you had better alight here. If not, and you fancy actually experiencing design and driving on a classic scale with an oily rag thrown in, well, hop in, belt up and let's drive off.

Lance Cole
Round the Bend
Somewhere Over the Hill

1
Plastique Fantastique
Alpine-Renault – The Essence of Getting It Right

Inside the glittering blue 700kg Gallic glass-fibre shell, I had to admit I was truly scared. A 'plastic' car wrapped around a central steel chassis tube or beam, is rarely safe or crashworthy. The occupants sit outside the chassis strength and are exposed to frontal, side, rear, and overhead intrusion when glass-fibre comes to the crunch. But let's not obsess on safety – well, not until we are lying in the hospital bed. All of which was miles from my mind as the Alpine Club of France gathered in Malestroit, Brittany and I joined them for lunch, a photo-session and a drive. Arrayed about me in a field were examples of the Alpine marque – true plastic fantastics.

In France this marque is Alpine (say it *Alpeen*), but in Britain, it is a Renault-badged affair (Peugeot-Talbot owned the name Alpine) and so often under the misnomer of Renault-Alpine, but we *must* call them Alpine-Renaults. They existed as blue, red, or yellow-hued moments of French design flair, something magnificent and confident that embraced the new. But on the day I encountered them in Brittany, nearly all these Alpines were wonderful iridescent blue and ranged from A108 to A610. Red and yellow variants populated the Alpine gathering, but it was the blue-hued A110s laid out on the summer grass amid the smell of fine food and French enthusiasm that delivered the moment. Alpine is clearly revered, and the Renault bit is the sub-culture. Alpine in its own right is something far more important to the French than others realise. This is no marketing con, no ad-speak brand mirage. There really is something special about these cars and the devotion they inspire. I accepted the offer of a drive without really knowing what I was in for.

Open the flimsy door, struggle down and in, park yourself behind the cluster of dials and sniff the smell of plastic, leather, oil, alloy, and sweat; it's just like being strapped into a Second World War fighter. The car (and its drive) is communicative, the way it is in a Lotus, an old Porsche, or one of those early Saab's Erik Carlsson rallied. On start-up, the noise is amazing, and the fear is palpable; there's no safety cage here. No matter; the drive is the thing. The little blue Renault Alpine A110

Berlinette wheezed, shook, rattled, and came to life. I moved off gingerly, creeping through the gears and, the car hated it.

'Stop poncing about and floor it!' said my tutor.

So I did, and we were instantly launched into a warp factor experience as the scenery came careering towards us.

'Don't brake!' came the warning. '*Steer*, bloody steer! Change gear, add power, now!'

I did and the lightweight plastic blancmange responded and hurled itself down the lane. I caught the oh-so-slightly tail wagging car with a tiny hint of opposite lock, then we were off again, power back on. There was plenty of feedback – the car seems to talk to you telepathically and I learned that it will let you know when the swing-axled, engine-hung-out the-back, rear end is about to let go in readiness for a bigger moment. The front brakes felt light and snappy, but not as useless as they are in a Lancia Monte Carlo. The steering seemed to feel every angle and aspect of the road passing under the tyres. Although the car bobbed and nodded, the front-end never went 'light' to a point where I did not know what it or I was doing. All told, this was obviously a superb tool; the little car simply flew along, skimming across the tarmac like a round flat pebble scythed across water. Hell, it was fast. You could set it up for the road ahead and sweep from bend to bend, it was so utterly involving.

Just for moment, delusions of competence pervaded my mind. Here was a car you *had* to take by the scruff of the neck. It needed a firm, determined hand, otherwise it might bite. And this was on a dry road. What was the Alpine like on ice? What on earth was this thing like plunging down an ice-strewn 'Col' in France or Italy? Imagine that at night for the pucker factor of all time. This drive reminded me of my first attempt to fly a really powerful single-engined aircraft. Utterly frightening, yet at the same time enthralling, addictive and very rewarding if you mastered the beast; but you *must* master the thing, or it would do for you. Indeed, in the A110 you could die quite easily on ice on a mountain road with precipitous drops lying just beyond the gutter. Clearly talent, talent far beyond my own, was required.

The sound was amazing, the sensations rushed at me. This one had 1442cc and went with *vitesse*. Road-going production cars are not like this anymore. You would have to drive a rally car to get these same reward of sensations. I got out of the dart-like, A110, with its ability to change direction like a wasp, feeling hot, sweaty, utterly wrecked and deafened but also elated. This was a true, experience, it was *real* driving – of the type that is so fast receding from view in today's cars. A drive I will cherish.

Renault (and Lotus) discovered early on that glass-fibre or GRP was light, as light as you wanted to make it. Lotus abandoned a 'safer' glass-fibre monocoque with separate 'crush zones' when it gave up on the advanced, multi-panelled and reinforced body of its first composite car in the Elite and reverted to a single-piece moulded hull for the Elan and subsequent models. Knowledge of composite bodies had stemmed from experiments in building glass-fibre bodies for the Supermarine Spitfire and Messerschmitt Bf109 – early iterations of moulded plastics technology; the Horten brothers had built a 'plastic' glider and, a plastic composite jet fighter so advanced that it was seized by American forces in April 1945 and towed across Germany and France to be shipped back to America before VE day! Soon the new plastics-based stuff was all the rage for making curved forms in aircraft, yachts and cars. Daimler mirrored Chevrolet's original GRP Corvette by building the SP250 Dart, a 'plastic' car so floppy that the doors opened on corners and bracing had to be added. At Standard Triumph, Sir John Black ordered the building of a glass-fibre Triumph Herald prototype in the 1960s with an eye to the overseas market where cars were built up from completely-knock-down-kit (CKD) construction deals. The Turks built an Ogle-designed glass-fibre Anadol – a Cortina Mk1 in plastic drag! So resin, plastic, glass-fibre or GRP cars were not solely from Lotus or TVR. And the French were at it early on – before these cars were made.

Perhaps the earliest recorded attempt to physically 'mould' new technology for car body making purposes did not come from Germany or Britain, but from France, as early as 1926 from Carrosseries Nagal of Bordeaux. The Nagal concern of Monsieur Gustave Carde exhibited at the 20th Annual Salon d'Automobile in Paris in October 1926 to demonstrate their coachwork 'Moulees' – a 'fibro' moulded complete one-piece body for a Ford Sedan. Fast-forward to Bakelite in the 1930s and the moulded glass-fibre plastic stuff would soon be seized upon in the 1940s by aircraft builders. But Fibro of 1926 makes the plasticised Duroplast of the Trabant body construction seem new! Today, composites are all the rage, yet our tools for examining them as they age and deteriorate are minimal and antediluvian, yet we still stick simple 'plastic' tail fins on airliners and await the inevitable.

Over twenty years ago, the last Alpine-Renault, an A610 model, rolled off the Dieppe production line. Now, there is a new Alpine from Renault; in between, the company produced some amazing cars including the mid-engined R5 Turbo, the Renaultsport Spider two-seaters in the Alpine tradition and a rash of tweaked-up Clios including a Williams variant and a mid-engined V6 of 'widow-maker' threat, as well as the A310, GTA and A610. But they all lie in the afterwards and firstly, we need to visit the before.

Imagine a Renault 4; remove the boxy body, strap a thin glass-fibre jelly mould shell to it, and throw in tuned suspension, engine and brakes. Then evolve it into something more powerful, but just as light. The result, via the first iteration of such tuning – the Renault-based 747cc engined A106 of 1955-59 – was the Renault Alpine; nothing, by the way, to do with a British Rootes car of the same name.

This happened in 1955 and the Alpine A110 – or the *Ah cent dix* – is what emerged by 1960, when a Dieppe Renault dealer's son had spent some time rallying Renault 4CVs and then tinkering with stock Renault parts and the new-fangled glass-fibre stuff, with help from the Chappe brothers who were pioneering its use in France. The car's creative genius was Jean Rédelé and so good was his work that Renault soon absorbed the project under its brand, buying the Alpine name in 1973. Rédelé was the son of a long-established Renault dealership owner and Emile Rédelé senior had (latterly) been mechanic to the 1906 Renault works driver Ferenc Szisz – who had won the 1906 grand prix at La Sarthe – better known as Le Mans.

Decades later, the Rédelé family turned out tuned-up Renaults as Alpines (Alpine was founded in 1955) and the secret to the Alpine was this; it was a bit Porsche 356-like in layout, but blessed for want of a better word with four, not six cylinders of the later Porsche 911 – its main rally competitor. The French car's advantage lay in the lightweight build. It was named Alpine after the icy rally known as the Coupé des Alpes. The Alpine was to become the Renault brand's latter entry into modern motorsport, so it's fair to say that the little plastic car made history. The newer Renaultsport Clio 197 model had some plastic panels too. Little did anyone know that at Le Mans, in 2016, an Alpine-Nissan badged car would win its class – Renault owning a share in Nissan being a later curiosity.

The first A106, Michelotti-styled and using a Renault chassis, won the 1956 Mille Miglia in 43bhp in a 'plastic' body styled for a car Renault failed to truly productionalise – a two-door fast-backed coupé designed to lure American tastes of the 'Fifties. But it set a fashion for glass-fibre and lightweight, rear-engined power. Soon there came the definitive A108 and A110 as special-bodied Renault Dauphin-based developments.

Rear-engined, with the GRP body strapped to a central chassis tube, tuned, with go-kart chuckability, yet also fragile, the Renault A110 boasted great traction and an aerodynamic Giovanni Michelotti-designed body, whose carefully shaped rear end was designed to meet the needs of airflow efficiency and engine cooling.

Renault would buy Alpine as a brand and running motor sport entity from the Rédelé family in 1973. yet the brand name was retained for obvious reasons.

Close your eyes and imagine Cibie headlamps slashing through the dark; smell the ice and snow and hear the howl of that tiny engine; watch a French racing blue-hued shark, sweep past in a flash. You're on the Monte Carlo Rally, and the A110 is scything to victory circa 1970-something; Jean-Claude Andruet and Ove Andersson take the victor's podium. An A110 came third too – an Alpine 1-2-3. So, an A110 had won the 1973 World Rally Championship on 1647cc. Decades later in 1994 an A110 won the RAC Britannia Rally.

From 1963 to 1977, with increasingly bigger engines going from the 954cc, 55bhp original via 1.1 litres up to the 1.6-litre unit that came from the Renault 16TX, the A110 turned into a 125mph-plus speed sledge. There was even a rare four-seater version. A blue, aerodynamic Alpine 'special' with a front end seemingly cribbed form a Ferrari GTO and a rear Kamm spoiler grafted on, shot round Le Mans in the 1970s and Alpine would continue to build Le Mans cars and to win. In 1978, Jean-Pierre Jabouille and Patrick Depailler drove their yellow Alpine A443 V6 Turbo to what looked like a certain victory in the twenty-four hours event that was Alpine's focus – hopefully rewarding the massive amount of money Renault had thrown at trying to dominate Le Mans. Yet circumstance and controversy would ruin the day when an engineering tweak designed to preserve the engine's life by reducing its power, rendered it broken beside the road and victory denied for the A443 – and handed not to Porsche but to a fellow Alpine-Renault A442B driven by Didier Pironi sitting under an aerodynamic perspex canopy that added speed to the open-cockpit car.

Only Porsche's 917-derived 936 Le Mans cars seemed to equal the audacity of the A443 'long-tail' Alpine A443 design for 1978. The dynamic team management of Renault's Gerard Larousse – the true driving force of the attempt – which included seizing British driver Derek Bell from the certainties of Porsche's Le Mans team, Alpine, was a huge success.

Back with the Alpine road-going iteration, with tuning tweaks taken from the Gordini and Mignot outfits, the original plastic fantastic had grown into a hallmark brand that was also manufactured in Spain, Brazil, Mexico and Bulgaria. From a 1.3 Gordini, to a special-edition 1.8-litre factory car the Alpine provided many with a rush of speed and patriotism. The car won the Monte three times, took the 1973 World Rally Championship and was placed in 2,000 other events. Fettled Alpines appeared with boot lids propped open to allow the engine bay heat to escape and with heavy roll-cages somehow fixed to the ultra-thin shell. In Britain, they found favour with privateers with names such as Hollier, Coleman, Roger Clark and Pat Moss – Sir Stirling's sister and Erik Carlsson's wife.

The records say that nearly 8,000 A110s were made, but it is the pure French factory cars that are really worth big money now, especially real race cars. A110s also exist as non-French 'copies' (including the Mexican 'DinAlpine'), although most of us would be unlikely to turn an A110 down just because it was Spanish or of other origin. 'Real' Dieppe-built A110s (with thinner and therefore lighter glass-fibre) with history now sell for £50,000+ and are rising fast. .

But the A110 was not the end of the Alpine story. Renault turned it into a 1980s and 1990s supercar – larger, less nimble, yet still rear-engined, made of plastic and with a power-to-weight ratio that made it very quick. These were the last of the Alpine line as the A310 (from 1972-1984), and the later GTA (1984-1990) and 1990-1994 built A610s with its pop-up headlamps. They were wedge-shaped supercars derived from related parts that partially side-stepped the purist principles of their antecedents, yet which still gave Renault something special to play with. They even had floor-mounted pedals, racing seats, and the point and shoot abilities of their forebears. The gearbox and its change quality remained close and slick, the handling, particularly at the rear was safely planted – no swing-axles here! The front suspension was finely tuned and the steering 'weighted-up' if you ploughed into a bend too fast.

The A310 – no relation to the Airbus of that name – took on the Porsche 911 and A310s four-cylinders gave way to a six-cylinder engine in 1976, yet it remained an acquired taste. The subsequent GTA model, had a C_D of 0.28 – at that time the lowest drag figure for any production car in the world.

Alpine-Renault had really thought about these cars and today they remain a 'sleeper', a fantastic modern classic, still cheap, still a secret gem forgotten by most, except those in the know. I have always adored the GTA and at the time of writing, suggest that it is a sure fire investment as a classic car-slow-burner, but investment is not what we about here; it is the design and the driving of the Alpine that captivates.

The last Alpine-Renault GTA Turbos into the British market were all painted a rather dull maroon hue, some with black roofs. They were 'Le Mans' special editions and twenty-six right-hand-drive cars were sent across the Channel. They had a *douze soupape*/twelve valve 2458cc (latterly expanded to 2,975cc in the A610) and the ubiquitous Garrett T3 turbocharger bolted to the narrow-angle 90-degree V-6 engine of Peugeot-Renault-Volvo ancestry that had been used in the mainstream Renault 25 range. The result was 200bhp at a 5700rpm in a car weighing only 1180kg. Later cars hit 250bhp. So the top speed of 150mph/241kph and 0-60 mph/0-95kph of 6sec, was of the Porsche-eating variety and in its latter version that hit 165mph/265kmh. Turbo-lag was minimal compared to the 911 930 Turbo series and the drive was simply exceptional – hugely 'responsive'. Yet if you forked out £24,000 for one when new, today's low values seem odd.

In the original 1960s-era Alpines we have a real classic car; in the later GTA Alpines, we have something accessible as a modern classic that delivers a true driving experience for a fraction of the price of a Porsche 911. You might agree that these are some of the finest classic cars – old and new and that they reek of engineering, design, and above all, of driving. If you are a true car enthusiast, surely you cannot, *not* 'get' what A110 to GTA (and the A610 it morphed into) are and represent.

Alpine built 251, A106s, made 348, A108s, and 7,879 of the A110 – the 'essential' Alpine. Yet A310 sold 11,616 examples, GTA 6,054 (including the first-ever right-hand-drive Alpine) and only 818 A610s were produced. [Ref 1]

Hail the humble Renault turned into a legend; cars that make a Lotus Esprit or a Porsche 911 look a touch less unique. For me, and for many, GTA/A610 may have been one of the last, pre-drive-by wire, mechanical experiences of the modern age and A110 may have been one of the greatest moments in 1960s realisation of the car as a driver's device. Suddenly, all these Alpines really are important cars, not just vital French cars.

Renault, under Carlos Ghosn as chairman, has realised that there is more kudos and cash to be made from the legend of the Alpines and the bleu and jaune eras of 'Alpeen', so there is a new Alpine concept – the 'Vision' that is, we are told, going to launch as a new Alpine-badged production car in 2017; styled to ape the original A110, unlike the fattening of the Porsche 911, Renault's new Alpine remains trim and chuckable – but safe and sound from a structural standpoint. According to Renault's Vision project's lead designer, Antony Villain, the new Alpine is what an evolution of the Alpines might have looked like if the brand had not withered. He is correct, because the Vision and the new Alpine that it will become, is, thankfully, not a retro-pastiche, but a nicely organic shape seemingly grown from an A110 cutting with a bit of GTA thrown in; all the elements are there in a 'just right' package and it is a 'real' design and, importantly, it is not fat like a 911 has become.

However, Renault had better make sure the new Alpine drives like a mechanical device, for if it does not, and feels like a fly-by-wire marketing con wrapped around a halo of past exploits that ultimately fails to deliver real driving reality, Alpine will stay dead, and Monsieur Rédelé may well become even more a legend in his own Gallic lunchtime. But it was Renault that gave us the 16TX, the Renault 5 Turbo from the prosaic Renault 5 (Le Car in the USA), the Clio Williams, Clio V6, the Renault Sport Spider (built at the Alpine works in Dieppe) and the Megane 275 RS Trophy/Cup, so we know that they can do it. But can Alpine come back from the dead? If only, then that might encourage Fiat to do the same for Lancia.

Could we then see Alpines competing against Lancias on the world's rally stages? What joy that would bring to so many people. One thing is clear, original A110s are classic car jewels and later Alpines up to the 1990s, remain certain investments.

For the new Alpine of Renault, well, the truth will be in the driving. And the French and others, notably the Rosbifs on the other side of the Manche, will howl loudly if the new Alpine iteration is too idiot-proof. It's up to you Renault.

2

Lancia Lamentation

The Great Waste

Lamentation, a depressing theme. I can think of no car manufacturer now more deserving of lamentation than Lancia. In the heart of Lancia lies triumph, defeat, innovation, genius, spirit, soul and probably some of the best cars ever to grace this soiled earth. From the dawn of motoring to a more recent time, Lancia was something special. Many place it alongside Maserati as a great marque. Yet Lancia was to suffer a fate worse than death, long and drawn out leaving it hobbled like an old soldier teetering at the gates of remembrance. To think that its last modern mark was of a badge-engineered Chrysler varietal upon which a Lancia grille was grafted, is sad. By 2017, Lancia's only car will be a skin-grafted Fiat 500 carrying the name Ypsilon, a seemingly pointless marketing exercise. Like many, I truly mourn the death of Lancia. Only the worrying reality of the latest Fiat two-seat spider of barchetta style being a re-skinned Mazda MX-5 that it is, comes close to causing similar bile to rise against the corporate-speak bean counters that now dictate what cars are. A Fiat convertible should surely reek of Italian excellence, be a car to inspire and delight, yet the new one is a re-skinned Mazda, which although a good car, has little soul. No wonder people prefer old cars!

We should perhaps recall that Juan Manuel Fangio drove a Lancia Aurelia B20 GT coupé as his personal transport. Dutch aircraft design legend Anthony H.G. Fokker ordered a Lancia Lambda. Mike Hawthorne (who owned a Citroën SM) also favoured the Lancia. Various Lancias have been the choice of Princes, Presidents and rich people with taste. Italian skiing legend Albert Tomba owned a black Delta Integrale HF1. The Earl that runs the Goodwood legend, Lord March, is as you may expect, a true car fanatic. Amongst his stable there lies a Lancia – an Aurelia GT coupé; he may agree that the Aurelia GT was a 'car of the century'. Mussolini drove a Lancia, a Castagna-bodied V8 Astura and this car was restored by Brian Dearden-Briggs. Peter Ustinov loved Lancias (and Citroëns and Saabs too). Ronald Barker the revered motoring writer, loved his Lancias. So too did Leonard Setright. Australians loved early Lancias and Australian Prime Minister

Malcolm Fraser owned a red, 1960 Flaminia Sport Zagato – one of only 90 made and one of only three right hand drive variants.

There was something about a Lancia, yet that 'something' was changed by the more recent Delta Integrale into a modern legend, only then to be cast to the seas of corporate-speak; H.G. Wells could have predicted Lancia's fate with certainty, I feel.

Lancia, purveyor of 'proper' cars, *did* modernise, it did become contemporary. Sadly, the British public remember only the stories of rusty Lancia Betas and the death of the brand in the UK. Yet Lancia remained an iconic marque in Europe for many years after the British myopia manifested. Eventually, Lancia came back to Britain, not least with a Thema, (say it, Tay-ma) including a Ferrari-engined variant and with a car called Dedra, which was nowhere near as dreadful as its name implied, but remained a Fiat underneath. Before that, there were the Gamma, the Delta and an ancestry of sheer greatness. Today, a decent Aurelia coupé might cost £100,000, but a very nice Fulvia 1.3 could easily be yours for £12,000 or a bit more for the 1.6 V-4.HF. A Fulvia HF Lusso, rebuilt by Omicron (the Lancia experts) sold in 2016 for £24,000, so it is time to buy.

Driving the delightful Fulvia HF, with its creamy little V-4 and delicate handling can bring great joy and many smiles. Like the Aurelia B20 GT, the Fulvia's engine was free-revving and light. So too was the car. Fulvias could be a bit fragile in the body, but provided they were kept rust-free, they went with verve and style and sheer Italian class.

The Lancia began on 29 November 1906 when Vincenzo Lancia legally founded and filed his company in Turin in agreement with a partner named Claudio Fogolin; both men had met working at F.I.A.T. This was only eight years after Vincenzo had, at the age of seventeen, decided he did not want to be an accountant! In those eight years he had raced early Fiats, at that time more correctly known as F.I.A.T.. Vincenzo worked and then funded the money to create his first car. He used Greek words to name his cars – the first being Alfa. From a bi-block engine to mono-block, the company soon turned out a 5.1 litre four-cylinder engined Eta model in 1910. The first car in Europe to have electrically powered headlamps was the Lancia Theta – a 4,951cc car. Having filed a V-engined design under Italian Patent in 1915, by 1919 Lancia was seizing on V-engined engineering principals and turned out a massive 6.1 litre behemoth known as the Kappa for 1920. A V-8 named Tir-Kappa arrived in 1922. The famous Lambda range of the 1920s sold over 13,000 examples across nine model variations through to 1931.

Innovation had become Vincenzo's company's theme. He realised early on that the benefit of the six or twelve-cylinder engine lay in the fact that in its actual mechanical action of combustion, the inertial forces, it could be smoother and more harmonious because at any one time, half of the pistons are acting in the same episode of the combustion process in an opposing cylinder head. Likewise, the ports and valves are better phased. Unlike a rough, straight-four or an unbalanced straight-five, a six or twelve was smoother, and in the V-configuration the block is much stiffer and more resistant to torque twist – but only if properly designed; only a horizontally opposed boxer-type engine is dynamically smoother. Lancia believed the V-engine configuration could be made smoother if configured with the two banks of cylinders connected in pairs via co-axial crankshaft mounts, Lancia's patented idea. In V-configuration (with Lancia-style twin-connecting rods) the pistons, the cylinders, and the valves are more in synchronisation than in other engines types – no need of a balancer shaft! So Lancias had smooth V-engines (latterly even V-4 engines that were narrow-angled at 10° or 13°), all were alloy head built with a three-bearing main crank and overhead cams for each bank; the latter Lancia V-4 was smooth, unlike some V-4s which can be a touch rough. The Aurelia's 60° V-6 was the world first successful production V-6 engine and stemmed from 45° and 50° prototypes devised during the Second World War.

Before this research occurred, Lancia's early exceptionalism was also part-guided by an Italian engineer and racing driver named Luigi Gismondi who we might suggest was vital to Vincenzo's plot as would be Francesco de Virgilio as engine designer.

The early 1920s Lambda was powered by a narrow angle V-4, had a one-piece unitary steel tub body, patented independent front sliding pillar suspension with enclosed coil springs and refined handling. Lambda became the Dilambda for the 1930s and moved into true luxury car territory. With a lowered body height and a 100bhp, 4.1litre V-8, it was a fast car. Lancia was making serious money. The company changed its car model naming policy to use the names of great ancient Italian and European highways for its cars. Most of these of course had been built by the Romans. So came the Astura V-8, a smaller V-4 as the Augusta. Vincenzo Lancia died on 15 February 1937, but not before he guided a car that was truly modern, into life – the Aprilia. Vincenzo's son Gianni would be unexpectedly thrown into running the company.

Aprilia to Aurelia

The Aprilia should have earned the same level of profile as Citroën's Traction Avant, but André Citroën was it seems, a better marketer. Like Citroën, Lancia was the man, the sole powerhouse behind a brand that bore his own name. And the new Aprilia had it all, a steel monocoque, an alloy V-4 engine with chain operated camshaft, independent suspension all round and notably, actual development of the body's aerodynamics in an Italian aviation institute's wind tunnel. The car was without any hint of hype, a significant event in car design, yet was also obscured by the coming the Second World War. Even more obscured was the Pinin Farina-styled Lancia Aprilia Coupé Aerodinamico of 1936 (a revised variant emerged in 1937) which was a fundamental moment in aerodynamic car body design and development, and one outside of Germany and the Stuttgart Institute. Indeed, did not subsequent German and Porsche design reflect such themeology of this aerodynamic pathfinder?

In 1939, Lancia then came up with the little 903cc Ardea streamliner saloon, the engine for which was a tight, peppy, narrow angle V-4 ohv unit driven by a silent chain mechanism. Incredibly, post-war, Lancia bounced straight back with the stunning car design – the Aurelia B10 series from 1949 and the Appia luxury small saloon from 1952. Appia had a 1090cc V-4, soon expanded in capacity. Starting as a saloon, the B10 had a Vittorio Jano designed engine (he who would grace Ferrari engineering) that reflected De Virgilio's work on V-angles and crankshaft and crank pin efficiency. The choice of V-angle – 60° or 65° was subject to intense calculus. Jano was assisted by the often-ignored Battista Falchetto. The overall engineering was realised by Gianna Lancia. Engineer Francesco de Virgilio was the man who spent hundreds of hours making sure that the Aurelia's V-6 engine ran smoothly with balance. Aurelia saw a range of engine capacities (as V-6s) installed across bodystyles – the most notable being the elegant two-door coupé that became the defining 'GT' of B20 series across the 1950s.

Aurelia GT was an exquisite form, a tailored car – a fine suit in steel. The records have it that the Aurelia as a saloon was shaped by F.M. Boano inside Lancia, but that the GT coupé was shaped by Battista Farina's carrozerria house. We may never know just how much collaboration there was (or not) between Boano and Farina over the perfect form of the sculpture that caught the light so beautifully that was the GT. Surely it is obvious that Farina's 1947 Cistalia and his 1948 Facel-Pininfarina-Bentley Mk V1 Cresta Coupé proposals both hint at Aurelia B20. But we can say for certain that Aurelia GT was and remains, in terms of scale, balance and seamless integration of three dimensional shapes, probably a defining example of car body design of the twentieth Century.

Underneath its body, Aurelia saloon and GT had the new 60° V-6 as a design milestone (the B10 prototype had tried a 50° V-6) which made the most of thermo-dynamics research by prof A. Capetti, at Turin Polytechnic – which Lancia had supported. The engine was low-stressed, had 32.9bhp per litre and a good, flattish torque curve. Add wet-liner construction, two thermostats, a Lancia-patented double cam chain tensioner operated by oil pressure sensor, throw in independent suspension, a unique transaxle gearbox to aid weight distribution, a strong and rigid structure, great aerodynamics and Aurelia as saloon and principally as the later GT, became the epitome not just of Lancia engineering, but of a great era of Italian design. The car went on to rally and race success and a dedicated owner following, notably in Great Britain and France. Le Mans, Mille Miglia, Targa Floria, Monte Carlo, all saw Aurelia B20s on the podium. Some experts believe that this car created the original 'GT' formula and it is unlikely they were wrong – grand touring – Gran Turismo defined.

Aurelia lasted through more than six 1950s models series, later cars (by then 2.5 litres) were given window quarterlights that somewhat destroyed the purity of the design, but the elegant bodyshell retained its impact, not least as a convertible and, as a 'one off' 1952 Farina special – the PF 200 'Spider Aerodinamica' designed to reduce drag and make the most of the Aurelia's new 2.0 litre engine upgrade. It is believed that in fact, six or seven of these special bodied variants were constructed. With their 'jet age' nose intake and curved forms, they caught the moment and the American, Harley Earl, GM, Mitchell, wave of styling themes at the dawn of the age of aerospace.

Aurelia in shape, powerplant and handling, was the pathfinder of change of the 1950s. The facts remain that this car encapsulated the best of advanced thinking, and a new appreciation of what the market and the car buyer could be offered – a future defined and delivered as production reality.

The 1950s were rich years for Lancia and in 1953 the company made its first steps into designing a single-seater racing car for the world of grand prix racing – Formula One. This first grand prix car was the D50 – with a front-mounted 90° V-8. Amongst other typical Lancia innovations, this V-8 racer boasted parallelogram front suspension that reacted to all wheel dynamics and stresses independently of the coil springs' action. Upon its first competitive outing at the 1954 Spanish Grand Prix, the D50, driven by Ascari, shot into the lead only to be sidelined by a failure of a small part in the clutch mechanism. It would be 1955 until the D50 won a race, the Turin 'Valentino' Grand Prix, which seemed fitting. Following the death of Ascari in a crash involving a new sports car during testing in mid-1955, Scuderia Lancia walked away from Formula One. In doing so, it gifted its entire repertoire of knowledge and D50 cars to Ferrari. Curiously, in 1937, the Maserati brothers had also walked away from grand prix racing upon the death of their youngest sibling in a crash. Maserati fell into other hands and the Maserati family went off and quietly created an obscure car marque in post-war Italy – OSCA(FM) – Officine Specializzate Constructzione Automobili (Fratelli Maserati). The Lancia-Ferrari Formula One cars quickly won the 1956 Formula One world championship. So, Scuderia Ferrari owes Lancia a very great deal.

From decades of Lancia innovation grew the beloved Italian marque that catered not only for Italy's upper class, but which also offered aspiring, socially mobile Italians a dream car to work and save for. So was set the post-war highlight of Lancia. The company's cars were heavily influenced by Pininfarina as arbiter of Lancia's style for the 1950s and 1960s. Lancia's Appia model of 1960 was styled by Zagato, but the Appia Coupé of 1961 was of Pininfarina's sheer brilliance. Pininfarina set a new post-war fashion by avoiding a prolonging of the curved, jelly-mould, or perhaps even Baroque style that had been set by the emergence of American industrial design's styling themes of the late 1930s; French styling themes of that era also having been proponents of such chrome encrusted ideas. Instead, Farina set a new clean-limbed, look with 1948 Cistalia, the Aurelia GT and then created the more angular genre of elegantly tailored 'three-box' shaped cars. Sergio Pininfarina would rise to the fore as would Lancia with what we can only cite as 'architectural' body designs as framed by such cars as the Flaminia, Flavia, and significantly the 1957 Florida II, which were the great original 1960s masterpieces of Italian car design whose legacy reached as far forward as the 1970s Fiat 130 two-door, yet which were eclipsed by the 1980s fashion for aerodynamics. The 'look' established by the Farina-styled Lancias cascaded down into Peugeots, Austins, and beyond into German saloons and emerging Japanese designs.

So came the last true era of Lancia.

As a young driver in the 1980s, I briefly ran a flaking, mouldering two-door Lancia Flavia 2000 coupé. It was pale silver blue metallic with tan leather and a wooden steering wheel. It sounded amazing, reeked of style and class and just oozed charm. How I loved that car. At this time, in a dodgy Lancia 'moment', I took myself along to the Chequered Flag Lancia dealership in Chiswick, West London and sat in their rally team's Stratos for far too long. The psychometry was strong; zooming, flashing images of near-death on a rally stage seemed to play on the windscreen in front of me. Did I hear the howling Ferrari-engineered quad-cam Fiat Dino motor? Could I smell the car's past and the fear captured in that cramped, obliquely aligned cabin? Was this the car that one of my heroes, Bjorn Waldegaard used to drive sideways at incredible speed in Graham Warner's Chequered Flag Stratos team?

Stratos was Lancia's seminal, Bertone-Gandini styled mid-engined moment of brilliant, lunatic madness. Launched in 1974 as a showroom excuse to officially 'homologate' as per the F.I.A. rules, 500 examples for rally use, the Stratos was edgy, hot, difficult and potentially lethal, yet it was the possibly the purest example of man and mechanised machine in action. Stratos was packed with exquisite engineering, as Lancias always had been. There was a Ferrari-built Lancia 'SC' *Squadra Corse* Dino V-6 bolted to the mid-body girder frame, a massively curved and expensive windscreen, a short-wheelbase and ultimate 'flickability'. Lancia built a long-wheelbase Stratos to try and tame the handling. It had a KKK turbocharged Dino 2.7 engine, about 500bhp and entered by Team Esso Aseptogyl and driven by Christine Dacremont and Marianne Hoepfer it did compete in several events but has now been forgotten by all except enthusiasts. Thankfully, unlike later 'Group B' type rally cars, the story did not end in a ball of flame, twisted metal and seeming F.I.A. inaction to better police the rallies – which was hardly the Group B cars fault was it. However, Stratos was a true, real legend, a Supermarine Spitfire with wheels, it remains a holy grail of car design, a car that defined a rally car era and influenced a road-car chapter.

Also in the showroom was a Fulvia, the two-door, a rare 1.6 HF no less – another Lancia available as a rally car and of which only 1,280 were sold. A narrow-angled chain driven and unusually smooth, alloy-headed V-4, a light body, and front-wheel drive that was well and properly set up, despite the rear end being suspended (somewhat surprisingly) by leaf springs and a beam axle – but properly sorted. All this and more made the Fulvia, even in base 1.3 spec, or better still as 1.6 HF, a sweet little device, a true gem. Today they remain cheap to buy, except as an HF and to lesser extent, as a deluxe variant, the Lusso. Lancia's lovely Fulvia was styled by Aldo Castagno and Pierro Castagnero, the engineering lead for Fulvia was Sergio Camuffo. With evocative names like these, Fulvia, either as a saloon or a two-door coupé, had no excuse than to be anything other than utterly Italian.

The rarer, fastback Zagato-bodied Fulvia Sport with lines drawn by Ercole Spada, remains an addictive, quintessential element of Italian genius, a car that simply just communicates in every way. It had that 1.5-litre V-4, a transaxle and a high, 10.5:1 compression ratio, and advanced technology, coated spark plugs. The gearbox was not just alloy cast, but mounted via its own subframe through rubber joints to the monocoque's reinforcing rails. This was properly thought about engineering carried out by passionate experts. Early Fuliva Zagatos had all-alloy bodies but a change to steel was made. To drive, the Fulvia in standard and Zagato form, needed proper command and informed use of the gearbox. Lancias were not for sloppy drivers. This was the era of true Lancia drivers cars and only the likes of the Alfa Romeo Junior Z could match it.

As the 1970s waned into the 1980s, there came the last 'real' Lancias – Beta,

Lancia Fulvia Sport Zagato: Sheer classic perfection

Montecarlo, Gamma and then, latterly came the Fiat-derived Delta. Despite being owned by Fiat, Lancia *was* allowed to create cars of its own identity. Before that happened, the Montecarlo really was a Ferrari-esque device, but front brake design issues blighted it and production was suspended for a re-think. The car re-emerged, not least as an emissions-strangulated 'Scorpion' for the US market. But rally and race-bodied variants of Montecarlo carved massive niches in their respective arenas. The Beta range was brilliant, and fully designed in every aspect, yet ruined by the rust issues that became apparent. The Beta Coupé derivative, especially as the longer wheel base, High Performance Estate or 'HPE' three-door, seemed to reflect the idea of Tom Karen's brilliant Reliant Scimitar configuration but on a mass produced scale as a car with the room of a small estate, yet with power and luxury – an early 'sports wagon' of the concept of which Audi would later make such a success. Beta HPE was wonderful to drive, steered and went like a true Lancia and made the BMW Touring seem a bit bland. The Lancia was a more modern, roomier and better drive, but it was the BMW that stayed in tune longer and resisted rot just slightly better. By the time the Beta range had given birth to an 'HPE Volumex' with a supercharger and series three styling, the death knell of Lancia and the wretched rust affair, had begun to sound.

There was also the Trevi saloon of 1980, yet by this time, Lancia outside of Italy and southern Europe was almost dead, which was a shame as the Trevi was a well sorted, better-made car of great character. Ours was gold metallizzato with beige seat trim and had a weird Swiss-cheese styled dashboard with white-faced dials peering out of orifices set in a marshmallow moulding in chocolate brown. It felt like being inside a Tunnocks' tea cake.

The Gamma (notchback) coupé was possibly the most elegant car of its era, the Gamma fastback saloon, utterly regal and so *very* Lancia. Sadly, there were issues with aspects of the four-cylinder 2.5-litre engine design. From 1978 to 1984, Gamma remained as a large, classy, big-engined, last-of-the-line Lancia that did indeed feel like a Lancia of old. The link with Lancia's past was tangible– *really*. My Gamma was navy blue and had that sense of occasion that defines great design. Arrivals in a Gamma were subtle yet pure class.

Bertone bit back to try and gain some Lancia business from Fiat and presented, in 1978, the amazing, brown-moulded form of its Lancia concept, the Sibilo which seemed to be a Stratos on plastic steroids turned into a saloon car for the composite age. It was a Bertone highlight, which given the recent closure of Bertone and sell-off of its stable, seems all the more poignant.

Lancia faded but came back with the Delta – a classy Guigaro-shaped hatchback that was strangely non-aerodynamic (C_D 0.46) yet blessed with true Lancia engineering because beyond its Fiat Ritmo/Strada floorpan, it still had a variation with the Lampredi-designed twin-cam Lancia engine. Delta arrived in 1979 as a 1300 or 1500 model. By 1983, a classic and usually Martini-striped 'HF' with turbocharged 2.0-litre engine arrived. It soon had four-wheel drive but the earlier, two-wheel HF Turbo was a car that sang and drove like a true Lancia sports car with poise and balance when pressing on. It left other hot hatches scrabbling it its wake. In 1985, a true monster, the Delta S4 group B rally car project with both turbo and supercharger, signalled a special-build future and a tragic end to life.

The four-wheel drive production series Delta HF arrived with a Torsen diff and viscous limited-slip system that divided up the drive 56% to 44% front to rear – as such the true precursor to the true Delta Integrale in 1987 – of which 7,500 road car version were sold. From 1989 to 1994 the car evolved into 'Evoluzione' iterations with various technical improvements, not least to the set-up of the four-wheel drive differential. In 1992, The Delta-based, privately built 'Hyena' was a Zagato designed attempt to create a coupé of true Lancia bloodline that a Netherlands based enthusiast, Paul Koot, was responsible for. He sold twenty-four. For 1993, the Delta HF Evo 2 signalled the end to Delta production and gave rise to what is now a collectors' item.

Delta Integrale took rally after rally win and multiple world championships, the road-going showroom version which in the end was a 16-valve 215bhp point and shoot weapon with 232lb/ft of torque at a useful 2,500rpm from a 1,995cc engine, was a driving experience beyond the ability of many. Sadly, Deltas kept in moist conditions can rust from the inside out and the cost of renovation can exceed value. Many have been crashed and repaired. *Caveat Emptor*.

Delta Integrale showed the passion and IQ still then contained within Lancia, taking dozens of wins. This car and its Lancia rally team under Cesare Fiorio as manager and Marrku Alén as its longest-serving Delta S4 driver, proved what passion could do. The termination of Group B rally cars in 1986 after so many accidents and deaths (not least of Lancia drivers Henri Toivonen and Sergio Cresto, with Attilio Bettega perishing in a Lancia 037 a year previously), meant that a race was on to find a replacement formula and it would transfer its halo into Lancia's road cars just as Peugeot's own ill-fated 205 16 Group B rally car had done in France. But were the Group B cars – the pinnacle of rallying – really to blame? Many think that the F.I.A. had blood on its organisational hands. But Lancia carried on winning with the Delta as driven by Massimo Biason in 1986. Heroes like Stig Blomqvist and Walter Röhrl, survived and today lament the end of the Group B story, one that had more to it than met the eye. We should also recall that Jean Todt made Peugeot great again through Group B and rallying.

Shoe-horning everything into the existing Delta gave rise to the wider body and extended wings of the road-going, customer-friendly Integrale. The result was a car that went and gripped with fluidity and sheer scything joy. Even today, Delta Integrale remains the grand-daddy of subsequent 'boy racer' hot hatches and apparently serious performance icons of Subaru or Mitsubishi WRX and EVO badging and legend – Audi's Quattro and the Peugeot 205 16 not being ignored.

By 1995, Delta production was over and Lancia began its decline, punctuated by the rare moment of the Ferrari-engined Thema, derived from the Type Four

Fiat-Saab-Lancia project. The legend of Lancia faded, subsumed into a Fiat-based, badge-engineered brand that reminded some observers of the fall from grace of Rover. For the want of strategy and strength, the Italians destroyed the golden halo that was the innovative and stylish Lancia. How such clever people allowed this situation to transpire, remains an enigma.

If you thought that a low, mid-engined supercar with three seats and a driver centrally positioned was pioneered by McLaren in their recent F1 model, go back to 1965 and see Pininfarina's Ferrari three-seat prototype to see who thought of it before McLaren – except Lancia aficionados will quite correctly point out that Vincenzo Lancia pioneered such a 'tre posti frontali' configuration on the 30 April 1934 in his Patent Application for an aerodynamic car, which was granted as Ufficio Della Proprieta Intellettuale on 28 September of that year. [Ref 1]

The true car enthusiast, the driver and the design aficionado, should all lament the loss of Lancia, always, for with it went one of the greatest stories of man's motoring.

3

Rear-Engined Entities

Lincoln Lovely: Tatra Temptations

Despite the death of some great marques, today, like many classic car fanatics, I keep on absorbing new aspects of car design and of driving. Rear-engined cars still hold a fascination for me and many others, not least as something far beyond thoughts of Volkswagen's rear-engined devices. We still have rear-engined deities of course – Porsches. And the new Renault Twingo! Doesn't the brilliant Suzuki SC100 Whizzkid remain, out there, too? Best not discuss the De Lorean though – which seems less rear-engined and more of a stern wheeler of a Mississippi ferry.

Old Renaults, Volkswagens, Skodas, Hondas, Fiats, and Hillman Imps and the still-born Rootes Swallow; rear-engined contraptions have an allure. Yet there are two such devices that aimed higher to a rear-engined nirvana. One comes from America (no it's not a Tucker, nor a Corvair,) and another comes from old Bohemia, yet both share links of thinking and bloodline. I suggest that amid all the varieties of rear-engined cars, these two stand as shining lights of thinking, two apogees of the amalgamation of the rear-engined preference. They are, to enthusiasts of such configuration, true deities. They are of the 1930s and 1940s, they are the American Lincoln-Ford Zephyr concept, and the Tatra of Ledwinka and Jaray in what was an Austro-Hungarian-Czech arena.

Edsel Expects

The rear-engined device, at *Ford?* Indeed, it is so, for no less a man than Edsel Ford, born in 1893, had thoughts of taking Ford into a new era of technology. To do so he envisaged a car so different from the Ford formula of the day, that thinkers flocked to create it for him. In 1933, a Dutchman, pilot and aviation enthusiast named Johan Tjaarda van Starkenborgh – otherwise John Sterkenberg Tjaarda found himself in America, working in the emerging world of the new art of industrial design at the GM's new design school, and names like Norman Belle Geddes and Harley Earl began to make their respective marks. On hand was Henry Ford's son Edsel – who wanted to create something new and competitive and who was running the Lincoln marque after Ford had purchased it. Also in the frame was Eugene Gregoire, the Ford car designer of Model Y fame. Circumstance and fate threw these men and a lot of money together to create a car powered by a 4.4 litre, 75° angle, V-12-engine from the runes of the Ford Flathead V-8. This V-12 engine had not met with a welcome when first used in the 1932 Lincoln KB model. The next Lincoln V-12 powered car was to be an aerodynamic, large, saloon that could become an upmarket American icon. But could Ford could be persuaded to accept a rear-engined configuration?

Tjaarda had previously sought to design and build his own rear-engined car and with that project stalled had then been associated with a development of his original thoughts (the Sterkenberg series) as a rear-engined 'aerodyne' prototype via a series of consultancy roles for American car makers and specifically, the Briggs company, itself a concern which worked with the major US car manufacturers on body-design development. By now, Tjaarda's rear-engined fetishism was obvious – had it been Jaray inspired? At the same time, back across the Atlantic in Europe, Saab's later car designer, Sixten Sason, was also drawing rear-engined aero-weapon saloons. Hans Ledwinka was thinking his thoughts and adding in Jaray ideas. The strands of John Tjaarda's thinking, of Walter Briggs' acumen and Edsel Ford's desire, manifested in a project for Ford's Lincoln brand to create a concept car or 'Dream Car' proposal. This was to be Tjaarda design at its most biomorphic, curved, smoothed and chamfered and with heavily spatted rear wheel enclosures. The idea was that the concept was to be exhibited at the *Century of Progress* exhibition in Chicago as an example of future thinking and as an example of what the Briggs company could do. So well received was this one-off, that it became a proper Lincoln design prototype upon the entry of Eugene Gregoire – Ford designer with a mind touched by French influence and exotic strands of Voisin, Lefebvre, Delage and Citroënesque thinking. Gregoire amended and added to Tjaarda's aerodyne design, including a longer and more imposing frontal treatment of boat-shaped prow (Gregoire had trained in boat design) – and a new chromed-up graphic of American style and glitz. The car *was* rear-engined – but only briefly as a single prototype (a front-engined variant was also constructed). The Lincoln Zephyr had sheer style, a strong visual graphic and a 'face' that endeared it to the public, despite its expense and elite nature. In such success, it exceeded the failure of Carl Breer's excellent yet visually braver Chrysler Airflow and its controversial waterfall grille (later modified).

But *whose* was the Zephyr's body design? Tjaarda or Gregoire – perhaps both? Irrespective of that question and an answer, Edsel Ford pressed the car into reality – the Lincoln was developed in 1934, but the rear-engined prototype was, although exquisite, a step too far into the unknown for Ford. A front-engined version was therefore sanctioned and built. By 1936, this was badged as the new top of the range 'Lincoln Zephyr'. It was stunning, but not quite the precursor to a wind of change that its name might suggest. Despite intriguing details in its body construction that featured a cruciform braced passenger cell, despite its sleekness and C_D reputed at 0.44 (much lower than the then norm) and its sheer elegance, the car *was* a modified, front-engined variant of a rear-engined original. As such, it was said to be compromised in a way that a purer, flagship design might not have been. It was lumbered with dead axles on elliptic leaf springs, having lost Tjaarda's suggested rubberoid suspension system of independent action and thus far too expensive for Ford. [Ref 1]

However, by the close of 1935, Lincoln as a halo-brand under the Ford Umbrella had a grand V-12 car of class, style, utter distinction and the ability carry up to six people in comfort on long distances. The new car sold over 17,000 examples in its first year. Chrysler's V-8 Airflow Mk2 offered something similar yet the Lincoln was bigger and more imposing to some. Buick's 1938 V-8 surly aped the Zephyr's effect. Over 130,000 Zephyrs were sold prior to the model's withdrawal in early 1942. Despite the compromises, this Ford has to be not just a great Ford, but a milestone in American car design and thinking. The car also formed the basis of Lincoln's 'Continental' model range from 1939, itself a great moment in American automotive design.

Ledwinka's Legend

Fascinated by the Lincoln-Zephyr, I looked backwards into the influences upon Tjaarda and the roots of advanced European design. Enter Jaray, the Voisin brothers, Lefebvre, Rumpler, Ganz, Porsche, Gerin, Steyr and of significance, a certain Austrian named Hans Ledwinka and his amazing Tatras; Ledwinka really hit the gold spot early on.

Tatra? If you don't know it, is I suppose, too simply framed as a sort of pre-Saab-Citroën-Porsche iteration of central European design genius and is one that deserves a bigger following. Tatras are simply captivating – *if* you 'get' the Tatra thing. Imagine, a rear axle-line mounted, air-cooled engine (perhaps a V-8) enclosed in a torpedoesque body of interesting structural persuasion; then add spice and distinctly Bohemian feel. Cross a light aircraft with a land yacht and the Tatra aura is approached. Tatra was Europe's third oldest car builder and how many people know that so enamoured was Ferdinand Porsche of Tatra's ideas,

Volkswagen would in a post-war environment allegedly pay a one-off million-Deutsche Mark royalty to Tatra in 1965?

However, in 1930, Hans Ledwinka and Joseph Ganz are both designers who seemed to have missed out on history, but Tatra is at least recognised (Ganz more so recently, after Paul Schliperood's book on the man). Think, if the Iron Curtain had not descended upon Tatra, who knows what might have transpired. Maybe a Porsche Panamera would be a Tatra; now, *there* is a thought. Indeed, we should recall that Leopold Jäntsche who was project leader on the 1960s Porsche 901/911 engine design team (with Hans Mezger being significant) had gone to Porsche *from* Tatra – the 1955 Tatra 603's V8 engine he was associated with had weighed only 380lbs (174kgs) and was air-cooled and boasted two-axial-fans to do it. Sound familiar? [Ref 2]

The Tatra company was founded in 1850 in Nesselsdorf, Moravia and by 1897 had become a car manufacturer; in fact, Tatra made the first motor car in this part of Europe. Tatra hailed from the melting pot of central European ideas and bloodlines. The company's founder was Ignác Suchstala (or Šustala) and he employed Hugo Fischer von Roeslerstamm as technical director in 1890. After the death of Suchstala, von Roeslerstamm directed Tatra's affairs and in 1897 he bought a German Benz – from which he was inspired to think of car making. Tatra, based at Nesselsdorfer as it then was known (prior to renaming as Koprivince), was an Austrian dominated concern; Edmund Rumpler went on to form his own aviation and car company and his Tropfen Wagen was an early attempt at streamlining (he also built an almost-all-wing aircraft). Originally cited as Suchstala's own company, then renamed Nesselsdorfer Wagenbau-Fabriksgesellschaft, having become a railway wagon and carriage manufacturer, Nesselsdorfer changed its name in the 1920s to Tatra – after the Tatra Mountains. Like Saab, Tatra would go on to build highly aerodynamic cars, trucks, and its own aircraft.

Tatra's later focus, even under later Communist rule, was to create upmarket luxury cars of a technically advanced nature; V-8s became the norm. In the early 1930s, Ledwinka and his German engineer Erich Übelacker, had built a V-12 saloon of upright style but then began building advanced, streamlined cars after reaching agreements with the local expert – the Hungarian aerodynamicist, Paul Jaray, late of the employ of Zepplin A.G.1914-1923. Tatra would also licence-build a German, H.G. Rohr, air-cooled, 1,486cc flat-four engine which had links back to Porsche and Adler – for whom the forgotten Joseph Ganz of Hungarian-German origins, would design a car now seen by many as a precursor to the VW Beetle. [Ref 3] Ferdinand Porsche who founded his design bureau in 1930, was of course also an Austrian – Bohemia was full of car and aircraft designers, not to mention the car companies of Larent and Klemin, Skoda, and Praga. Austro-Daimler, Auto-Union and Mercedes-Benz were not too far away either. Intriguingly, Ledwinka worked for Steyr from 1917 to 1923, a company that would soon employ Ferdinand Porsche to design it a streamlined and beetle-shaped car.[Ref 4] In an act of reverse-engineering, Adler would also produce rear-engined, aerodynamically-honed cars bearing the imprint of Ledwinka's old friend Rumpler and then create a little teardrop of a saloon bearing the Porsche or Ganz hallmark depending on whose claim you accept.

Before all that, in the 1920s, the work of engineer Hans Ledwinka with his aircraft-fuselage inspired ideas for a backbone-tube chassis-cum-shell in place of the then conventional collection of struts and sections of traditional chassis-building and flocked bodywork, had created the Tatra as a 'frameless' car, if not a true monocoque. Earlier Tatras were front-engined, both air-cooled or water-cooled and were cars of limited aesthetic or dynamic appeal. But this would change when, in late 1933, Ledwinka drew up and built a rear-engined V570 prototype with an air-cooled V-8 mounted at the rear. So was born the Tatra theme we now remember; the body was aerodynamically styled with a low frontal area and sleek, swept form leading to a beetle-insect like curved shape at the rear. This car was to become the defining Tatra 77.

To Ledwinka's colleague Paul Jaray, directional stability and reduced drag were core themes, as was the control of wake turbulence off the roof and the back of the car, but this particular aerodynamic factor was perhaps better focused upon by Wunibald Kamm and Reinhard von Koenig-Fachsenfeld in the 1930s. However, Jaray patented his ideas as early as 1922 and a smooth pontoon body with a tapered cabin were his hallmarks – as deployed into the T77 by Ledwinka. The T77 was claimed to be the world's first production-status aerodynamic, air-cooled V-8, safety-bodied car. Others such as Lancia and Citroën were experimenting with low-drag bodies, but we might argue that Ledwinka's T77 of Jaray influence exceeded them all in aerodynamically technical competence. Skoda would also produce its own Jaray-esque fastbacked, 'six-light' large saloon-coupé 935 prototype with a dorsal fin in 1935. The British Tatra agent Fitzmaurice got the Harrington coachbuilding company to build a streamlined one-off body on a Tatra.

A claimed C_D 0.2455 for the T77 was rather ambitious as it referred to a scale model devoid of production surfaces and subject to the benefits of scale-effects in a small wind tunnel. Thus this figure, so often cited, must be treated with extreme caution; there was no doubt however that the Tatra *was* sleek, low-dragged and not known to suffer too much adverse lift. Maybe C_D 0.34 might be nearer the mark for the road-going item; tests of a full-size T77 at the Stuttgart Institute did indeed reflect such a possible figure. But one thing is likely, with its large cross sectional area, the T77's C_{DA} might *not* have been outstanding. The T77 had a windscreen A-pillar rake angle of 45° which was then the most raked such production car design – exceeded only in 1947 by the UrSaab. Saab 92 design's 47° as another aerodynamic pioneer of a car and one with a decidedly Tatra-esque rump.

After the T77, came a range of rear-engined big Tatras and, often forgotten, occasional diversions into front-engined attempts as the 52 and 57 series. But it was the 1930s Tatras, T77, T87, and T97, that set a motif. Tatras with V-8 engines (and four-cylinder 'boxer' units) and huge curved bodies with aerodynamic detailing, wind cheating windscreens, and airflow-inducing ribs down the spine to the tail, all became Tatra hallmarks. So too did unwieldy swing-axle handling that gave rise to a series of accidents to unwary drivers. Tatra's post-war iterations continued in 1947 with the Tatraplan 600 series, itself a smaller brother to the T87, featuring a horizontally opposed four-cylinder engine (rear-mounted) and minor styling changes. Ledwinka had been imprisoned by the Communists and was not immediately released, so the Tatra company was run in the late-1940s by Julius Mackerel. Over 6,000 Tatras were manufactured.

During the 1950s, T600, T87/97 would run-out and be replaced by the less 'purist' form of the new 603 model – still however with a rear-mounted 2.5 of over 110bhp in a stylish amalgam of European and trans-Atlantic themes. Single-seat Tatra racing cars provided an intriguing 1950s tangent. [Ref 5]

What was it about these cars that caught the attention and affection of those who admired them? Whatever it was, the allure continues and Tatras have a huge following and rising values. As late as 1975, a modernised 603 with hints of BMW in its Vignale/Michelotti styling, emerged; this was the 613 that lasted for over a decade, yet was still rear-engined and of distinct design. The 613 was restyled in 1996 with input from G. Wardle, a British designer who believed the car could sell to wider audience. A very small number of these last-of-the-line Tatras with 3495cc V-8 powerplants delivering approaching 200bhp, were hand-built up to late1998, when Tatra, builder of cars and as offshoots, aircraft, really did die, only to leave a truck-making legacy for the Millennium. [Ref 5]

For me, and for others, the Jaray-influenced body shape (with a nod to Jacques Gerin's amazing 1920s aerodyne design) the flat-floor, the gills or air scoops on the rear pillars, the dorsal vane or rib, spats, fastbacked cabin and curved front wing line, the tumblehome and the stance of the T77-T97, all add to a distinct icon of highly personal design. Add in the engines, structural effects, semi-trailing suspension and an air of Bohemian chic, and they all just seem to create a car that reeks of Saab, Citroën, something German, a touch of Italy, and ultimately to define something individual that is *none* of these things, nor of those cars. Ledwinka's big torpedoes are wonderful, and unique and came *before* such marques excelled in design and wind cheating recipes. You seem to strap a big Tatra to you, it feels like sitting in a bathtub but it is far more agile. These cars smell old too – tin, steel, enamel, horsehair, glue, vinyl, chrome, Bakelite, wood and damp wool. The trim and fittings have a sort of Porsche 356 aura; the cabin is Citroënesque with a hint of Bugatti too. The steering is direct, the sound of an air-cooled V8 amazing in an aeronautical vein and, there is that rear-engined stance while all the while there is the sound on reverb: *Throbiddy, throbiddy, throb-throb*.

In my T77 moment I had many thoughts. At start-up it seemed to pulsate and flex – just like an aircraft standing on its brakes. The steering was light, the torque had grunt; the feel of the thing was of limousine mixed with tractor, with a bit of aircraft thrown in. It had style, it had a sense of rare occasion. Here was a stepping stone from vintage car to modern mid-twentieth century car. Here could have been a future. Was it a car, an airship or something betwixt the two? Sitting behind the Tatra T77's wheel, I felt as if I was at the controls of big prop-driven airliner – more DC-6 than DC-3. This was a piston-engined cockpit in a fuselage of a car that flew along the ground.

Was the Tatra dangerous? Only in the hands of a fool or a virgin, but it was not to be trifled with. Legend has it that the renowned motoring writer Gordon Wilkins once stated that driving the Tatra was akin to shampooing a lion. So you have been warned. The one I drove was simply stunning in its tangible sense of genius. It also frightened the so and so's out of me on a wet road, but so has a 911, an Allard L-Type, and a Bavarian girl named Karin. What a wonder the Tatra was. Once you have got the Tatra bug, the huge step in engineering and design that was the Tatra's 1930s genesis suddenly seems really important. These Tatras really are terrific classic cars, vehicles with a defined design language that truly speaks. They were Bohemia's car; a class car from a region that yielded up massive advances in automotive and aeronautical knowledge, yet was a place lost amid a lost time and the misadventure of opportunity. Today, Tatra is also a 'lost' car, but it *was* once the embodiment of its time, its place and that design knowledge – so often denied by the Allies on the other side of what was a Nazi colony and then a Communist outpost behind the Cold War's Iron Curtain. Space rockets, missiles, discoid flight devices, delta wings, all-wings, advanced swept wings, gliders, aerodynamic cars, air-cooled engines, they were all originally brewed in or by Bohemia and its blood lines, only to be stolen by the madness of Hitler, then absorbed by the ruthlessness of Allied advance that claimed such genius as its own under new nameplates.

Think Lippisch, Vogt, Voigt, the Horten brothers, von Braun, Messerschmitt, and of Multhopp to name just a few.

The Tatra Club thrives in Britain and across Europe, so I am not alone in my Tatra fascination. *Octane* magazine's Delwyn Mallet has a wonderful T87 and a T603. Sam Glover at *Practical Classics* was a Tatra 613-4 man before the photographer Sam Frost then enjoyed ownership of the 613-4. Cuba's President Castro owned a white Tatra 603. Sir Norman Foster the architect and auto-aero enthusiast owns a Tatra. King Farouk of Egypt owned a Tatra. Even Communist Ministers owned Tatras. Sensible men all – for they recognised Tatra's Bohemian rhapsody.

4

Madame Itier's Bugatti and a Carrossier Conundrum

The problem with provenance is that it can rely on opinion, or disputed history. One man's 'proof' is another man's conjecture. Perceived wisdom is a powerful antidote to an open mind. So when a 'mystery' car has been subject to 'Chinese whispers', it is difficult to cut through prejudged opinions. Such is the tale surrounding Madame Itier's lovely Bugatti and its status. As a Bugatti luminary best left unnamed, said to me of my theory about this car, 'Where is the paperwork to prove it?'

Fair point, but many of the greatest artworks hanging on museum walls in Paris, London, Amsterdam, or New York have been attributed by an opinion or a committee's opinion, often with no paperwork or actual 'proof' at all! And what if the paper trail is itself incomplete?

The only thing to do is compare brushwork, details, technique and location; so I have done so here. But things are made even worse when the waters are muddied by the fact that the car in question is a rebuild of a rebuild that was originally a factory 'special'. Yet what if the truth is that this car's unique and still-original 1938 re-body – albeit recently re-chassised – is a forgotten work of a great master?

Enter the 'Itier' Bugatti roadster owned by Henrik Schou-Nielsen.[Ref 1] It is a wonderful blend of Art Deco and Bugatti motifs, yet it is also an enigma. Opinion within the Bugatti movement about this car and its recent reincarnation remains divided. All I know is that there is another story to be told here amid the wheels of faded remembrance. This car started life as a Type 51A, that according to research by Bugatti expert Pierre-Yves Laugier for the owner, began as a Grand Prix racing type in March 1933.

The car was, say the Bugatti records, ordered by Anne-Cecile Rose-Itier, straight from the factory. By 1930, she was one of the best known female racing drivers in France. That she would soon be a rich divorcee Bugatti owner (and revert back to her much-cited Itier surname), only added to the story. Having previously driven Bugattis, Itier ordered the 140bhp twin-cam straight-8 Type 51. It seems that the then 'new' car is reputed to have been based upon an earlier works chassis, but built as a Type 51A configuration as a new car. Such practice was common at

Bugatti when they sold 'works' cars across Types 35-37-39-51 with little chassis modification required. Itier raced her Bugatti at Le Mans on five occasions and took numerous club and regional victories and placings. From 1933 to 1938, she campaigned her 140bhp twin-cam straight-8 Type 51 across France and Europe. She crashed out of the Eyemoutier hill climb in August 1935 and in 1936 raced the Bugatti against a radial engined monoplane at Montlhery. After competing in nearly forty official events ranging from Poland to Italy, she retired after competing in the 1937 Grand Prix at Berne.

Then came the riddle in the exhaust plume of Bugatti history. Upon her retirement Mdme Itier sold the car in Paris in early 1938, whereupon it reappeared some months later with a new roadster body of supreme style; yet no one knows who designed and built this re-bodied car, which seems a very strange anomaly in the annals of Bugatti. Surely by now, given rising values, someone might have worked it out? Post-war the car had re-appeared as the property of a Suzanne Lenglet, another Parisian woman. Quite how the car was kept from the clutches of the occupying forces during the war is probably a story on its own.

In 1946, a Scandinavian chapter began when a Dane named Erik Nielsen purchased the car in Paris. Next, a Swede, Allan Sodeström added the Bugatti to his private collection in 1964 and the car disappeared from the consciousness of even the classic car cognoscenti for over three decades. Fast forward to the modern era and Henrik Schou-Nielsen purchased the car at the end of the last century.

'When I bought the roadster, no one was sure what it was. Its racing past was forgotten with the passage of time. Nobody paid much attention to old stories of an earlier lady owner – including myself!' says Schou-Neilsen who became intrigued. In 2010, Bugatti expert Pierre-Yves Laugier started digging into the car's history, discovering that the roadster was, prior to its 1938 modification, a Type 51A racing body. But the aficionados controversy centres on the fact that in 2010 Schou-Nielsen decided to 'revert' the car back to its Type 51A racing form. This left the 1938-rebuilt body (and T38 engine) 'spare' to become another reincarnation as a 'new' Bugatti out of these original parts. Some purists decried this move, others were in accord. But that debate is not the concern here.

Two for one is not bad, and given that the car was *rebuilt* in 1938 anyway, doing the same thing again may not be so inappropriate as some now suggest. Of course, the roadster is now, horror or horrors, 'non-matching numbers' – but that was *also* true in 1938! Yet crucially its body *was* an original. So the 'mystery car' is not in its second, but its *third* incarnation. Hence the 'whispers' that seem so unfair to this car. But who shaped that amazing 1938-dated roadster body? Who built it?

'No one knows who designed the body.' says Andrew Ferguson of Historit, based at Bicester Heritage Centre who lovingly care for the car in the UK where the owner is keen for it be seen and used. 'If you have any idea, tell us!' adds Ferguson, whose father is librarian to the VSCC.

It couldn't be one of the circa 1937 Van den Plas-bodied Bugattis could it? Doubtful. A Jonckheere body? Unlikely. Sodomka? Van Vooren? Surely not. Neither is this the work of Gurney Nutting. You might cite Geo Ham, Letourneur et Marchand, Gangloff, Ventoux, or Iakov Saoutchik. Were Ēmile Darl' Mat's cars a parallel thought? But could it be an Eric Giles, Corsica of London design? *Maybe...*

Inspecting the car, I immediately thought I knew who had designed that body, because I have studied the designer's works for decades. Yet was I correct, or was I just another opinion wrapped up in the own arrogance of perception? I contend that here in the 1938-dated roadster rebuild stemming from an unknown Parisian carrosserie, we have the 'lost' Bugatti work of the late, great, Georges Paulin. Not only that, it is an earlier work, styled *before* his more famous Talbot Lago T150C SS Marcel Portout-built Aerocoupé – that design being first constructed in 1939, with a second in late 1940. Did Paulin shape this car during his close association with co-designer and fellow carrossier, Joseph Figoni, who may well have assisted after he had built the earlier Talbot-Lago Aerocoupé 'Teardrop' cars?

If I am wrong, the post bag will howl with criticism. But bear with me, for Paulin had started his career as a dentist but had a passion for the new art of industrial design – into which he launched himself in the early 1930s. He was a 'natural' and through various opportunities, he styled special bodywork on a series of cars for the Parisian carrossier Marcel Pourtout and, for Figoni et Falaschi, the Darl' Mat, Peugeot-based bodies being early works. Paulin excelled in 'one off' body design and one of his ideas became a Louis Delage-commissioned coupe based on a Delage D8-120S chassis. We also know that Paulin had considered a Bugatti chassis Type 57 for a special body in 1938. But there are scant records as to what happened. So well-known was Paulin that is it said that the occupying Nazis asked Paulin to go to Germany to design a car for them – he refused. Paulin shaped the influential, ordered-in-Paris, Andre Embricos-sponsored Bentley – with all that entails in terms of design and legacy; Paulin was close to Rolls-Royce's Parisian office in 1939 and placed to influence Rolls-Royce design when war intervened. Paulin, hero of the French Resistance in Paris died aged forty on 21 March 1942 at the hands of the Gestapo and his talent and records were lost. Maybe he left us this riddle to solve?

He was also fascinated by furniture and product design, boats, jewellery, fashion, sculpture – as were the Bugattis, notably the Jean Bugatti, prior to that, Rembrandt

(Bugatti, not van Rijn) had followed similar yearnings. So did Paulin yearn to 'do' a one-off Bugatti? And is *this* it? Or is this a Gangloff work? And what of Corsica in London? They built fourteen Bugatti bodies. [Ref 2] Years ago, in conversation at French autobrocante event, a wrinkled old Frenchman, a wheezing, gnarled old coachbuilder-stylist, told me that Paulin *had* styled a unique Bugatti in Paris, but he thought Le Tourner might have built it. But the tale was just an anecdote, utter hearsay. I forgot it. But today, it rings clearer with the clarity of visual reality.

Here is the evidence: Look at the details of this Itier Bugatti and other Paulin designs: compare and contrast – examine the brush strokes. Note the front wing and rear wing shapes of this Bugatti notably in side profile. The front wings are a particular indicator of Paulin's hand. Note the frontal aspect and the angles and radii of the blend around the grille, front valance and wing intersection. They are almost identical to Paulin's Talbot-Lago coupes of Figoni et Flaschi and those of Pourtout construction. The chrome strip along the bonnet that rises into the twin-pane vee-windscreen is a also masterpiece, yet does it resemble anything? What about Jean Bugatti's rib or spine seam that ran the length of his Type 57C Atlantic coupé design? Many think this was a rivet line for that car's elektron magnesium alloy that was too difficult to weld, but now we are told that this was unlikely and was a styling feature in the production cars' pure aluminium bodies.

Then note the bonnet vents. The downswept side vents are very close indeed to those of the Figoni-built 1937 Talbot Lago Type 150C 'Teardrop' series (coupé and notchback) that preceded the 1939 Portout-built variant of the Talbot Lago Type 150. The shapes around the scuttle to bonnet panels and door shut lines are also pure Paulin; they match closely to these other cars. Even the dashboard design and instrument layout reflects the designs used on the Portout Talbot Lago Aerocoupés and significantly, the Atlantic Type 57C coupe. Indeed, the layout of dials and four switch in-line, is pure Bugatti.

Then, and this is crucial, take a close look at the longitudinal strake that runs down the bootlid and into the rear end. Again, the relationship to that same feature upon the Paulin/Portout/Figoni Aerocoupés, is *so* close, that if the author is not the same, then a copyist has been at work. But the same feature also occurs on the Jean Bugatti Type 57 Atlantic aero coupé.

So Schou-Nielsen's roadster's body design categorically car reeks of Paulin's hand and eye. The brush strokes are undeniable. The application of scaling, stance and graphic, are all Paulin. Indeed, imagine a fastbacked hardtop added and the car becomes even more obvious as of the 'Gouette d'Eau' or 'drop of water' school of design. Maybe, given that he and Joseph Figoni worked so closely together, there is the touch of Figoni as well. Who built it? Figoni – rather than Pourtout? Or another? Whichever, this is a roadster borne of grande routières design and then slimmed down. It is a sportier iteration of carrosserie aerodynamique. As such, *is it a unique and vital piece of Bugatti history?*

Think about it, a forgotten, Paulin-designed Bugatti! Unless of course, another pen was responsible? If you do not agree that this is a Paulin design, then there is only one, and perhaps even more exciting alternative; that is that the design was a Jean Bugatti-designed 'one off'! To my eyes, Paulin seems more plausible yet it could be that Jean Bugatti shaped this car. But wasn't he in Molsheim, Alsace, running the factory whilst his father Ettore was in Paris designing trains?

However, we know that Jean designed the Type 57 SC Atlantic tear drop coupé and that it had Figoni synergie. We also know that Jean created some one-off show cars for the Paris Motor Shows of the 1938 and 1939 and that these were modified into other cars. If Georges Paulin did not *not* shape the Itier car's body, then did Jean Bugatti? And again we must ask, was Ettore involved as well? Was the Itier car one of those possible motor show cars that had been created? Is Jean the possible alternative author of the car – if Paulin was not?

Purists may carp at the reincarnations inherent, but suddenly, a Bugatti with an interesting 'designer' history, and a unique possibility, could be amongst us. A real 'sleeper'.

5

Malcolm Who?

Malcolm Sayer – From Bristol to Baghdad
and Back to Browns Lane

Great names often get their due credit – and sometimes the contributions of others to that greatness, gets forgotten. Many people have heard of the Jaguar E-Type, and Jaguar's Sir William Lyons is recognised not only as the man who created Jaguar, but also as the man who shaped Jaguar's elegance; the 'Lyons line' was how the was legend recorded. People argue over his greatest designs, but many think that the one-off 1938 SS 100 coupé design concept was the shape that made the most important mark for what became Jaguar, and the XK 120 as its first post-war lodestone.

Sir William, like the Supermarine Spitfire designer R.J. Mitchell, had a team, men whose names are sometimes obscured. Lyon's earlier forays into making his cars' shapes (usually frombrain to clay sculpture without making definitive drawings) were made with engineering help from his team. They were: Cyril Holland, coachbuilder; William Heynes, chief engineer; Robert Knight, drivetrain engineer; Claude Bailey, engine designer; Robert Blake, an American bodymaker; William Rankin, publicity man and sculptor; Walter Hassan, engine guru; Norman Dewis, development engineer and tester par excellence. These were the men who helped Lyon's craft his sculpted, animated car shapes and the superb engineering underpinnings of Jaguar's output into the 1960s.

But what of Malcolm Gilbert Sayer, Jaguar's aerodynamics pioneer?

Malcolm Sayer shaped the Jaguar C-Type, D-Type, the crucial E-Type, the XJ13, touched the XJ-6 and created the once maligned but now adored, XJ-S. Yet Sayer's name and works tend to be unknown by many but the Jaguar lover and a few classic car enthusiasts. Lyons was behind the 'look' of his own *earlier* cars as the XK series – the 120,140,150 and the early saloons – he would sculpt their forms on large bucks himself and then display them at his home before deciding which design feature to go with. However, the opinion and work of Sayer seems to have occupied hallowed ground with Lyons and he *was* allowed to suggest and influence

Lyons' ideas; He may have been the only man to have done this, although senior engineer Bob Knight often achieved comparable implementation of perfection on the cheap.

In interviews with retired Jaguar staff, it became clear to the me that Lyons' strength of character might have been intimidating to some who were less confident, but that Sayer's depth and detailed abilities offered a mooring point that was of benefit to Lyons and thus to Jaguar as an entity. Lyon's was of course, a man of vision and tenacity, in a different way, so was Sayer. He however, led a less conventional lifestyle.

In the arrogance of the now, many modern designers – notably of cars and aircraft – assume that as they know everything about computer-aided design, if an old car or aircraft exhibited advanced aspects of design, it did so by luck, accident of chance or unintended outcomes or non-specific knowledge. Indeed, it seems that today's digital 'experts' invented all that we know about automotive and aerospace aerodynamics in the late 1970s onwards to date, or so they say. But Sayer's knowledge *was* advanced, he did not 'style' cars with a sketch pad (although he *was* an artist and did draw his cars shapes). To create the shapes, he used an aviation-industry method that he had learned in the 1940s to plot co-ordinates of multi-formed, multi-dimensional shapes using advanced mathematics and elliptical modifications to aerofoil and surface shapes and definitions. In doing so, he forensically calculated the shape of the body and its resultant highly efficient aerodynamics as controlled airflow – deliberately so. He investigated mathematical techniques of aerodynamic surface development – issues such as skewness and kurtosis. So he was years ahead of today's computational dynamics digital gurus and wind tunnel men and their certainties. His shapes were superbly aerodynamically efficient and it was no accident, no fluke. Indeed, cars benefiting from his theories raced at, and won, Le Mans – topping 200mph / 310kmh on the circuit and, his E-Type design was safe and stable at 150mph on the motorway in daily use; lift, so often the problem of low-fronted and fast-backed shapes was tuned out as far as was possible. So contrary to some suggestions, Sayer and Jaguar *deliberately* and knowingly created early aerodynamic advances, and did not achieve such by 'accident'. How he learned to do this, offers an intriguing tale.

Sayer was born in May 1916 and died in 1970 at a tragically early age. A Norfolk man, he came from the sleepy coastal town of Cromer and was educated at Great Yarmouth Grammar School, where his father taught Maths and Art. He won a prestigious 'Empire' Scholarship and went on to Loughborough College (now Loughborough University, a renowned engineering hub) studying in its Department of Aeronautical and Automotive Engineering. Sayer was initially interested in aerodynamics as well as engineering, earned a first class degree. At the College, he drew, sketched, designed and got involved with motorsport and music. He supplied cartoons and illustrations to the College's publications and developed his artistic side (creating the university motor club logo, and tie) as well as learning sound engineering 'nuts and bolts' thinking in what was an essentially conservative engineering environment. But it was at Loughborough that he encountered speed, structures, airflow, design, and cars. From there, in his early twenties, he got to the Bristol Aeroplane Company, commencing work on 22 September 1938.

After the Second World War, leaving a 'reserved' occupation with Bristol, Sayer travelled to Iraq in 1948 to work at Baghdad's so-called 'University'. It proved to be less than defined opportunity as the 'university' was not actually established. While in Iraq, legend has it that he met a German aeronautics professor who, it is said, helped him recognize the mathematical relationship of curved co-ordinates expressed to physical panelwork, as can be defined in a fluid motion test body. Was this tale one of Sayer's jokes? Or was it true? We shall never know, but few are aware however, that Malcolm Sayer had in fact become immersed in the mathematical expression of aerodynamic, elliptical and advanced curvatures and localised and boundary layer airflow effects long *before* he supposedly met that German professor – who *may* have provided the final page in the steps to Sayer realising his method.

He was a forensically minded technician yet also an artist and a musician – playing the piano and the guitar. His was an unusual mind, mathematical, calculating, yet not tied down in rules or perceived wisdoms. Sayer was creative, sensitive, free-thinking, adventurous; his designs transcended fashion or themes, not only creating a new motif, but standing the test of time. Although Sayer was hired by Jaguar Cars in 1951, before that happened, there were certain influences that shaped the man and his later works. His father had taught maths and art, an unusual blend of normally opposing brain function and personality construct – one that Malcolm's own work reflected. From his educational scholarship and qualification in engineering, he went to work in the aviation industry. Despite being under thirty, he devised the ground breaking wartime theory of reversed airflow cooling system for an aircraft engine – as used in the Bristol Blenheim and the Beaufighter. This process realised that more obvious, natural mechanism of air feed-driven or ram-air could be become blocked or choked in an aero engine and its intake (and also as applied under a car bonnet) and that this would render apparently beneficial inwards airflow, inefficient. By tuning the airflow's pattern and solving local turbulence issues by unblocking the air's pathway, Sayer increased the cooling efficiency by the apparent paradoxical method of changing its natural flow direction, and increasing its effect (of cooling) hence the 'reversal' effect. Through such lessons, he was also later able to attend to the vital under-bonnet and under-car airflows of the Jaguars he would design.

Soon, Bristol would build cars that would also advance the art of automobile aerodynamics. These techniques as applied not just to Bristol aircraft but to cars, led to long low bodies with tailored rear ends, shrouded wheels and detailed attention as to how the airflow behaved over, across and under the car, and how it separated cleanly off the rear of car – known as the critical separation point or 'CSP'. But what inspired Malcolm Sayer to the curved and ellipsoid forms? Was it solely the oft postulated (yet possibly fictional) chance encounter with a 'German' aeronautics mathematician in the curious landscape and circumstances of old Persia?

The answer may lie in the sky.

In 1938, a man named Beverley Shenstone – the quietly spoken and unknown Canadian who *circa* 1934-1936 calculated and shaped the Supermarine Spitfire's wing and its aerodynamics (notably the modified twin-axis ellipse, blended double-aerofoil sections and wing fillet), started a period of work at the Bristol Aeroplane Company, focusing on Blenheim and Beaufighter concepts: Shenstone brought with him the highly advanced mathematical tables and co-ordinates techniques he had learned shaping the Spitfire's modified ellipse – that he had first absorbed from working with Alexander Lippisch on the realisation of the swept, delta wing idea in 1930-'31 (Lippisch was guest lecturer at the RAeS in London as late as December 1938 with Shenstone as his interpretor).

As war dawned, Shenstone worked on the development of Bristol's twin-engined fighter bombers and on their engines – having previously used advanced mathematical formulae (with the help of the forgotten name of Professor Raymond Howland of Southampton University) to predict the Spitfire's airflow behaviour long before today's computer aided flow analysis. Techniques of logarithms, of elliptical axes, of boundary layer flow and lift distribution and wake turbulence, and of blending multi-formed surfaces together to reduce induced and parasitic drag forms, had become Shenstone's area of expertise. With the Spitfire's unique wing, Shenstone (in his mid-twenties) created the world's most advanced, modified elliptical wing, a wing that blended two ultra-thin aerofoil sections together and deployed forward sweep, double washout, advanced surface lift pattern techniques and, reduced induced drag as well as providing low and high transonic speed stability without the need for any 'spoilers' or slats or 'fences'. This wing was unique, revolutionary and in *not* in any way aerodynamically similar to that of the Heinkel He 70 as has been so erroneously claimed by some writers.

What has all this got do with Bristol, Jaguar and Sayer?

The answer is that Shenstone spent over a year working at the Bristol Aeroplane Company where he worked alongside a certain young man in his mid-twenties – Malcolm Sayer. Bristol aficionados and Sir George White might not know it, but there *is* a link between the Bristol Company and the design of the Supermarine Spitfire – and at high level: can we suggest a link in reverse – from Spitfire to Bristol via Sayer? What about from Spitfire to Jaguar?

The circumstantial evidence is strong – via Shenstone and Sayer at Bristol. Think about it, Spitfire was a revolutionary elliptical shape achieved using advanced mathematics and, also used elliptical structural members in a monocoque sub-chassis construction. In shape and build, Spitfire was perfect and ellipsoid. Its aerodynamicist (Shenstone) worked with Sayer at Bristol and just a few years later Sayer produced a perfect, elliptically sculpted car designed using the same mathematical techniques and also built from elliptical structural members in a monocoque sub-chassis context.

The car was the Jaguar D-Type and it was the Supermarine Spitfire's blood brother in form, structure and in aerodynamic function. It's designer had worked with the Spitfire's aerodynamicist and shaper.

Sayer and Shenstone – it's obvious really isn't it. And D-Type gave birth to E-Type – another perfect, ellipsoid, dream machine.

There is more evidence – because the young Beverley Shenstone had in 1929 trained with Junkers as a proponent of the all-wing planform (and then with Alexander Lippisch), and became a fan of the so-called 'flying wing' – or all-wing shape, that is an airframe without fuselage, and often without tail. At Bristol, the senior director Mr Butler, mentored the all-wing proponent Shenstone – who lodged with Butler at his home at Durdham Down. Shenstone also became professionally close the Bristol's other director – Sir Roy Fedden. By 1944 Fedden was presenting his own all-wing design theories and by 1945 he was racing across Germany trying to scoop-up advanced German aerodynamics research as war-prize material – Shenstone being of use with his fluent German and knowledge of Lippisch's works. Bristol and Fedden, learned much in Germany and had of course of course had a prior relationship with BMW and its smooth running engines. Indeed, Fedden went to see his old BMW colleague Dr Amann in Munich during the officially titled 'Fedden Mission' of June-July 1945.

Was it was Shenstone whom had sowed the seeds in Sayer's mind, in the same office at Bristol? Shenstone – even cited as 'co-designer' of the Spitfire (a tag he rejected) had a specific expertise – that of using advanced mathematics to plot aerodynamic co-ordinates on multi-dimensional surfaces and new swept-wing shapes. Log tables, seven and nine digit plots, and advanced predictive techniques were all used to create and blend multi-dimensional shapes for the Spitfire's wing and body. This was revolutionary stuff and, the facts are that *Sayer* later used similar techniques. It is more likely that Shenstone's works and Spitfire-wing fame, are where Sayer encountered early learning in this field prior to his own personal technique – rather than the 'German professor in the desert' scenario.

Shenstone had also studied boat hull design and loved sailing and used a unique, pioneering sail-like wing-fillet panel to great advantage on the Spitfire (the Hurricane and Me Bf 109 lacked such device), he then went on to advise the sailor and emergent yacht designer Uffa Fox in the early 1930s prior to Fox's rise to profile; Fox lived near Shenstone and wrote to him seeking advice on the designs of gliders and yacht hulls in April 1934.

The Spitfire's wing-to-fuselage 'fillet' is its other major aerodynamic advantage and such 'sail' panels or 'fillets were not to be forgotten by Sayer at Jaguar – XJ-S would have just such sail fillets in its bodywork.

At Jaguar, for Sayer, curves, the ellipse and their plots and calculus became *his* unique field of expertise – but allied to his own artistic skill and ability to think in three dimensions. Shenstone meanwhile, had moved on from Bristol's to a senior directorship at the Air Ministry prior to spending time at Wright Field (now Wright Patterson AFB) Dayton Ohio in the mid-1940s and thence to Avro in Canada prior to returning to British aviation in 1947. By 1962 he was President of the Royal Aeronautical Society (RAeS).

Did, *circa* 1938-1940 Shenstone and Sayer compare notes on elliptical design, aerofoil work via mathematical co-ordinates, all-wing design and engine configurations deep inside their office at Bristol? It is unlikely that they did not, given that they worked on the same project at Bristol together. Shenstone and Sayer each went their own separate ways, but any knowledge transfer between them would not be wasted.

Of significance, Malcolm Sayer embarked on a car body design exercise while working at Bristol when he and some friends devised a sporting car for the post-war market; this lightweight and lithe car was named rather curiously, after a river in the city as the 'Gordano'. Made in Clifton, Bristol, the backing came from outside Bristol's, from two local businessmen: Mr Fry of the confectionary manufacturer; the other being a Mr Cesar a noted driver and builder of 'Specials'. So Malcolm Sayer's first foray into car design was the weird little 1940s, Gordano open two-seater that looked like a hill-climb special crossed with a sports car of the era, somewhat Allardesque perhaps.

Despite the car's simplicity, he managed to include some interesting features into its design. The front wheels were enclosed in 'cycle' type wings that were aerodynamically shaped and of note, turned *with* the wheels. The body was ovoid in cross section and tapered in profile: at the rear an elliptical tale featured a horizontally mounted spare wheel that stuck out to act as a de facto aerodynamic aid – an airflow separation point as a 'spoiler'.

Although the Gordano failed to sell widely, several were made including a more streamlined saloon-body version.

At this time the Bristol Company had not produced its first car, but it *would* soon do so and the legacy of Sayer's ideas may be evident therein prior to his departure from the company in 1948. Bristol (and specifically Roy Fedden) had had close pre-war links to BMW, notably via engine development and Bristol's first cars showed clear hints of Bayerischen Motoren Werke engineering and Frazer Nash thinking – with whom Bristol had collaborated.

The first, post-war Bristol car (the 400) echoed 1930s 'streamliner' styling themes, it represented only a small design step in the way that it began to enclose, previously separate, front and rear wing/fender panels into a single bodyshell shape: it remained a 1930s BMW/Frazer Nash -inspired vision. Coachbuilding and body shape input came from the Autenreith concern. The next Bristol, the 401 of 1948, featured a smoother all-in-one 'pontoon' type body and a very aerodynamic treatment to the front and rear of the car. This car shape was we are sometimes told, the work of Carrozzeria Touring of Milano (with *Superleggera* lightweight all metal construction), but if that is the case, Bristol's must have been concerned to discover that it bore a very close resemblance to a 1947 Alfa Romeo 2500 body shape previously designed by Touring. It is however accepted that it was Bristol's own aerodynamic experts – at Filton (in the wind tunnel) who tuned the shape.

As with subsequent Bristols, the names of the company's own 'aero' men, Dudley Hobbs (a wing designer) and James Lane, are cited as the lead design influences. Bristol subsequently turned out the super-aerodynamic 404 sports coupé, which at prototype stage sported *three* rear fins. The later, Hobbs-styled 405 – a fastbacked saloon-coupe was the first car to use a 'bubble' wraparound rear windscreen design (known to French sylists at the *hayon bulle*) which subsequently dominated 1970s coupé design trends.

In the Jaguar D and E-Types, as icons of design and in the ground similarly occupied by the Supermarine Spitfire, we can say that they share a known lineage and an influence from the war-time studies of two men – Shenstone (the older) and Sayer (the younger) whose paths crossed at Bristol's in 1938-1940. Amazingly, *both* men's resulting designs became timeless icons of British industrial design. Jonathan Glancey, the writer, design critic (and author of his own superb Spitfire book which is a must read, for any classic design enthusiast) expressed in print and to me, that the essential ethos of the era could be seen in such devices, and that the Spitfire was like Sayer's D-Type, or the 'Flying Scotsman' locomotive, in its animated and charismatic purpose.[Ref 1]

Sir Nigel Gresley shaped the A4 'Pacific' Class locomotive design with its streamlined form of slanted nose and side fillet 'sail' panels. He had visited Ettore Bugatti in Paris in 1935 cars and noted Bugatti's use of such wind-cheating shapes prior to adapting similar ideas for his locomotive design. Bugatti gets the credit for the 'shovel' front that directed air over (rather than around) the front of the car, and Gresley did likewise with his locomotive; many argue that Bugatti (and as a corollary, Gresley) was aping such thoughts as first expressed by Gabriel Voisin and Andre Lefebvre in their earlier, 1920s Voisin *Laboratoire* cars.

Jaguar Defined

Sayer got to the Jaguar 'Types' after leaving Bristol, via the brief period at the curious interlude of a strange, so-called 'teaching' position at Baghdad's yet to be established University and then, after a period out of work in Great Britain, to Jaguar at Brown's Lane Coventry. It was William Lyons himself who hired Sayer, and introduced him to Jaguar's racing manager, 'Lofty' England. Sayer went to work on the modifying the Jaguar XK120s that would run at Le Mans in 1951 and win the race. Slippery, cooler-running and faster, the Sayer-shaped XK-based C-type was his entrance examination to Jaguar. He passed (despite some cooling issues during the race that stemmed from use of smaller diameter pipes due to the revised 'aero' bodywork) and thus became Jaguar's aerodynamicist/designer. His initial work at Jaguar on a short-term contract was overseen by chief engineer W. "Bill" Heynes and, from that to designing the aviation-spec D-Type with its aerodynamic outer skin, rivetted monocoque construction, under-body cooling and stressed skin construction, was but a surprisingly short step. Thus from C-Type came, D-Type (with and without a 'fin' empennage), a developed 'long-nose' D-Type, the XKSS, and then, the fighter-jet-on-wheels that was the XJ13; therein Sayer created a design language for Jaguar whose highlight say many, must be the E-Type.

A look at the XJ13 (a 197mph/ 309kph capable car) might just point to its influence of many, later cars and even recent Jaguar design concepts. And if XJ13 suffered a bit of lift at over 160 mph, it was a reminder of the steps into the unknown that were taken. Two of the 1950s Sayer-shaped Jaguar models won Le Mans more than once, thus proving his design theories. The E-Type stemmed from such cars.

For the E-Type, it was aerodynamic cleanliness and efficiency that its supercar performance, stemmed from. One of Sayer's main areas of focus was that a design functioned both aerodynamically *and* visually – the two often conflicting in car design. Some of his contributions to the process, included the introduction of slide rule and seven-figure log tables to work out formulae he invented for drawing curves. Today, we rely on advanced 'CFD' computer aided design techniques to solve such issues. Of note, Sayer's cars – including the Le Mans winners, were aerodynamically stable, did not produce an excess of dangerous 'lift' yet were devoid of the usual, large, 'stick-on' aerodynamic spoilers – because the body shape was intrinsically correct in the first place and did not need add-on fences, splitters and panels to achieve aerodynamic efficiency in any form – be that frontal, cross-sectional or planform.

This is *not* to say that he was against movable or deployable aerodynamic devices. Just as with the slats, flaps and speedbrakes/spoilers on an aircraft wing being extended at certain speeds, Sayer was not adverse to the idea of a movable aerodynamic device being fitted to a car – to be deployed for a set function. What he and other experts, such as his contemporary Frank Costin (who designed the Lister-Jaguar), *were* adverse to, was the idea of 'fixing' a flawed aerodynamic shape with 'stick on' wings and spoilers. Such need would indicate a failing in the *original* design. Some rear end lift was inevitable if a designer deployed a sleek, shallow-angled swept rear canopy that altered airflow speed and air pressure, but Sayer worked out a way to reduce it using tuned side-vortex flow. Of significance was Sayer's pre-E-Type 'EA' prototype as a 'one off' bodyshell. This was narrower than the production E-Type, smoother skinned and of note, the one-piece bonnet only extended half way down the wing line – different to the fully enveloping bonnet panel used the on production series E-Type.

Ellipsis

The ellipse in its physical deployment as a shape or form, offers unique aerodynamic and hydrodynamic advantages in reducing drag – notably 'lift' induced drag and parasitic and interference drags. The ellipse also offers benefits in structural design – reducing stress points and more evenly spreading load in a structure. The Vickers Viscount airliner offered a 1950s embodiment of all the advantages of both the aerodynamic and structural elements and benefits of ellipsoid design; in the automotive world, Saab's little 92.001 and 92 did, circa 1949, act as an elliptical design precursor. Jaguar's D-Type and E-Type moved the elliptical art further forwards. Use of ellipsoid shapes – plotted using advanced mathematical process, yielded an advance. Sayer also deployed elliptical structural forms in the D-Type's self-supporting alloy central 'tub'. He used aircraft industry lightweight magnesium alloy welding techniques too, but it turned out to be too porous, and there was the risk of it combusting in a fire, and so magnesium was dropped.

D-Type in short or long-nose variants must be the most beautiful, road-legal racing car ever made and represents a step-change in design with its aerodynamic excellence, disc brakes, alloy-braced monocoque and lightweight suspension mountings supporting everything from double wishones and torsion bars (front) to Panhard and radius rods (rear). Via the 3,442cc D-Type, Jaguar triumphed at the 24 Heures de Le Mans three times (including under Ecurie Ecosse colours) 1955,'56,'57. The 1955 version having a 7.5 inch longer nose and a vertical rear fin to provide directionally stability at 175mph+. The 'productionalised' D-Type variant – the XKSS might have achieved wider fame if the disastrous 1957 fire at Jaguar's factory had not culled the run; only 16 were finally produced: Steve McQueen had one for private use, more recently, the Lynx Company's own XKSS offers well-heeled modern enthusiasts the experience. Jaguar are now building their own 'continuations'.

Sayer's D-Type offspring was the E-Type, and both in hard top or fixed head coupé and soft-top roadster (convertible) forms, is regarded as the greatest car shape not just of its type, but across all car design. Even Battista 'Pinin' (little) Farina thought that the E-Type had ascended Italian automotive couture.

In the 150mph E-Type we saw all of Sayer's C- to D-Type learning, the low form, the shrouded wheels, the delightful use of 'tumblehome' curvature to create a hull shape, the attention to vortex flow off and around the car, and the detail of the rear end 'deck' and tuned wake and exhaust flows. Despite the long nose and short tail, the car did not suffer from extreme 'lift' nor from unstable longitudinal stability – because Sayer had tuned them out as far as then possible. He also created the various 'lightweight' and 'low-drag' E-types – notably an alloy-built, riveted together, sleek, low-backed coupé with a very pretty and highly aerodynamically efficient rear canopy. Of intrigue, today, Jaguar has started to produce a new-build identical lightweight E-Type in just six examples, each costing a reputed £2million. The Sayer-shaped low-drag E-Type coupé can now also be purchased as something more than a 'recreation' via the efforts of the Eagle Company's Low Drag GT coupé.

We might wax lyrical over Jaguar's V12 engine (as fitted to the E-Type from 1971), but the earlier 'straight' six of the Series 1 3.8 (1961-1964) and 4.2 are the hallmarks of the first E-Types and the short-roofed coupés seem more elegant than the taller cabin turret of the later 2+2. With external bonnet catches, 'flat-floor'

Sayer's buttress or sail panels on the XJ-S; Supermarine Spitfire influenced? (Jaguar)

footwells and faired-in headlamps, the early E-Type defined Jaguar and Sayer's skill. He worked with engineer Bob Knight a man who by 1960 was in charge of Jaguar's engineering development and was the key figure in the E-Type's chassis development. Both men were qualified, forensic and perhaps obsessed with achieving detail perfection in their respective arenas. Knight was the man who developed Jaguar's ride, handling and drivetrain standards to be the best in the world – in the case of the 1966 launched XJ6 saloon, better than a Rolls-Royce. It was Knight who created the disc brake system, first seen in a Jaguar via the 1953 example of the C-Type; such braking improvements advanced the art of sports car handling. Knight also worked his magic on the E-Type's suspension, ride and handling compromises. We might suggest that Knight and Sayer were the unsung heroes of the E-Type's realisation and of turning Jaguar's nascent, low-budget expertise, into the basis of a global brand's core ethos – while not ignoring Sir William's previous efforts that created the marque and its ingredients.

The later 1970s destruction of Jaguar's standards of design and build quality under British Leyland must have been a particular wound for Bob Knight who unlike Sayer, lived to see what 'BL' did to the once great marque. Gladly, Jaguar was to be reborn via the efforts of Sir John Egan and his 1980s successors. Today, Jaguar's cars really do reflect not just the Lyons' legacy, but the work of men like Knight, Sayer, and the small team that made Jaguar a great marque. Keith Helfet, later sculpted the wonderful XJ 220 under chief engineer Jim Randle and somehow the car said it all about Jaguar; the latest Callum-influenced Jaguar F-Type and coupé, also reeks of absolute Jaguarism and Sayer-esque heritage perfection of integrated form. But let's not forget that it was the XJ6 saloon of 1966 which provided the stepping stone from famed sports car status, to major, global, large-car manufacturer renown. After that and subsequent events, it was the likes of such Jaguar men who saved the great marque from extinction.[Ref 2]

XJ 13

The Jaguar passion is a personal thing and we all have our own favourites. I focus on the XJ13, as what I suggest is the genius of Sayer let rip even more than in E-Type. If E-Type was style it was also a static sculpture that is waiting to pounce whereas XJ13 seems to be moving when it is standing still – it has 'thrust'. XJ13 was something even more. XJ13's lead project engineer was a young man named Mike Kimberely, his name should be familiar because he went on to lead Lotus and touch Lamborghini, he also had the unenviable task of productionalising that errant flight of fantasy that was the Mr De Lorean's project.

Kimberley (with Walter Hassan) turned Sayer's XJ13 into a real car. He was assisted by engineers Gary Beddoes, Brian Martin, Frank Philpott, Peter Wilson, and test driver David Hobbs.

Sadly, XJ13 with its incredible, animal-like biomorphic shape, quad-cam 'barking' Jaguar V12 and sultry green paint, crashed on a test run (Norman Dewis lived to tell the tale) and was rebuilt to slightly different form and specification, yet it remains a defining moment in Jaguar engineering and in automotive design and sculpture. A 'new' XJ13 project to create a series of recreations has been the passion of Neville Swales and he has managed to build the first of what is hoped to be a series of 'Building the Legend' specials. Sam Sayer and Ceol Sayer (grandson and great-grandson of Malcolm) were on hand to witness the launch of Swales' 'new' XJ13 at the London Classic Car Show in 2016. In America the Sports Car Factory turn out 'SCF XJ13' composite replicas.

So Malcolm Sayer's evocative, brilliant XJ13, might just shake off its bad luck and become a daily driver for those who can afford it; all we can do is lament that back in 1960-something, Jaguar did not create a road-going, softer-trimmed, production-series XJ13 with which to wipe the Muira and assorted Ferrari's from the sales charts of European supercardom – although just such a design proposal did exist prior to the XJ-S shape being defined. Derrick White was the chassis engineer on the E-Type who had worked closely with Sayer at that time and latterly, was also part of the team that developed XJ13. George Buck also being closely involved. From such inputs, came the mid-engined road car derivative of XJ13, that then morphed into the final outcome that was the XJ-S itself.

What of the next big Jaguar GT car – the project XJ27 – which became the XJ-S as an E-Type replacement? Did it really start out as a front-engined, long-bonneted, short-cabined GT car of the dimensions or configuration of the XJ-S? The answer is no. A series of studies and clay models were made, latterly a long-nosed GT of dimensions and scaling akin to those of the later Jensen Interceptor. Yet few people realise that Sayer's (and thus Jaguar's) *first* suggestion for a GT supercar to take on the great marques, was not a GT type of touring car, but a mid-engined, two-seat supercar of a more purist style aimed at the Lamborghini Muira, and Ferrari 512 BB: potential Le Mans attempts and high-speed aerodynamics were also considered.

Sayer's first XJ 20-series design was therefore a direct and distinct child of XJ13 whose form and scaling it closely aped; indeed, imagine an XJ 13 with a long low, shovel-fronted nose, distinct front wing lines, a vertical rear windscreen set behind the cabin and lying between two straked buttress panels. Thrown in a distinctly Italianate canopy shape and Sayer's pre-Ferrari 512 'look' to this mid-engined proposal was radical, futuristic and a true super car. It died as a still-born full-size clay model that was discarded in favour of the larger, four-seat, front-engined, XJ21, GT concept that was to become the XJ-S. Indeed, Sayer's early sketches show a recognisable XJ-S shape, yet with deep side windows and a taller cabin – something less squat than the production item itself. Yet the idea of a small upright rear windscreen behind the cabin enclosed by two de facto buttress panels survived into production.

Prior to XJ-S as Jaguar-coded prototype X-27 and amid the revised XJ13 styling proposal, there was also XJ-21 as Sayer's first attempts to re-work and modernise the E-Type. This looked rather Italianate of Frua-esque impression seemingly allied to an E-Type reiteration as a long-nosed, swept-back, two door coupé that if it had been made, many would have hailed as the great styling of Guigario or some such Italian master. Yet it was too tame, and something of more presence was needed – something with a stronger designer 'graphic', something, that, just as with a Rolls-Royce, made you remember its form as it passed you on the road. So came XJ-S and its more unusual sculpture. Indeed, Sayer quickly went to clay model sculpture to develop his shapes and work with the small engineering team to make the idea reality. In this late 1960s' era he was assisted by Bob Blake, Cyril Couch, Jeff Joyce, Roger Shelbourne, and Phil Weaver, who all contributed to the prototype development process. And what of XJ-S and its so-called ' flying buttress' (more accurately, 'buttress') rear panel work resembling wing fillets or sails – were they an echo of 1941, Bristol and Beverley Shenstone's Spitfire work? The angles, 'washout' twist, and edge-blade to these devices were exquisite examples of Sayer's mathematical sculpture in reducing wake drag and defining airflow / pressure stability and yaw angle effect.

What of XJ-S' small, low cabin 'turret' and carefully tuned side panels? Suddenly it looks timeless and elegant; those in the know also realise that its combination of swept rear 'buttresses', sharp edged, aerodynamic critical separation point at the top of the rear windscreen, and ovoid front and rear lobed forms, do represent the now computed, optimum expression of aerodynamic entry, exit, and cross-sectional, yaw angle, airflow design details. The buttresses also enhanced structural rigidity. [Ref 3]

Jaguar's XJ-S is often hailed as Sayer's last design (he died before it took to the road), but the facts are that in its original prototype form, it was his, but with known

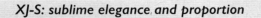

XJ-S: sublime elegance and proportion

contribution at clay model stage from Sir William Lyons and, at latter stages from several designers including Douglas Thorpe. Sayer's first XJ-S sketches entitled 'Fastback Concave Lines' do show a deeper windowed, thinner, more elegant prototype; in production form, it was lower, squatter, and a perhaps a slightly bastardised design because the additions made to it by new legislation which corrupted the original shape – US-spec 5mph impact-bumpers spoiled the looks, added weight yet rather surprisingly, prove to have benefited the aerodynamics; the addition of a higher bonnet line and oval headlamps further affected the original Sayer shape. Many feel that the oval headlamps were a success over the original quad-lamp set up (latterly seen on US specification variants). The post-Sayer rear lamp treatment finally settled upon can only be described as an unfortunate compromise, but was remedied in the later facelift exercise by Geoff Lawson who went on to lead the re-birth of Jaguar design prior to Ian Callum's more recent wonderful re-working of the Lyons line.

I once slightly exceeded the British speed limit on the A303 in a newish Jaguar XJ-S, it was just like flying fast at ultra low level. The sound of that V12 as the air cleaved over Malcolm Sayer's sculpted yacht of a car was exquisite. How I remember squeezing that throttle pedal and the big Jaguar scything forwards with a silken urge of thrust; the long bonnet rising and the car squatting on its haunches and lunging ahead sweeping lesser cars aside as its silvered, ellipsoid form glinted in the hastening light. How the memory of that Jaguar still lingers. It was steel grey with a hint of green and had a good stereo – upon which I played Willie Nelson singing of the vast American west, and Carlos Kleiber performing Beethoven as no one else ever did.

As Devon and Wiltshire flashed past the windscreen in a blur of high definition landscape format, we flew along with the grace and pace of Jaguar's hallmark: the V12 with Mr May's 'HE' tuned engine breathed heavily up hills and then exhaled as the anticlines and synclines of the great road unrolled beneath us. Exeter to Andover passed in a moment of utterly classic driving. Chrome glinted in fading light; heat, soaked back through the bulkhead; the V12 sung and the Jaguar cocooned and then careened its elegant progress across the ancient highway of a land marked with the leylines of history.

The whole car, the ultimate package seemed to gel that day, the engine, the handling, the seats, the design, the drive. This was Jaguar at its most sublime yet serious, devoid of race pace or a howling hull flashing down the main straight at Le Mans, yet an XJ-S moment that seemed to track back to those glory days of Jaguar's past; a car with character and soul. Somehow I could sense the personalities of the men that made it. XJ-S or XJS as it became, remains a quintessential talisman of a car. Indeed, proof that this Jaguar *is* timeless comes in the form of a company called KWE which now re-manufactures the XJ-S and offers them as a tantalising blend of old and new. The point about the XJ-S was its presence, its shape on the road, the effect that its passing had, and of the drive from within it. In these, we can now see that it was a stunning success. Add in the option of the clever styling adaptations of Paul Bailey upon the XJ-S (the 1989 'Monaco' and others) which were so redolent of an earlier Jaguar, and XJ-S then and now, emerges as something truly clever in its timeless form whatever you do to it – within reason. Of the TWR XJ-S and the wide-bodied Lister XJ-S? No complaints will be tolerated.

We might wish to cite 'integrated styling' in reference to XJ-S but Sayer is said to have disliked the 'styling' term or context: XJ-S as originally shaped (for a global grand tourer market, notably in the USA) by Sayer, was lighter, crisper, more elegant, although no E-Type. XJ-S, achieved drag coefficient of C_D 0.38, yet this *could* have been so much lower. But a low C_D figure was not the be all and end all of aerodynamic design. Plenty of low C_D cars have dangerous lift, dirty rear ends, and poor cross-wind stability. Sayer's cars did not suffer from such failings.

Sayer's years at Jaguar produced a series of intriguing styling proposals. These included a range of XJ21 designs, notably the perhaps Frua-esque shape referred to earlier. Oliver Winterbottom also suggested a very stylish interpretation that was not uninfluential.

Malcolm Sayer's grandson, Sam, himself a graphic designer, proudly says of his grandfather:

> 'The unique blend of maths and art shaped his career – many people assume he was solely an aerodynamicist – he was a talented artist and produced many works of art for his family and friends in his lifetime.
>
> 'Everyone knows what an E-type Jaguar is, and they still draw awed stares some 50 years later. I get a flutter in my stomach when I catch a glimpse of one on the road, still struck by its beauty and elegance. It's always been a humble honour to know 'my grandfather created that' and remains a proud part of my family legacy." [Ref 4]

We should not forget that no lesser a person than Enzo Ferrari stated that the E-Type was the 'most beautiful car ever made'.

If anyone deserved a medal, Malcolm Sayer did, for he defined Jaguar, not just as a racing success, notably at Le Mans, but also as a British car marque of a distinct and recognisable style. But he neither received a medal, nor sought one, nor got his due recognition. Yet he was an early creator of 'design language' – as was Lyons.

Yet a 'blue plaque' in Sayer's adopted town, a bronze plate at Loughborough University and references in books, are the few passing clues to his work and its effect. Jonathan Glancey's BBC Radio 4 programme about Sayer, broadcast in 2014, did at least, carry Sayer's name into the nation's homes.

Few can surely doubt that Malcolm Sayer was the most important engineering-design figure to a post-war Jaguar, and therefore a major contributor to the British car industry and yet he remains an enigmatic genius of British industrial design. Alongside Sir George Edwards Vickers VC10 and Concorde airliners, and Sir Nigel Gresley's A4 Pacific Class streamlined locomotive, the Jaguar E-Type must rank, not just as perhaps the greatest example of 20th Century British industrial design expressed as aerodynamic art, but also as an example of a fleeting moment in time when all the world's other designers were eclipsed by such genius.

We can only wonder just what he would have contributed to today's Jaguar cars if he had not suffered a fatal heart attack, the last of a series, one month before his fifty-fourth birthday. One thing is for sure, if we look at recent Jaguars (notably the new F-Type) and certain other cars, they seem to reflect the lean yet lithe forms of Sayer's sculptural yet aerodynamically excellent, scaling and shaping. So the scale and stance of today's Jaguars does contain elements of the Sayer-inspired functional elegance and the F-Type coupé and roadster avoid being retro-pastiches yet retain the essential motifs of Jaguar's design language – the act of design at its best.

Fewer people today, might recall, that upon its 1961 launch E-Type stunned the world and stopped the traffic in the streets of many global cities: pedestrians and drivers simply came to a halt and stared at its incredible and yet sublime beauty. Perhaps no other car shape did what Sayer's E-Type did. It was a 'Concorde' moment. If anyone deserved a knighthood more than an overpaid celebrity or corporate fat cat, it was Malcolm Sayer. We can only wonder if he felt slighted at the establishment's ignorance of his contribution to British design and to Great Britain PLC. I propose that their should be a fitting memorial to the man – in the form of a bursary and internship for a young British aspiring car designer trying to enter that difficult world; let's call it 'The Malcolm Sayer Award' and make Jaguar and Loughborough University sponsor it. Address your letters in support of the idea to Chas Hallet, Jaguar's PR chief.

6

Sydney Allard's Towering Achievements

The last time I broke down in a classic car was recently, in a 1949 Allard. We happened to fail to proceed outside Waitrose in Cirencester (as you do if you are traversing the Cotswolds). A very snotty woman in a quilted green jacket and beige ensemble expressed horror at my overalls and greasy hands. Apparently, I was a 'horrid mechanic type'. How dare Waitrose let me in. Call security and get this oik out! You can hear her now. I had a wife like that once.

What beasts we grease monkeys must be, but armed with superb sandwiches from said supermarket, my mate and I cleaned out the carburettor, blew the fuel lines through and went – nowhere. Then the AA man arrived and did the same thing with better skill. And we drove home. Incompetence, there's a lot of it about.

The AA man at least, knew the origins of the car he was fettling, origins that lie in a complex set of circumstances and design characteristics that created the genesis of the Allard car marque. It was a gestation and lifespan stemming from circa 1928 to 1959. From those years came not just a unique range of cars, but also a record of competition driving and victories that are legends in the annals of motor sport. Today, if a major car maker was to enjoy such a record, it would be plastered across advertising boards and national newspaper pages with a multi-million-pound marketing budget. Back in 1950-something, Sydney Allard (known as the 'Guv'nor' to those close to him) and his men, just got on with it – winning and often featuring in *Motor Sport* and across the motoring and national media, by result. Against drivers that included Stirling Moss, Carol Shelby, Briggs Cunningham, Alberto Ascari, and other famous European names, down into the clubmen and the amateur enthusiast ranks, the bespectacled Sydney Allard and his cars from the factory and from private owners, formed, for a few brief years, a core of competition results that proved he had got it right.

However much of a cliché for those in the know, it bears repeating for those who are not; it remains true that Sydney Allard is still the only man who competed in and won outright, the Monte Carlo Rally in a car of his own design and manufacture and, competed in the Le Mans 24 Hours doing the same thing – in a car badged

'Allard'. Allard won the 1952 Monte Carlo with Guy Warburton co-driving and navigator Tom Lush, to beat Stirling Moss driving the works Sunbeam Talbot. Sydney was also third (overall) at Le Mans – on his first attempt at the gruelling race. Incredibly, he led lap one at Le Mans in his 'home-built' car – leading the famous names of Moss and Ascari. Were these not incredible feats for a bunch of men who did not boast the resources of major brand such as Ferrari, or Jaguar? Allard also won the British Hill Climb Championship and numerous national events. Men in sheds never had it so good.

How many chief executives of branded motor manufacturers go out and drive their products to the edge of competitive safety in major championship events? Few, ever, even as a hobby or a PR stunt. Yet Sydney Allard created and built a car company from doing just this and then continued to do it in his own-branded cars. The key fact in Allard's success was that the product defined the brand – *not* the brand defining the product.

The Healey marque did of course achieve success, but Allard did so on a wider scale across many contexts. So, in 1950s motoring Britain, Allard was big news and a regular media story. Allards competed all over the British racing calendar and across the American racing scene with a strong following that remains to this day.

Even some of those in the know about Allard may have forgotten what happened at Le Mans in the early 1950s. Allard competed at Le Mans against famous names and cars such as the Mercedes-Benz 300SL, C-Type Jaguars, various Ferraris, Aston Martins, Lancias, Porsches, Talbot-Lagos, Panhards and Renaults. The names of the drivers, Cunningham, Macklin, Moss, and Ascari were writ large. Amongst them was also Sydney Allard. On Allard's first visit to Le Mans in 1950, the marque came home third overall and was the first British car in its class, and with a new record. On the third visit to Le Mans in 1952, Sydney Allard and Jack Fairman were running in fifth place overall by soon after midnight and, Frank Curtis and Zora Arkus Duntov (later to become the Corvette engine man) in the second Allard were also running well. Yet both were to have to retire from Le Mans that year – so near so far...

For 1953, Allard returned to Le Mans with its new sleeker JR variant with a lighter chassis and equipped with a V8 giving a claimed 280bhp. The big names of car manufacturing and racing were there too – with even more resources than ever seen before at Le Mans – including Alfa Romeo with its 'Disco Volante' cars. Stirling Moss in his C-Type Jaguar awaited his fate.

Few would have predicted what happened at the start of the Le Mans race that day.

Just after 4pm on that Saturday 13 June, the greatest names in motor racing of the day sprinted away from the start. They roared off, over sixty of them. Then a silence prevailed on that French afternoon. Anticipation hung in the air. A few minutes later, the crowds in the grandstand turned towards the other direction, eagerly awaiting a famous marque driven by a famous name to emerge at high speed from the haze, leading at the end of the first lap. Soon it came, a throbbing sound, the roar of induction in a heavy breathing engine; other engines were howling and wailing in the background. The silence was broken by shouts and cheers. Hail the leader of Le Mans, lap one, 1953! But the shouts were not for Jaguar, nor Alfa, Ferrari, nor Aston Martin. The shouts were of another name, 'Allard! ... Allard! ... Allard!

The Allard name rent the airs of the La Sarthe circuit, shouted by thousands, many thousands, people of British, French, German, Italian and American tongues, even in the pits where many Italians were stupefied by the turn of events. The place erupted. The little team, the independent *garagistes* of Allard, were *leading*. Here was the Le Mans crowd hailing a lone Englishmen in a car of his own design and manufacture, built in Clapham and bearing his own name upon its crimson badge.

Alfa, Ferrari, Cunningham, Porsche, Aston? Jaguar and Moss? *All* were behind Sydney Herbert Allard of London, as he rocketed past the grandstand at 150mph in *his* Allard, leading the field at Le Mans; behind him were red Ferraris, snarling Alfa Romeos, and giant, burbling Mercedes. Yet an Allard driven by bespectacled Mr Allard, was leading Le Mans. The crowds were cheering his name, again and again. It was moment of history yet it seems a stunning moment that has been forgotten and obscured by the passage of time and PR.

Sadly, Sydney's JR had suffered the beginnings of a rear axle mounting-bracket weld failure on the next lap and had to be pitted and withdrawn from the race for fear of further breakage. But what a moment, what a memory for the man, his team and for Britain. Allard led Le Mans; heady stuff in the heyday of British motoring and motor racing.

A golden age that really was.

From major headlines and wonderful PR profile across nations, notably in America, to being a forgotten brand (except by enthusiasts) seems a tragic journey. Yet Allard is no tale of smoke and mirrors, no story of a brief puff of bold claims followed by bankruptcy after failing to produce a single car – a scenario so familiar to many motoring observers when someone says that they are going to start, or resurrect, a marque. Allard made just under 2,000 cars and was a big British success and influence. The death of the Allard marque by 1960 was *not* the result of profligacy or of incompetence but, rather, the result of difficult decisions amid changing circumstances in a new society and marketplace. Yet in a moment that lasted just over a decade, one man (assisted by his wife) and a band of brothers operating from a south London garage, did not just take on the greats, they created a niche marque of unique cars that shocked the old guard, the industry and the big names of motor sport and the motor industry.

Sydney Allard first began making his 'Specials' when he used parts from other cars that he 'improved'. His first such attempt at a Special was a four-wheeled iteration of a Morgan three-wheeled chassis with which he began his nascent competition career and sporting car mindset in 1928. This Morgan-based device was a true one-off or special type, but it was not the first true 'Allard Special' and the eleven cars of that ilk latterly made. Bits of Earl Howe's Bugatti Type 43 also found their way into the first, Allard Special, but it was the Ford name that would become a core supplier. Yet Ford remained at arm's length to Allard; after Allard stopped building cars, the company built tuned and modified Ford Anglias and manufactured parts – Sydney's son Alan becoming a major figure in drag racing, and supercharging design and application.

But what *is* an Allard? Who was Sydney H. Allard? How and why did his cars become what they were? How could the once famous tale of Allard and his cars have become submerged into the confines of the world of classic car enthusiasm, leaving a massive public and PR profile of worldwide fame to the memories of history? In the years after its car making demise, Allard withered to become a little known name in the minds of even dedicated petrol heads, but just sixty years ago, Allard was a household icon, a great British brand and a major name in competition. Few know that Allard was the first official British car manufacturer to use the de Dion suspension layout design – a minnow of company outpacing the big names to a system the major marques later adopted. Yet Allard was a small, family firm, created at the behest of one highly driven, personality.

Allard was also the rock upon which the development of drag racing in Great Britain grew from, Sydney's son, Alan, at one time being Britain's record-holding fastest drag racer. Today, Allard as a name and car brand is resurgent with the launch by the Allard family of cars that are not re-creations, but restorations and, continuations, of Sydney's thinking now framed by Alan and son Lloyd, with his brother Gavin curating the brand's archive.

In the intervening years a widespread Allard enthusiasm has grown all over the world via the Allard Owners club and the Allard Registry.

This, it seems, is a story full of questions. But today, many people – except the classic car tribe, have forgotten Sydney Allard and his cars.

Allards were exported to America, and worldwide, with nearly 1,900 made. It seems a small number today, but if you look at what Allard did, 1,900 cars sold on a global stage is a huge achievement for any small company, let alone a small 'start-up' brand affair whose competition success and resultant profile was mostly at the hands of one man. Around 500 Allards remain – scattered across the globe, in varying states of repair. The values of some models have reached interesting levels.

Allard called themselves 'Britain's premier competition car'. A worthy claim at the time yet one stemming from a small works sites in south London, not the better known locations such as Brooklands, Feltham, Malvern or Coventry. But Allard's reputation was significant. Trading ventures by Allard in America and Canada also existed. Neither should we forget that the likes of Carol Shelby, Tom Cole, and the de Larringa brothers all raced Allards. The 1951 de Larringa car was a Le Mans-type J2 updated to X specification with which Sydney Allard and Rupert de Larringa competed in British hill climb events in 1951. This formed the basis of a further modification to form a 'JR' competition car with sleek, all-enveloping bodywork covering a tubular chassis and a 5.4 litre Cadillac engine. This car was shipped out to North America in November 1955 and continued its competition career, carrying the Allard name across many states. To see a bevy of various Allards at Watkins Glen became a normal scene on the world's stage, such was the allure and legend of Sydney Allard and his cars, the brand writ large across the motoring scene.

So it seems that Allard and his cars were a great British tale. Today, there is a healthy and growing worldwide interest in Allard, a strong owners' club (actually founded in 1951 with Sydney's personal support), the Allard Register in the USA, and enthusiast groups. In America, Allard is something of an icon amongst those in the know; the J2, J2X, K2, K3 and JR models being of particular profile. There is an Allard resurgence, which proves that true, race-winning design, performance and handling ability never go out of fashion, they just wax like the moon until their time comes again.

Allard enthusiasts or 'Allardistes' – as they are sometimes termed, know what is what, and opinions vary as to which Allard is the best or perhaps the 'purest' Allard car to reflect its progenitor's ethos.

Each Allard model has its dedicated band of followers, but as landmarks, we should consider that the J2 marked a hallmark of Allardism, but also consider if the later Palm Beach model and its derivative, the GT or Grand Tourer of 1959 with its hard-topped coupé styling and pre-Jaguar E- Type effect, symbolise the greatness of what Allard became, and what was lost. Imagine the style of an Austin-Healey crossed with a Jaguar, sprinkled with something unique and built upon a hefty

Allard chassis with either Ford 2.5 litre or Jaguar 3.4 litre power, and the lost, 1960s sales potential of Allard's last car of which only two were built, is obvious; Sydney's 'GT' design was his contemporary modern up market, sporting coupé with massive marketing potential. Sadly, it failed to reach production and Sydney Allard's own GT (registered as UXB 793), marks the end of the company's own creations. Between these models, were the J-M Types, all different yet all Allards and with a competition history that few other marques could match.

Allards had pace, style (if not exactly grace), and a certain panache, a wonderfully British look. Using American engines was not unusual – it was to be good enough for Bristol, Jensen, and cars of exotic Latin origins too. Allards offered guts and power long before the fashion for Italian Supeleggera (lightweight) constructed cars took over. Of course, not everything went well for Allard and the cars came in for increasing criticism for their poor fuel economy, somewhat 'brutal' design and under-developed fittings as the 1950s car market progressed from re-warmed 1930s products to more finessed affairs. For example, Allards lacked windscreen demisting and adequate ventilation. However, Sydney's deal with Jaguar (via Lofty England) to secure that company's engines for new Allards, could have been a stepping stone to success.

The real underlying issue was that the 1950s Allards – sleeker, bigger, less sporting and more comfortable, were still based on old, mud-plugging, Trials-derived chassis designs of strength but also excess weight. Converting the lighter 'motorcycle with four wheels' ethos of the J2 and J2X into a grand tourer or softer roadster, was also always going to be a paradox. In a way, the Allard had become neither one thing nor the other and avoided more efficient monocoque body construction and lighter components; such issues had financial and sales implications.

Allards were not flimsy, nor specialist-built one-offs. They were production items, a British icon with a client list that today's marketing would have loved for its 'celebrity' status. We can safely assume that this would have been furthest from Sydney's mind; customers were customers.

One of the best known names of Allard was that of Godfrey Imhof who, from a secure financial position of his own, had time to follow his passion for cars, engineering and design – he became a key contributor to Allard car design and was also an early form of brand ambassador to the marque. David Hooper was Allard's chief engineer and Dudley Hume was the quiet man behind Allard design details and model development. David Davis, a salesman, chased the American market for Allard. Other men in the small team also played a vital role and their contributions are framed herein. From these men and their labours under Sydney's leadership,

Allards at Silverstone

came the profile and allure of the crimson enamelled badge with its silvered script that was one word 'ALLARD'.

Today, any passing minor nonentity gets the chance, via their celebrity-conditioned status, to do things that others with equal or more talent, miss out upon. But back in the 1950s, 'celebrity' meant something different. Some drove Allards.

The broadcaster Richard Dimbleby owned an Allard M-Type, as did the composer Eric Coates. Donald Campbell's wife owned a 'Bluebird' blue Allard as did the fictional radio character Dick Barton (played on the radio by RNVR sailor and Antarctic hero Duncan Carse, and in film by Don Stannard). Other famous

Allard owner/drivers include Dirk Bogarde, General Curtis Le May, General Lee Griswold, Bill Marriott of the hotel group, Tommy Sopwith then of Armstrong-Siddeley Motors and Phillip Schwartz, the head of the Colt Gun company. It is reputed that the infamous Kray Brothers were rather keen on Allards too. Lady Mary Grosvenor (whose family owned large tracts of London) purchased the Allard 'Special' with the registration number FGP 750 and she drove it in post-war events.

An Allard J-Type appeared on the cinema screen in *Written in the Winds* with Lauren Bacall, Rock Hudson and Robert Stack. An Allard K-Type featured in *Genevieve*.

The actor Richard Wilding told a lovely tale of stopping his Allard at a West London garage in the 1960s and extravagantly asking the attendant add 'a fiver's worth' of fuel. The fuel pump man replied, quick as a flash, with, 'In the tank or straight into the carburettor sir?' Perhaps an Allard would not have been suave enough for Ian Fleming's James Bond, but then the real Bond was not intended to be as suave as certain later interpretations. Did Ian Fleming toy with putting Bond in an Allard J2? It is rumoured ...

"Allards? They're Lancaster bombers of cars!" Such words from an enthusiast somehow captures the Allard allure.

Jerry Thurstan has owned Allards and several media figures, notably classic and vintage car guru and *Classic and Sports Car* magazine's editor-at-large Simon Taylor is an Allard enthusiast. The Porsche specialist of international repute *Autofarm*, has at its founder Josh Sadler, who is also an Allard enthusiast and Allard Club luminary. And, just to prove the effectiveness of the Allard idea – let's recall that no less a man than Carroll Shelby drove an Allard as did Peter Collins, the Ferrari team driver.

Famous names in motoring journalism loved Allards and John Bolster praised the J2. J2X and other Allards for their fine handling and thought the J2 handled superbly, but was less enamoured of the softer-sprung Palm Beach. Douglas Blain (now publisher of *The Automobile)* was also a believer in the Allard 'hot rod' and 'mud plugger' combination and said so in no less a journal than *Road and Track*. In more recent times, the talented racer and writer Tony Dron became an Allard fan and profiled the marque and its exploits in *Thoroughbred and Classic Cars* in the 1980s. Even more up to date, the highly experienced John Simister 'got' the Allard ethos when profiling the restored Palm Beach MkII in the excellent *Octane*.

To a current Allard fan, or educated Allardiste, it might seem incomprehensible that someone would not know of Allard cars and their character, yet the truth is that beyond the classic car movement, Allard has become obscured by time, bizarrely, most of all in its British homeland. Yet just half a century ago these cars were a household name in Britain, America, and beyond. The 1950s photograph of HRH The Queen Mother at the Allard stand at the London Motor Show rather makes that point. Slightly more recently, the dragster movement knows of Allard's role in its birth in the UK, but for many, Allard as a company and the man behind it, have become an enigma.

Sydney Herbert Allard, born June 19 1910, died on April 12 1966 at home after a six-month illness with stomach cancer. The story of what he achieved in those fifty six years is a great tale. Allard – the amazing marque of a lone man, amid an era swamped by the temptations of automotive fashions concerned with more easily explained appeal, and the domination of global car making.

'My father just wanted to race, he had no interest in fame or vast accolades, he simply wanted to race cars – cars that *he* had designed and built.' says Alan Allard, confirming that Sydney was no egotistical motor industry megalomaniac as some of the automotive world's figures have been. Instead, Sydney Allard was, as his grandson Lloyd says: 'A true petrol-head, a real car man, an all-round good bloke who just wanted race and look after his blokes.'

Like his father Alan, Lloyd has raced professionally and is known for his 'hot' Golf. He recently drove an Allard around the Nurburgring.

Sydney Allard can now be seen as an engineer and designer of unrealised potential. Surely Ford would not have worked with him if he had been anything less. In the 1960s, Ford let Allard sell his tweaked Anglia's and rarer Cortinas. From mud-plugging 1930s Allard Specials, to a GT car, Sydney was above all, a pure, classic, British motor industry talent of the very best type. His name should be more widely remembered and revered. Something more than a blue plaque is required.

7

Riley to Rootes

BMC and Badge Engineering

Perhaps one thing we can now say about British badge engineering of the 1960s, was that at least it meant that various Austin, Morris, MG and Riley badged bodyshells can now share spare parts – beyond their badges. The British Motor Corporation as BMC really excelled in mix and match, bodge and badge affairs. Some of these cars will appreciate in value. Riley's 1950s Pathfinder was a re-badged shared BMC bodyshell and as such was not a 'real' Riley after arguably the last independently designed and produced Riley, the RM-series of 1945, had died. But the new BMC Riley Pathfinder varietal *did* at least have its own unique Riley engine. Were 'real' Rileys last seen in the 1930s? Some might say so, some might not, not least as the late 1940s did indeed see the last real Riley-derived car as the RM series, but looking back, can it not be seen that Riley was one of the greatest and most innovative British car brands?

Anyone in doubt about the excellence of the Riley, might wish to recall that none other Robert 'Bob' Lutz – auto industry luminary who has led at BMW, Ford, Chrysler and GM – chose to own a Riley 1935 MPH two-seater convertible for over fifty years. Given that the man had access to any car he wanted and was a qualified jet pilot, his choice of a Riley for his personal enjoyment and statement is significant. One thing I do know is that if today we look back at the BMC-based Riley Pathfinder and imagine a Trilby-hatted old codger wafting along in a melange of tweed and decay, then we have got the wrong Riley. Prior to such stereotypes of BMC Rileyism, there was a different world of Riley cars and drivers. So, forget badge-engineered Pathfinders and the execrable Mini-based Elf and Hornet and focus upon *real* Rileys. For imperial progress with skirts gathered up and a cabin of faux Edwardian wood, try an Armstrong Siddeley Sapphire. Rileys were the more sporting saloons that, if the marque had been correctly managed, might have given a post-war BMW something to think about as an 'ultimate driving machine'.

Is Riley a sleeping thoroughbred, best left undisturbed? At least its dignity remains intact and not subject to an affair such as that of the Rover 75 of recent years. However, perhaps we can we agree that of all the 'retro' branding exercises,

Riley may have been best forgotten to avoid such a retro-pastiche fate in the twenty-first century?

Prior to 1939, Riley had it all, sporting pedigree, salon elegance, pure engineering, and sheer style. Quite how Riley got lost and then got forgotten, stupidly constrained to the parts-bin of history, is a bizarre and sad tale of typically British mismanagement. Riley, bicycle and light car makers of Coventry from 1898, had a long heritage starting with cycles, tricycles and a voiturette. By 1908, Riley was building 2.0l engined cars. 2.9 litres was a highlight but after the Great War, Riley developed high-output and very efficient 1.5 or 'Riley 1½ litre' engine. It was Riley who patented demountable wire wheels and sold them to nearly 200 car makers the industry emerged into the great age of motoring. Riley engineered its own engines, chassis and bodies, Percy and Stanley Riley being in direct charge of the company's expansion after the First World War. Riley boasted large capacity side-valve engines with hemispherical combustion chambers and twin-camshafts placed high in the block. The valves were inclined and much thought had gone into the engine porting characteristics. A high-revving engine with good torque for its capacity was the key to creating sporting cars with performance with the late-1920s fabric-bodied Monaco saloon being particularly successful.

From Riley's Redwing four-seater to the two-seat Imp which in 1934 was so stylish, to the revered Nine, to later cars with engineering touched by names like Railton and Parry Thomas, through a range of cars of the 'Thirties, Rileys were a massive brand and a hugely respected. They were seen at Brooklands (winning the 1934 British Racing Drivers Club 500-mile endurance event) and major British and European race locations. Rileys got larger and heavier and sold as gentleman's sporting cars such as the Lynx 9, yet Riley also created cars like the Sprite two-seater. From entries in the Monte Carlo Rally to finishing fourth at Le Mans in 1933 and second and third in 1934, Rileys were famous. A powerful 1½ litre Riley-designed engine that was reliable and had an excellent long-stroke torque delivery formed the basis of not just Rileys, but Riley-engined other marques; Frederick Dixon was the man behind the tuning and development of Riley engines that influenced ERA single-seaters.

1930s highlights included the 'aerolined' (as Riley termed its version of streamlining) Kestrel series and Monaco model with lowered floor and cabin between the chassis. The Kestrel in its 1933, 14/6 Mk1 sports saloon iteration could in terms of its engineering and design, be said to be Britain's top sports saloon of the time, with the proven Riley Nine six-pot in-line engine, at 1.4 or 1.6 litres respectively, a four-speed gearbox for relaxed cruising and a 'low-rider' chassis to improve the handling. By 1936, the Kestrel had an optional, smaller, new engine as a four-cylinder 1.4 litre and, whichever engine was chosen, a new, curved fastback body that was and remains, oh-so elegant. Details from the Riley Sprite roadster were also added to create a fast, sports saloon with the crisp handling to match. Was this, almost a 1930s 'Air-line' style, touched with an Art Nouveau derivative of the more Art Deco inspired Kestrel Mk1? Some observers think so and we can certainly see a British interpretation of mid-1930s 'aero' design themes. The swept and drooped lines leading to a down sweep for the rear side windows create an emotional statement, a graphic that was so clever. The 1936 Kestrel MkII is just so quintessentially English. Throw in an RAF officer's uniform, a black Labrador and a willowy woman in a headscarf and they and the Riley seem to encapsulate an era amid a vignette from lots of films you may have never seen. Underneath the show, the Riley was also, go. Wasn't this the best upper-middle class British sporting saloon for years past and years future?

Four and six-cylinder Riley engines powered the large Riley saloons of the late-1930s – notably the Falcon range. A confusing range of model names gave us the Riley Adelphi, Stelvio, MPH, and an array of engines ranging from 1.5, 1.7, 2.5 four and six-cylinder units, and a V8. Riley also produced the two aerodynamic Kestrel fastbacks to great acclaim and it is these that are now the rare and favoured models amongst many Riley aficionados. At the time of their manufacture, these cars excelled over the contemporary saloons and fastbacks of the day, even if they did lack the new-fangled steel unitary bodies and relied on old wooden coachbuilding skills. And weren't Riley's a cut above the MG?

Riley's pre-selector gearboxes had ushered in a new relaxed driving era, and yet Riley had also remained a major name in motor racing. Sadly, such diverse production and design abilities led the company to financial impediment on the grounds of engineering and tooling costs. This wonderful family firm, an absolute hallmark of 1930s British brilliance, was absorbed into the William Morris Nuffield Group in 1938. After the hiatus of the Second World War, Riley's open-tourer the RMC three-seater had stunning lines with cut-away doors and many were sold in America. Riley built 507 of the RMC as a two-door convertible, but then built 502 RMD saloons and a cleverly re-engineered 'drop-head' cabriolet-type folding fabric roof. The 1945 Riley 1.5 saloon and RM series of up to 2.5litres (from 1947) are perhaps best seen in two-tone paint and in final 1954 run-out series specification, devoid of running boards and given smoothed-in 'pontoon' type bodywork. The RM had independent front suspension and the more direct rack and pinion type steering and an age of worm and roller preference. These cars were the last true, timber-framed Riley-family influenced outcome prior to Riley engines being transplanted into badge-engineered steel unitary Morris bodyshells for the Morris-Austin-MG-Wolseley merged British Motor Corporation (BMC) of the mid-1950s. The Riley name was latterly ill-advisedly stuck onto the Mini – the last iteration of a great marque. We can surely be thankful that in the Honda and BMW eras of Rover ownership, Riley's name which had rested within the Rover group and the rights that went with it, was not debased by a shared-platform or parts-bin retro-themed car.

Riley truly was revered and not just within Britain's island shores. So highly rated was the marque that overseas sales were strong. Of peculiar interest was that in 1949, Swiss carrossier Walter Köng drew up an idea for an exotic targa-type-roofed two-door grand touring coupé based upon the chassis of no less than the Riley RM, known as the 'Transformable'. The car's creator wanted to shape something modern and aerodynamic and the resulting special 'one-off' looks distinctly American in its style and, in its girth and multi-channelled, multi-panelled form, is unlikely to be as aerodynamic as its designer hoped. Indeed, the 'Transformable' looks as if it came off a 1950s Hollywood film set, having just driven in from Palm Springs by a suited driver wearing a hat, accompanied by a blonde with something else on her mind.

That the famous car man, Bob Lutz, owned and loved a Riley Nine, says much about the abilities and quality of the car. Innes Ireland raced one, and today, the Nines remain hugely popular. Yet perhaps we should recall that in the post-war Riley rival, the 1948 Wolseley 6/80 was a tarted-up Morris 1000 with the Morris Six's extra length but wrapped up in an illuminated badge, a 'woodie' interior and a strange steering mechanism that defied logic or accurate piloting. So, what was good for Wolseley, was good for Riley – so said BMC. From 1953 to 1957, the BMC parts-bin-based Riley Pathfinder had a lovely Riley-designed 2.5 litre four cylinder unit of excellent torque characteristics and of twin-cammed response. The styling, or should we say, the generic BMC design, was modern, unadorned and still timeless into the 1960s. The man responsible was Gerald Palmer, a Rhodesian who had worked for Morris, Jowett (creating the post-war Javelin) and then BMC, where his ensuing car design work was as elegant and clean lined as any Pininfarina shape that BMC later went to Italy to secure. Indeed, might we suggest a touch of Lancia and Pininfarina about Palmer's designs for the Riley Pathfinder? Yet the Pathfinder's body was a generic theme applied across the BMC badge engineering party. Palmer latterly moved to Vauxhall's design department, where his intuitive 'aero' knowledge was given less freedom than it had been at Jowett and MG. Little known, is the fact that an ex- Lancia designer, Riccardo Burzi was working within Austin and BMC in the 1950s and he penned the Rubenesque wheeled sculptures of post-war Austin that contrasted with Palmer's cleaner-lined and somewhat Farina-esque elegance.,

Riley Pathfinders, (tagged 'Ditchfinders' if they had the Mk1 rear suspension set-up) even though they were BMC-derived, now sell in good condition for around £10,000, which seems to have become the entry point for many 1950s-1960s classics in a reasonable state and not requiring re-shelling or massive amounts of money to be spent. 'Proper' Rileys in restored state sell for anything from £20,000 to higher figures. Rebuilding the steel and wood of arguably the last 'real' Rileys – the RM series, suddenly seems a worthwhile proposition.

How many people recall that as the 1950s ended, a bunch of BL designers and engineers who had worked for the ERA company as it was absorbed into BMC – which itself had commissioned ERA to develop a new car design, would shape a rear-engined car of somewhat Issigonis character? Fed up with BMC's machinations the design team would decamp to the Rootes car company and there, design a large four-door saloon that had shades of the BMC Austin/Morris/Wolseley 1800/2200-series Landcrab. Curiously, this Rootes beast, intended to be labelled as the 'Swallow' (a most inappropriate name given the cars lack of curves and ellipsis), was rear-engined, angular yet clean-lined and built up from a base unit 'flat-floor' floorpan with very thin roof pillars. As such, it resembled a cross between a bloated (Rootes) Hillman Imp and an amalgam of Volkswagen and Citroën themes. Created by an engineering team led by David Hodkin, with Jack Channer, Richard Brown and with Rex Fleming as lead stylist, the car was far better than history records. And the early design proposals for this new Rootes large car were front-engined, transverse configured affairs. But along the way, the rear-engined small car from Rootes, the Imp, acted as a marker and management went with a larger version of that concept as a big rear-engined saloon for the late 1960s?

What were they thinking of — GM and the Corvair? Tatra, VW, NSU? Perhaps Renaults of old? In hindsight, it seems weird that top car industry men should have been suggesting such blind alleys in 1963, so close to the dawn of the great decade of car design 1965-1975, yet such words should not undermine the ideas within the Rootes Swallow. The Swallow was killed off in late 1963, as Rootes faced financial issues. In its place came the four-door 'Arrow' range. [Ref 1] Yet the Swallow and its ilk, convey the essential magic of the cars of that era through their design and its excellence. And then there was the Hillman Imp, surely the Citroën AX or Fiat Panda (Mk1) of its day.

The Rootes Swallow story provides an example of the behind the scenery of engineering and design that populates classic car history.

Futurism Denied

History is subject to the whims and opinions of those who write it. The victors have control of the epilogue of conflict. Is this why current views on the highs and lows of the British Motor Corporation and its outcome as the combination that was the BLMC and finally, as British Leyland and then Austin Rover Group, are so biased? Yet failures and bizarre decision do abound in the BMC-BL merger story.

It is easy to slag off BL's cars of the 1970s and 1980s, but at their worst, were their 'crimes' no greater than those of the output from Fiat, Renault, Citroën or maybe even Ford? And what of BL's best? Or the best bits of BL's so-called baddies?

Well, BL soldiered on with MGBs that they put on stilts with horrid black plastic protuberances. They spent money on re-skinned Mk4+ Marinas and titivated Maxis and, with inherited Triumph 1500s/Toledos and Dolomites, cars that shared the same body but offered differing rear-driven and front-driven drivetrains across all three variations! Think of the production costs. Then came the chance of the new and the offer from Pininfarina of two cars – one large, one medium-small and both of aerodynamic form. This was the 'Aerodinamica' suggestion, a design for a large (and a smaller sibling) streamlined car by Pininfarina's Messrs L. Fioravanti and P. Martin then resident at Carrozzeria PininFarina,Torino. But this chance was refused and a tamer course was taken by the men of the BLMC. Even that alternative course was then diluted by bean counters and men in suits. Latterly, BL having 'wasted' millions on a design called SD2 – a replacement for the tired Triumph range – then cancelled it and 'bought' a car design from Honda in order to create a Triumph Dolomite range replacement as just another chapter in the badge engineering that had become a BL ethos and perhaps BL's own personality disorder. Prior to that, there was a saga of shared components and wheezing old engines, of revamped Mk4, series five, tart-ups and of wasted potential.

Yet hidden in the story was the use by BMC and BL in its cars of self-levelling hydrostatic and hydragas suspension, early use of the hatchback, high torsional rigidity and a distinct 1970s 'wedge' styling theme amongst other innovations. Alec Issigonis, Harry Webster, Harris Mann, and many more lurk within the tale. Add in the effects of British Government policy towards BMC and then BL as a merged late-1960s entity entering the 1970s amid a revolving door of chairmen or chief executives and the BL story becomes a sad tale of what could have been, but never would be. The effects of merging Britain's car marques into one overall 'brand', with all the competing needs and demands of its sub-brands designs, sales and dealers, was doomed from the start – wasn't it? And amid such events, died

Riley, Wolseley, and eventually MG, Triumph and Rover. Here lies the great motoring history of the Midlands and the legacy of successive British Governments of alternating political hues and consistent failures: today, derelict buildings and workers lives lie in memoriam to a Midlands motor industry culture that is no more.

What of that easy 'Leyland-bashing' story – the Allegro? In fact, it was a car which, although it is currently fashionable to 'knock', was in reality, far better than more recent opinions have allowed. It rode well, steered with aplomb, looked 'new' and in tuned up, larger-engined versions, had decent performance. The 'flat-backed' practical estate variant was not as bizarre as its looks might suggest; it was in fact a worthy hold-all that gave excellent service to many families. No other car maker offered a medium-sized car of such space and ability in the market sector. And Allegro rusted at a slower pace than French and Italian offerings and was no more of an oddity than for example, the Renault 14.

The original Allegro as designed – a smarter and leaner device, could have taken on Citroën, Peugeot and VW and ensured a far more profitable outcome for BL; Correctly engineered, Harris Mann's Allegro *original* design could and should have wiped the floor with Europe's car makers. But in Allegro's reality, the brilliant and futuristic design for Allegro was fiddled with and that increased its girth. A higher front wing/bonnet line was enforced due to the engines used and appalling build quality was standard. The potential winner that was Allegro, became a beast of burden to its owners and perhaps, to its talented designer. Yet Allegro was 'sprung' with BL's excellent 'hyrdogas' system, not old steel springs, and contained several advanced design ideas. The senior managements' choice of a squared off 'quartic' steering wheel was seized upon as a marketing idea, then dismissed as a gimmick. For the want of more modern engines, the original sharper styling, a hatchback, and an interior devoid of excreta hues, Allegro might have saved British Leyland and opened a new dawn. The potential as a pioneering supermini-class design was there. Some say it was a blob of a car. Others can see that it was at least fresh and new.

Sadly, Allegro was quite literally 'dumbed down' and became yet another example of cheapest cost, highest yield, thrown-together BL car production of cast-iron blocked, vinyl-roofed short term myopia. You could hardly blame it on the designer or the workforce, however 'Red' the factory floor men may or may not have been. Still, the Allegro 1750 Sport went well and was nowhere near as bad as the court of public opinion as led by the media, latterly claimed. From two-door, four-door, and estate variants, Allegro provided a complete range, but somehow, through no fault of its designer, it missed the target. If it had had a hatchback, imagine the fuss! The motoring media lauded the AlfaSud, yet they drove new, press cars, they did not get to see what happened to a newly-purchased AlfaSud just one year into its life and after one British winter. I did, and it made Allegro look like a Merc! AlfaSud simply disintegrated – internally and externally, bodily and shoddily. But history prefers the AlfaSud, and it did indeed drive wonderfully, for as long as it lasted!

Sadly, some of BL's men in Birmingham seemed to have a fetish for brown paint, brown vinyl and, side stripes. Throw in spot lamps and, if brown did not appeal, a vomitesque shade of puce for the paintwork, and poor old Allegro was burdened at birth with such anti-design accoutrements. The car was trimmed up to have pensioner appeal, not youthful brightness; a Vanden Plas version with a hideous front grille, seemed just to encompass the evils of badge engineering and an almost Soviet act of standardisation stemming from sterilisation.

If it had been properly finished and hatchbacked, the Allegro could have been BL's VW Golf, or a GS and AlfaSud challenger – with all that could have followed. It did not happen and so was lost BL and, so too was gone, wider fame for the talented visionary for its designer that is Mr Mann – yet another unsung hero of the genius of British design. Citroën persevered with 'design', although it too, failed to provide build quality – a nemesis that eventually came home to roost. VW and Toyota fare of the 1970s achieved build quality and made more friends, yet could not be said to be cars of advanced design – more of refined design ideas finally put in into practice. Meanwhile Ford was still churning out its cheap-as-chips Escorts with their own brand of penny-pinching trim – but shinier.

BL's clever Mr Mann had worked for Commer and Ford on commercial and car products, notably contributing to the Capri and Escort Mk1. He followed Ford lead designer Roy Haynes to BMC and BL, having left, Mann then worked in wider industrial design creating shapes for trains, motorcycles, trucks, buses. The grandson son of an express steam locomotive driver (the LMS *Royal Scot* no less), and immersed in British industrial heritage, Mann could have offered British car design a new beginning, but his talent was subsumed amid the BL mindset of the era. Mann could have shaped great European cars maybe even big Citroëns; his design for the BL Princess range evidencing such futuristic requirements of style, scale, and aerodynamics. But it was not to be and another great British designer, Trevor Frost, known as Trevor Fiore, became the man who ended up being the English chief stylist at Citroën design in the 1980s. Harris Mann's name is unknown to many households, yet there is irony in the fact that he designed the most popular and most enduring, moulded plastic, garden watering can ever made!

Today, Allegros have their followers, and motoring writer Richard Gunn is known for his tastes in old BL cars (and Saabs). Gunn's driveway is littered with beached BL-era cars, none more evocative than the puce-hued Allegro two-door that he clearly adores. His colleague, James Walshe, as assistant editor at *Practical Classics*, is known for his passion for old Citroëns, but he too has the BL 'thing' – a lovely blue Maxi being his daily driver. Walshe says that Maxi is the 'forgotten game -changer'. Many men and women who read the words of the likes of Gunn and Walshe, also have a love affair with the cars of the idiosyncratic, yet essential, BL and a unique era of car design. And, if BL was not your thing, then what about an Escort Mk1, a Hillman Imp or a Sunbeam Stiletto?

Surely the old BMC originated, Issigonis legacy that was the Maxi, was brilliant in all but its austerity trim and cable-operated gearbox. Renault's 16 might have looked flashier and been more deluxe, but it was flimsier (having a lower torsional stiffness rating than the Maxi) and rusted. Maxi was a stiff-hulled old sod born of its ancestor – the ADO 17 or 1800 range – the use of that car's doors so hobbling Maxi's styling potential. Maxi soldiered on through several reiterations, even gaining plastic bumpers and colour keyed add-ons. Yet Maxi was old even when new and Donald Stokes ordered it to be facelifted *before* it was launched; a less old fashioned front end was added. And it seems that its development into a more modern car took place after it had gone on sale! Customers were the guinea pigs. Soon, a rod-operated gearchange replaced the launch cars cable affair. Launched in 1969, Maxi was still on sale in 1980 as a modernised and velour lined holdall of peculiar attraction to certain buyers. Geography teachers loved them. No matter, fold all the seats down and sleep easy. Other activities in the back of a Maxi were not unknown. Vinyl can tell many stories.

But even the Maxi's seats were 1950s throwbacks and such a contrast to the advanced seats Volvo or Renault offered at the time. Like later BMC/BL offerings, the essentials were right, so clever, yet utterly hobbled by what some say was an Issigonis legacy for clever but 'simple' low cost engineering. The idea of cabin comforts, sculpted seats with headrests, a slick gear change, fuel injection, alloy wheels, a centre console, or anything other than round headlamps set in a chrome weave of a grille, were an anathema to the apparent austerity 'rules' of BL. Maxi was so constrained, yet the later, BL wedge-shaped 18-22 series Princess *did* throw off such austere thinking and go 'deluxe' for the 1970s. But Maxi *was* front-driven, transverse-engined, gas-fluid suspended and hatch-backed. So, Maxi *was* advanced but it just did not look like it. The engines, the gearbox and the trim, let it down, down into a singular and peculiarly British homage to a past era of beige and brown, British Rail sandwiches, Liquorice Allsorts, and steamed up windows on rainy days amid rumpled corduroy and damp duffel coats.

The later BL designs of Harris Mann solved the 'design' problem and created a 'wedge' look whose effect we might compare with the 'carved' design motifs of Mr Bangle at BMW decades later. Like Bangle, Mann did not follow fashion, he set it. His original and stunning sketches for the Princess reek of a new age and a new style that was anything but derivative. Likewise, Mann's real Allegro design was lean and stylishly European. But it got hobbled by committees. Once again, if only …

We will never know why BL ruined the advanced art of the 1970s Princess range by larding it up with horrid faux-grilles and chromework, not least in its Wolseley branded guise. Why wasn't 'Hydragas' further developed and made of 'active' suspension design? So much was there for the taking and yet discarded, not least in quality faults that stemmed from the Cowley production lines and penny-pinching costings. Yet in BL's 18-22 Princess, notably the Austin branded variant, there could be found a visually advanced British car; underneath its skin lay aspects of elegant engineering, so the 1970s Princess, especially in Austin 'HLS' trim, could have taken on Europe's big saloons, notably those of Citroën and Renault. And could the Princess estate have competed with those of Volvo and Ford? But BL could not afford to build it. So none of it was to be.

Oh, for a ha'penny of tar!

BL applied its old, cheapest common denominator thinking, applied old engines (newer O-series units only belatedly being installed), old build standards and old ideas of trim and fittings to brilliant design, thus consigning the Princess to the dustbin of a vinyled and oily history, via a typically British face-lifted iteration named 'Ambassador' that belatedly gave the car the hatchback it should always have had. Ambassador truly was the last obvious, Austin Drawing Office 'ADO' car. BL reputedly spent £30million developing the Ambassador out of the old Princess, chopping a hatch hole in the rear then restoring torsional rigidity and lowering the front bonnet and wing lines – oh and adding a window in the rear pillars; this was complex and expensive re-tooling. This time BL's big car was made in just one version; no more with three different front ends as with Princess! This time it had alloys, luxury trim and it still had massive cabin space and great comfort. They made just 43,3000 Ambassadors and today, less than twenty remain roadworthy. More Maestros and Montegos remain extant than BL's near-extinct Ambassador. Back in its day, Cavaliers and Sierras would wipe Ambassador out, not least as company cars for be-suited 1980s salesmen. Yet Ambassador was a character car and a good one, yet which, like Rover's SD1, marked the end of a distinct period in British car design and ownership. There came the 'three-box' mindset, for saloon bar salesmen preferred the likes of the Ford Granada and its own Mk2 version of an already decade-old design yet one so cleverly re-skinned by Ford's top design guru Uwe Bahnsen.

As a design, BL's early 1970s Morris Marina was perfectly contemporary and 'new' yet it too was hobbled (in the true sense) by its ancient front suspension inherited from the BMC cost-cutter parts-bin. Using Morris Minor top-arm lever suspension parts in Marina had created a chronic understeerer, notably in the 1.8 litre heavier-engined versions. Both *Autocar* and, *Motor,* came close to labelling the Marina's handling as suspect, but behind-the-scenes, changes were made to camber angles in the suspension and, opinions were, shall we say, 'modified'.[Ref 2] That BL should keep Marina, first designed in 1967, on into its Mk3 guise and into the 1980s was an indication of an inability to command itself. Wasting millions turning the old and tired 'stop-gap' Marina Mk 3½ into the Ital was surely a crazy decision then, and remains so, now. Why on earth *did* BL pay millions to Guigario to fit a 'plug in' black slatted front grille, headlamp and bumper valance, new rear lamps, and a chrome 'disguise' trim kit around the side windows, to the dead-on-its wheels Morris Marina? Given that BL's own Harris Mann had designed a 'posh' revised Marina Mk4 (perhaps a Vanden Plas?) which was drawn up in-house and ready, paying millions to an external designer instead, to 'design' a black grille and some moulded plastic, seems utterly bizarre. And who knows what Guigario thought of BL using his 'Ital' name for the fiddled-with-Marina in 1980. BL also spent millions on a still-born Marina replacement too – the ADO77 a larger, plusher, more technically advanced, O-series engined car for the 1980s and that was binned as well and Marina soldiered on to its Ital death notice. ADO77 and the Triumph SD2 proposal both died as cash was scarce and nationalisation ruled the accountants' roost. One car (or none) would have to fit all across BL's myriad of marques. So came more design and prototyping, all to be cast to the memories of BL's mad moments. Incredibly, BL's later proposals were rear-wheel drive, despite the front-driven fetishism of the Mini, 1300, 1800, Maxi, and Allegro. A strange outcome yet it was not unique – after all, as GM readied its new front-wheel drive Ascona/Cavalier Mk2 for the 1980s, Ford was putting ancient rear-drive technology under the skin of its so-called futuristic, slippery Sierra. This was the car hailed by Ford and its Bob Lutz at its launch as a bright new future, as nothing less than the reinvention of the car. I know, because I was there, standing next to the man and Lutz would have none of it when the press pointed out the rear-wheel-drive set up, fuel tank under the rear end, and other 'old' technology that had been wrapped in a new 'aero' suit. And what about Citroën and Saab aerodynamics! Ford's marketing machine made Sierra a success – but not without some post-launch tweaking and the 'XR' developments.

There were other BL cars whose 'design' was 'lost' amid the torpor and the turbulence of BL's 1970s political lifestyle and its deployment of strategic irrationality. Many factors were at play, yet for the want of a bit more planning, BL could have been a huge 1980s success and a global earner.

Instead, BL gave us the MG Metro 6R4 and then topped itself and with that went the cars, the designs and the careers of some of the most talented British engineers and designers in the business.

But then the remains of BL became Austin Rover Group and gave us the front-driven LC/LM 10 types that were Maestro and its Montego derivative. Maestro turned out to be much better than expected or stated, but it too was poorly finished in a factory where morale was low and tempers short. My Maestro had a brilliant Perkins diesel engine and did 60mpg, but rust ate at the sills in months. Of the Metro minus a five-speed gearbox or safety enhancements and its reincarnation as Rover 100? Well, hindsight reveals that it was an obvious and typical BL 'moment' – one damned by events.

Did it all begin to go wrong in the 1970s when BL was unable, due to a series of circumstances, to cash-in on the great boom in car sales and car design? Blaming one man or one car is unfair. But the facts were that BL was unready and some its people were unwilling. Turmoil and torpor gripped other car makers too. Yet as with all things in the BMC-to-BL story, it came down to money, the lack thereof and the competing priorities of a multi-branded, multi-party organisation as a state-influenced entity. We might want to lay the same charges at the Peugeot-Talbot affair and its Sunbeam hatchback for the 1980s – underneath it was a twenty year-old car – the Hillman Avenger – even sharing its front doors and the drivetrain.

What of BL's Harris Mann? He also sculpted the TR7 – which was far more radical than its reputation allowed and in its day, an advance in terms of design, engineering, safety and comfort. Buy now before they all die. And there was a V-8 and a lovely coupé version of TR7; the 'Lynx' was planned and its prototype is on display at the British Motor Museum at Gaydon. Lynx was a four-seater coupé of great style and a unique offering that would have sold in massive numbers in America and Europe. Sadly still-born, Lynx was another case of BL and, 'if only'. That the Italian stylist Michelotti would contribute to the TR7 coupé projects shortly before his death, remains a hidden tale in the last days of the once great Triumph marque. TR7 could also have spawned SD2 – a new upper class Triumph based on TR7 underpinnings, engines and running gear; it was also developed at some expense, yet abandoned. The amicable Harris Mann later worked on the MG ZT and for BMW, also to teach at Coventry University's transportation design course. TR7 also gave birth to 'Project Broadside', another suggested coupé derivative and one that used Rover SD1 rear panels to save money. It looked bulbous and was abandoned on financial grounds.

We can also cite the MG XX, the Mini 9x and the various MG replacement prototypes also on show at the museum. Can BL and its legacy, the designers, or its workers, be blamed for the failure to get these cars into production? Of course not. Management (and the government) was in charge and Lord Stokes choices were just the precursor to a series of 1970s and 1980s decisions that were regrettable and at times, the unavoidable outcome of meddling by too many. Even the uncomfortable rational reality of BL's Michael Edwardes, failed to save the day for an industrial liner of a company that was already too far off course to be saved. As proof, we should remember that at the height of the 1970s-1980s car sales boom, the combined market share of Rover and Triumph in its own homeland of Britain was in 1976, a pitiful 1.6 per cent. There had to be a reason why. Jaguar too, was tainted with BL build quality and the lack thereof, but luckily Sir John Egan saved the marque and its reputation.

Meanwhile, Datsun, Honda, and Toyota as well as VW and Renault, made the inroads into our motoring that are now their achievements – not just the hopes they then were. Who can blame them.

8

The Porsche Passion

Elegance of Function and an Addiction

'911' is the magic number for the Porsche enthusiast and its appeal is undiminished, yet 911 has, in the opinion of some, morphed into something different. The problem is that the Porsche profile and Porsche 911 prices have gone through the roof and off into the madness of extra-terrestrial logic. But that is ok, because my nice clean, Porsche 944 2.7 in Grand Prix white cost me less than £5,000 and was to coin a trade phrase, a 'minter'. It may not have Hans Mezger's wailer of an engine design, but it can only ascend in value. To the purist, a front-engined device like a lithe little 924, or the very slightly more padded 944 and 968, can never be 'proper' Porsches. 'Van engines' are cited for 924s but the truth is that the 924 did *not* borrow a VW van engine – the 924 (and the much-modified motor in a VW van) stemmed from the engine in the luscious Audi 100 coupé. It is also easy and fashionable to decry the mid-engined air-cooled Porsche 914 and 914/6, but they too deserve more respect for their essential correctness, which was maligned by marketing and snobbery. As a VW-Porsche, only just under 120,000 were sold from 1969-1977. If any car qualifies as being the most misunderstood, the 914 is it; the concept of the 'entry level' Porsche is still with us too.

So, who are the purists to prescribe rectitude from a self-appointed position of ego where apparently lesser beings must be told to change their opinions and thoughts to match those of the preacher ? I mean, Porsche, it's not a religion, *is* it?

On second thoughts …

Of *course* I would purchase a 1970s 911 or a 'Pre-A' series 356, but I haven't got the price of large house lying about in petty Porsche cash. If *you* have, good for you. Purists, of course, would also object to the re-manufactured retro-look 911s produced by Autofarm, Paul Stephens, or Singer. Personally, I think they are fantastic and do not dilute, but enhance, access to the 911 and its merits in a sensible and rational way at accessible prices depending on your means. One of Mr Dickinson's zingining Singer 911/964 re-imaginings with 390bhp (or more) delivering 0-60mph in 3.3 seconds, would surely touch the spot – but should it be orange, or blue? Do I really waste my time dreaming of such moments and decisions. Like so many, I do, which I suppose, is rather sad; my wife just rolls her eyes and thinks, *oh no not Porsches again!* Then she shuts me in my study and leaves me to my Porsche mistress and my dreams of a faded ambition to design one – the sketching never ceases.

So what *is* it about Porsche that engenders the passion, the obsession and the current marketing-speak rubbish that goes with the Stuttgart legend? Can a lump of metal really result in an emotional attachment? It seems it can. But we are not talking about all Porsches here. Aren't we talking about old Porsches, not new ones? Now, to be clear, there is *nothing* wrong with a new Porsche and yes, I want one. But I want something balanced, small and nimble, not an over-sexed, wide-bodied barge laden with barnacles of trims, blings and a mulch of plastic, faux alloy and electric-trickery. I want a real Porsche, not an ersatz Porsche fit for the boulevard. So, my *new* Porsche would be a Cayman (GT4) – the hidden gem of the marque and the car that outshines the 'halo' branding of the 911. Is this heresy? Probably, but you see, the problem is that 911 is now obese, short-nosed, and larded with the accoutrement of celebrity. There is little wrong with it, but the *purity* as gone. Now, a 911 is turbo-only – so you cannot get a naturally aspirated 'wailer' *unless* you can get hold of a new 911 R – which is unlikely this side of the price of a flat in London's Docklands. Of course, the new 911 R with the GT3's non-turbo engine does answer the criticism to a degree, and no, I would not turn one down. But wouldn't you rather have the 997 GT3RS 4.0 litre?

Even a water-cooled 996 – the controversial Pinky Lai design, or a late model 'old' 997 – could provide a sniff of the real Porsche 'ism'. Oh, and there is the little matter of the new 991's electro-mechanical steering. It is not until you compare it to the old fully metalled mechanical set up that you realise what has been lost.

Some of us Porsche fans were not too bothered about the change from air-cooled to water-cooled – because the 'flat-six' still wailed. But now, the steps are too much. Turbo-only robs the engine of sound and lightness of pace, making it too smooth; electro-steering robs the 911 experience of its sexual tactility. To me, the PDK automated gearbox makes a car feel like a play station and sound like a snappy and rude one at that. But that's just my opinion, and may not be yours.

But the new 991 R proves my point, with Porsche desperate to regain some marketing ground.

'Oh, no, the last *real* 911 was the 964 series,' I hear you say, you wretched purist, but surely a 993 was the apogee of Porkerism?

No!

What of the 1950s 550 A or the 1960s 904/6? Were they not the last true race-to-road lithe little Porsches? Some may say, others will argue loudly that later Porsches are just as capable.

Look, each to his own. And what is wrong with the 928? Big it may well be, but it has the style, the sense of occasion, the great, last-of-the-grand tourers feel about it; 928 is the other forgotten gem. But back to my new Porsche of choice. There are two brilliant Caymans – the GT4 at the top of the model range and, the 'pure' base model Cayman (as a manual gearboxed choice) with the smaller four-cylinder engine at the bottom of the hierarchy. Both are chuckable, smaller, involving, and utterly delightful. So, get a Cayman devoid of PDK gears, devoid of ultra-low profile wheels, devoid of bling, but just make it sapphire blue or carmine red with a two-tone leather interior. Give it normal wheels and make it manual with a sports short shift 'box. You will need the 14-way adjustable 'cradle' driver's seat too. But that is it.

Yes, yes, I know, they have electric steering …

Thus suitably equipped, Cayman, be it base model or GT4, we will set off onto the finest A and B roads of the back bye ways of England. But in doing so, won't the memory always be of a telepathic, classic 911, traversing the tarmac in the before rather than the afterwards?

Classic 911 'Historika' at Goodwood Members Day

Driving the Old Wailer

The journey was from Newbury to Marlborough and beyond, along the sweeping, open bends of the old Roman route of the A4, and then a diversion onto the lanes across the roof of Wiltshire. This has to be 'push on' Porsche country. Few other cars seemed so as if made for such a stretch.

Climbing in, the cockpit was just right, everything fitted. I became part of this 1973 911 in an instant. There was delicate yet durable quality to the fittings, and why was the shape, the motif of the windscreen somehow so, emotional? The floor-hinged pedals were perfect, the hip-hugging seats likewise. The three-spoke steering wheel, utter, total, perfection of design. This car has something, you *know* that from the second you sit in it.

Starting it up was a real occasion. *Whrrr, whrrr,* chatter but no clatter. Then it talked to me with that unique air-cooled, flat-six sound, not a throb, not a burble but perhaps a distant harmonic that turned into the wail of a siren calling you to seduction. A whirring of a soul, an engine that men get all emotional over from the moment the starter motor engages and the opposing punches of the horizontally opposed pistons being, not a fight, but a boxer's dance. I say a few words of thanks to the men behind the Porsche 901/911 engine design – as directed by Hans Tomala and Klaus von Rücker; the project leader was Leopold Jäntsche (ex-Tatra no less) and the design was engineered by chief engineer Ferdinand Piech and Hans Mezger, with Robert Binder, Horst Marchart, Helmutt Rombold, Hans Honick, and Helmuth Bott as lead contributors. [Ref 1]

As the oil and alloy temperatures rose, I eased away, gingerly at first, then out of Newbury through Speen and onto the A4, westward ho. Traffic lined up ahead doing 45mph but there was a gap and you could see for miles. The 911 was warmed up now, so I looked over my shoulder, got the all clear, dropped to third and pushed the pedal. The 911 breathed its induction sound then flexed its cylinders, was on the cam, then it truly wailed – *WHANG*. We shot past a line of four or five cars, the push from behind urging our capsule on as the decibels rose to that howl that can only be rivalled by the haunting melody of a Vickers VC10 venting the closing of reverse thrust from its Rolls-Royce Conways. 911 screamed again as I went into fourth, then we darted back in, the steering direct, precise, telepathic over the white lines painted on the road. You could even feel the change in the grade of the tarmac. Light rain meant the front end felt different on wet tarmac; the steering really was that good.

Expansive open bends with clear, long sight lines opened up towards Hungerford and then beyond, towards Marlborough. We scythed past slower traffic in a flash of curves and chrome as that flat six really heated up and began to scream and smell of hot oil. This car could be placed so perfectly, set up so easily; the thrill, the sound, the mechanism of driving was all here. A bob, a weave, a shuffle, real communication. Isn't all this missing from today's digital bang-and-burp electronic gearbox driven devices Only a Noble M15 driven on these roads matched the old Porsche's analogue charm; manual gears, real steering, proper tyres with enough ratio of rubber hysteresis to actually absorb a pot hole or a bump, real mechanical driving – not some electronic synthesis of adaptive this, digital that, fake-feel steering with an uncouth double clutch semi-auto snapping away as the reactive computer-signalled suspension dialled out reality. No synthetic exhaust sound being fed through speakers here! Instead, this was real driving.

Beyond Marlborough, on climbs and dips, through S-bends, she flew as if gliding, lifted up slightly off her haunches, only to get down at the rear as power was applied in a series of cut and parry manoeuvres as we darted out towards Devizes and Avebury, then to head back towards Swindon on the A360. We turned right and took the switch-back, S-bends of Rockley Hill as if we were on a German mountain. Power, turn, squeeze the trigger, whoosh, *WAIL,* gone. Soon afterwards we turned around and came back down that escarpment; the 911 leaned and twitched slightly, the power was kept on and she settled her bottom down into the second gear corner before powering out onto the flat plains below. The steering, the suspension, the revs and the torque, just for once, I got it all correctly synchronised and the Porsche rewarded with the drive that is like no other. I continued on across Wiltshire, then back towards Hungerford, Inkpen, Kintbury, then across the valley to Lambourn and the curves and cambers of country backways where a Porsche could sing. The 911 never threatened, never faltered. She got hot, and once I entered a bend a touch on the back foot and she felt like she might shuffle on me, but a prod of power and a minute dab of steering, saved the moment. Once, just once we got fast enough for that special Porsche-flying-on-wheels sensation to assail us. It was real, so real, and there was always that sound, that noise that seeps into your senses and can be heard still as you drift off to sleep at night.

This was the mechanical act of driving. Pure and almost simple – as Porsche intended. You get it now, don't you?

9

Old Saabs and Old Sods

What is it about old Saabs? What is it about the diversity of their owners? Whether it is a turtle-shaped 92, 92, 96, or more modern 99, or 900, these jewels of Swedish design and ethos, have a massive appeal across many races and nations. And the owners seem to come from all over the social spectrum too – from bow ties to turtle-knecked jumpers, from Loakes to Clarkes. From conservative to LGBT – but not MGBGT. Saabs are as loved in America as they are in Great Britain with a big following in the USA and club gatherings ranging from smart events to watching a dedicated enthusiast like Tom Donney race a Saab Sonett across the Bonneville salt flats to reach 115.6 mph on a two-stroke engine. In the Netherlands, Germany or Australia, old Saabs rule. There are Saab in Africa and on remote Pacific islands. Saab seemed to have touched the hearts and minds of many people of differing creed and personality construct. Above all, Saabs (especially the older ones) were true drivers' cars. Many people agree that early Saabs had the feel also found in early 1950s Porsches or Lancias, and perhaps in other lithe little cars that performed heroics on small capacity engines.

What is it about Saab owners? Therein lies true diversity. Some are bearded old sods – great company – others are smartly attired, some are Lefties and some are not. Brighton's Gay scene is packed with Saabist couples. The Queen of the Netherlands loved her Saabs, as did Prince Bertil of Sweden. Saab owners are all different. So are the cars. Vote Conservative? Vote Volvo! Then there were the Swedish (and other nationals) as rally drivers from Erik Carlsson and Gunnar Palm, Aman, Cederberg, Eklund, Haggboom, Hertz, Karlsson, Kronengard, Lampinen, Lohmander, Nottrop, Orrenius, Petterson, Raino, Stone, Svedburg, Svensson, Stromberg, Sylvan, Trana, Turner, Wehman, and modern hero Stig Blomqvist, all men who threw Saabs across the rallies of the world. Women rallied Saabs too – notably Greta Molander, Pat Moss Carlsson, Helga Lundberg, Elizabeth Nystrom, Margaretha von Esssen, and Ursula Wirth.

Who can forget dear old Erik Carlsson? What a man, a gentle giant, kind, rude, forthright, utterly honest, a man who helped others as well as having the ruthless touch of a winner. He was Saab, Saab was Erik. He was born at just the right time. To use a well-worn cliché that happens to be true, we shall not see his like again.

Saab also raced at Le Mans. In Uruguay, Saabs were locally built by Automotora and its director Jose Arijon was a well-known Saab rally driver in his 96. Hector Marcias Fojo and Torres de Ozaalso rallied in a 96 Sports. Saabs were rallied everywhere and took on, and beat, the greats. Today, old Saabs touch the hearts of many. At *Octane* magazine, two of the editorial staff run Saab 96s. At *Practical Classics* Saabs are also in the writers stable, as they are at Hemmings' *Sports and Exotic Car* in the USA. So, the Saab thing seems to transcend many opinions, types, and choices. The death of Saab was a tragedy of Shakespearian proportions, a long death with many players. I still cannot believe that it happened. Blaming one man is missing the point – many hands toyed with Saab's fate. I believe that Mr Muller had the right intentions, after all he is a Lancia fan too – its just that he might have underestimated the forces he was dealing with. There were many plots in the affair of General Motors, Muller, Saab and scene twenty, act ten of a tragedy. Despite the death of the Saab car company in its original form, Saab clubs thrive all over the world and Britain hosts the informal yet beloved, 'Swedish Day' in the depths of the West Country where Saabs from all over Europe congregate. At the Saab Museum in Trollhattan, the Saab spirit remains wonderfully alive and Mr Backstrom provides a rock of ages. In Poland, a large Saab movement exists and the efforts of the Saabist Krystof Rozenblat (of the Rozenblat Foundation) in keeping the spirit of Saab alive, demonstrate the love Poles have for Saab and its cars. Krystof is an amazing man, and his mesmerising daughter is a Saabist too. They both flew in to Britain for Erik Carlsson's memorial event, because to us Saabists, Saab transcends everything. If he had still been alive, one of Saab's biggest heroes and a wonderful chap – Robert Sinclair would have turned up too. Sinclair was Saab's top exponent in America and guided the brand to its US highlights and promoted the idea of a 900 convertible.

Scratch and Sniff

Old cars have a certain something. They smell different too. Of all the car smells, old Saabs seem to smell the strongest. The smell of Saab is something unique, it is a personal tale of odour. Old aeroplanes smell, every classic aviation enthusiast knows that. Sit in a Spitfire or a Messerschmitt 109 and the patina of leather, aluminium, bakelite plastic, oil, grease, and canvas, lends a tangible reek, an actual smell. The same whiff pervades the interiors of Catalina flying boats, Lancasters, Douglas DC 3s and just about any old aeroplane. Even old, first generation jetliners have a smell – think Boeing 707, DC-8, Comet or Caravelle or VC10. A whiff of analogue history pervades.

When it comes to cars however, the smell thing seems less defined. Yes, classic 1930s race cars reek, so too do 1960s Alfas, Lancias and Morris Minors. But some cars have no smell at all, not even old ones; when did you last scratch and sniff a 1980s Honda or a plastic lined Ford hatchback, you didn't because they don't pong. All of which begs the questions – why do old cars, and specifically, old Saabs have that unique, special smell and what is it? And is it something to do with aviation? To answer the questions, I took my mind way back to days of yore, when Saabs were Saabs and note genetically modified 'GM' varietals..

My first car was bought in 1981 and was a 1968 early model steel bumpered, Saab 99 two-door. It had that lovely cockpit style fascia with a toproll coaming that arced back into the door side panels. The clock was off a Saab 96 and there was chrome detailing on the seatbelt buckles and some very fungal vinyl in the cabin. Above all, there was the smell. The car had this really strong pong and it smelt just like my grandfather's Auster light aircraft, a sort of vintage eau du armpit mixed with stale canvas, cigar, oak, horsehair, alloy and an air of classic French polished woodwork. The Saab smelled.

It was not an off-putting odour, but it was a definite pong. My mate had a 96 V4 – a white one – and we both suddenly realised that both cars smelt the same. We could not work it out so we just put up with it. I sold the Saab for a fat profit and (somewhat idiotically) bought a Citroën GS. Years later we had a dog poo brown 1976 Saab 99 and that also had a smell, especially when the heated seats released years of pungent farts from the trap of their molecules. Hmm, was a previous owner a purveyor of curries we wondered? Even more years after that, I owned my classic 900 five door GLI in blue with blue trim. And you've guessed it, that smelt of Saab too. But along came a new generation, General Motors-built Saab 9-3 and an early 9-5 – and the smell was gone. I have always wanted to know why my old Saabs ponged and what the smell was. On visits to Sweden, no one at Saab knew what the smell was, but they all knew that Saabs had a smell: 'Oh yes, definitely, Saabs smell,' they would say in lovely sing song Svenksa speak, but, 'No, we do not know what the smell is.'

So, what *was* that smell? The answer, I believe, partly lies in a mix of low tech glues that were used to stick trim in all cars and aircraft up until the late 1970s. From the 1920s to 1970s, seats and trim were put together in the same way – stuffed, padded, tied, strung, and stuck. And the interiors of cars and aircraft were made of alloy, tinplate and mild steel – even dashboards were metal – albeit covered in lovely rubbery vinyl (kinky stuff I know). And then there were veneers of wood, of fake wood, and more spreads of the marmalade of glues that were car (and aircraft) interiors before slush moulded, toxic lumps of dashboards and trims were bunged into post-1980 cars and began their leach of nasty chemical compounds into your car and your body. The glues used in old cars and old Saabs would have been animal based and, let us hope that they were organically fed! Interiors had bare metal, plastic vinyl, chrome, carpets and seats that may well have contained horsehair and glass-fibre in a combined heady mix, topped off by the whiff of ancient Bakelite (younger readers will have to look Bakelite up…).

Even the last Saab to smell – the 900 Classic with its moulded trims, new dashboard and its headlining monster, combined some of the old world craft of interior trim artisanship. Throw in the effects of damp and, the fact that even the late model 900 Classics had wooden panels in the back end of the cabin – plywood for something's sake – and the smells created a list of ingredients just like a 1950s Saab. The mouldering plywood has got be the secret ingredient in the fragrance. I reckon the mix of the above, all brought together as only the Swedes can, is the reason why Saabs smell. Newer Saabs and newer cars in general, have none of this – it's all moulded micro pores and polycarbonates – with no bare metal to stroke and nothing organic to smoke. Which is why they do not smell like Saabs.

So, there you have it, a theory on why old classic machines, and notably old classic Saabs, smell. And I recently found almost the same effect in a 1950s Bristol. This smell affair is a wonderful, nostalgic mix of animal, metal, mineral, all blended and smeared together to create an aura like no other. Called to ordure, as they say…

Ellipsoid Elegance

Saab's 92 prototype, the 'Ursaab', framed an often forgotten yet vital moment in design. When the Saab 92 was launched in 1949, the motoring press freely admitted that so unusual was the car's appearance, that it was difficult to quantify its shape or pigeon-hole the design lineage. Even *Autocar* were shocked by the new themes of design that Saab's 92 invoked, suggesting that the shape resembled that of a small yet exotic sports coupé. Here was something new, a new design language that left the re-warmed pre-Second World War school of late 1940s car design in limbo. While many other car makers churned out cars with bit-part bodies, the strange, one-piece Swedish car boasted a rakishly inclined front windscreen angle, a domed roof with an exquisite sculptured shape that eased smoothly back into a tail section that resembled the aft end of a fuselage. The production Saab 92 as Saab's first car, stemmed directly from Ursaab as the prototype. Looking back, all Ursaab needs is the addition of an empennage and some chrome, to look like a

1960s American 'space-age' design study from GM's studio of Mr Earl, yet it was conceived in the early 1940s. Or was it Tatra-esque?

Tatra and Ledwinka echoing around the room again as they always will.

Ursaab was an integrated sculpture of utterly new form and in designer-speak, it had a strong 'DRG' the down-the-road-graphic – the visual impression the occasion of its passing creates. In the prototype, variously known as 'Ursaab' 'Exprwagen' or '92.001', Saab produced a blend of ideas that reflected a recent past that had not yet defined a future. That it was to be powered by small twin-cylinder engine and then a three-cylinder unit of simple, unburstable design, was a predictable curiosity.

How did this aero-weapon of a car with $C_D.0.32$ ($C_D.0.35$ in production design) suddenly emerge? Under that airflow-tuned skin, there was front wheel drive, a transverse engine, a flat floor and reinforced A-pillars and a built-in roll hoop. All this was years before the Mini and the Citroën DS claimed the plaudits for their respective claims to innovation. Like other cars of the era, the Ursaab was shaped by a sculptor, yet one who was a pilot and aerodynamics expert; Sixten Sason. The car was called by the Swedes a 'Vingprofil bil' – a wing shaped car. Ursaab contained themes of Art Deco, Modernism, and a touch of the L'Esprit Nouveau. Surely Le Courbusier would have seen the Ursaab as a piece of architecture that just happened to have wheels.

The Saab car idea stemmed from Saab's need to diversify as the end of the war would bring a downturn in its business. Saab aircraft engineer Gunnar Ljungström was the true 'father' of the Ursaab and its 92 offspring, and Sixten Sason was the designer who shaped the Ursaab at Ljungström's request. Rolf Mellde, the engine and handling specialist, came to Saab just as the 1946-drafted Ursaab was emerging into its productionalised form. Ljungström was a time-served car fanatic and engineer who also designed wings and hulls for Saab the aircraft maker – and was not Ursaab or 92.001 a wing on wheels?

F. Porsche's VW 'Beetle' may have been teardrop shaped, yet it was an aerodynamic nightmare of airflow and ill-defined airflow-separation-point issues. But Saab's teardrop was more aerodynamically accurate. Saab was unhindered by a previous psychology; Saab the car maker could start with a blank sheet of paper and new ideas. Saab was an aeroplane maker and research was vital, but the DKW link was intriguing, for DKW's small cars had sold well in Sweden in the 1930s, so the starting point for Saab was to be a memory of a pre-war German car of Danish provenance. Key to the Saab car project was Swedish car dealer and former DKW agent Gunnar V Philipsson. He signed a contract for 8,000 of the new cars, and invested 1.8 million Swedish Kroner into the project in advance.

Surely Saab, the aircraft maker could take the basic idea of a car concept, apply its aircraft design and engineering ethos and create something more modern? The first Saab car design remit stemmed from a management decision that the Saab car should be both faster and more economical than the DKW. This could only be achieved through aerodynamic design and an efficient engine. Thus was set the foundation of the Saab car ethos. Ljungström choose a teardrop, but one that was front-engined and front-driven, of the valveless two-stroke cycle that aped DKW and Heinkel works. The taut hull, low-roll angle handling and buzzy 25bhp/18KW two-stroke delivered an unheard of driving experience for the Swedes and the production version 92 was an overnight rallying success.

The metal thickness used in UrSaab/92 was over twenty per cent thicker than on any other contemporary car; the metal of the roof skinning was 1.11mm thick, the body side walls 0.87mm and the crucial, box-section steel sills were 1.59mm in thickness. In a unique, chassis-less aircraft fuselage inspired design, all apertures were reinforced, closely welded and riveted and the roof was a one piece pressing with no leaded joints. There was also no boot opening and through such techniques torsional rigidity was exceptionally high, reputed at 11,300lb/sqft, an incredible achievement against a then industry average of 2,000lb/sqft (and even a more recent 6,000lb/sqft). As comparison, the 'soft' Ford Cortina Mk1 had a torsional

Sixten Sason's early Saab 92 badged as a 'Sonett'

Saab 96 as driven by Saab GB and rally luminary Chris Partington

rigidity rating of 2,500lb/sqft – compare that with the Saab's 11,000lbs/sq.ft.in! Now you know why Saabs were stronger.

Thanks to Ljungström's previous role as a wing stress engineer and the work of Olle Lindgren as stressman, and Erik Ekkers, the little Saab had that tough aircraft style hull that resisted intrusion. Project Manager Svante Holm guided the development of a wooden buck prototype at Saab's Linkoping base prior to car production at the new Trollhättan factory. Wood, horse dung, boot polish and the skills of a 70-year-old artisan woodworker were all employed to build up styling buck into an ellipsoid UFO of a car that Sason had created. For the new car, Erik Rydberg was the chief engineer of car production and production /tooling manager and Claes Sparre factory engineer. Ursaab's test drivers were Mr Garbing, Mr Nyberg and Mr Landby.[Ref 1] The first car in the metal, built by a team of fifteen men, some of who were just young apprentices such as Tage Flodén and Hans 'Osquar' Gustavsson, used second-hand parts including DKW and Hanomag items. An Auto Union fuel tank was used in Ursaab's building. Steel was in short supply and Saab had no previous parts-bin to source from. But Ursaab Prototype no.1 was completed on 1 May 1947 and the revised no.2, less than one month later. In 1948, Ursaab even sported a badge calling it 'Sonett', a name that Saab would apply to its composite construction two-seat sports car in 1955 and a later 1960s range of cars.

Ursaab had a $C_D 0.32$ at a time when the industry average was closer to $C_D 0.50$. Wind tunnel tests at the Swedish Institute of Technology showed that, despite lacking a Kamm-defined critical separation point bodywork ridge, Ursaab had good airflow characteristics and it even kept its airstream attached down its rump to reduce wake drag. Studies in the 1970s also showed that the 1940s 92.001's form, its windscreen rake angle and frontal curves or lobe, approached the near-ideal aerodynamic form for a car. Ursaab had to be lightly modified for production, the fully shrouded front wheels had to be partially exposed to permit proper driving on rural roads, and the wing aerofoil leading edge shape of the nose was too avant garde even for Saab – various proposals brought about twin podded lamps and more upright grille.

Was the front of Ursaab too bulbous, too excessive in cross-sectional drag? Later work on the ideal aerodynamic form indicates that the prototype Saab was more intuitively correct that subsequent claims made for it. But for Ljungström's new Saab, Sason had walked into the office and put down a sketch of a raked, stylish fast backed, teardrop that had shades of French and pre-war Bohemian styling trends. Above all it reeked of the ellipse and influences that lay deep within the substrata of the Ursaab's design consciousness. The roots of Sason's influences and styling preferences stemmed directly from his time studying sculpture and design in Paris circa 1936 and his tours in Germany and Italy at the height of the Art Deco years. Sason's knowledge comes straight from early aviation and the pioneers of aerodynamics and it was clear that the trends of the late 1920s and motifs of the 1930s, allied to the tangents of thought fro Jaray and Ledwinka. In the early 1930s, Sason had gone to Paris to study sculpture. Also fascinated by sculpture in Paris at the same time as Sason, was the Italian Francophile, Flaminio Bertoni, the man who went on the shape the Citroën DS after he had previously sculpted the Traction Avant out of clay in a few days. In terms of smooth saloon-coupé modernity, perhaps the late-1950s Citroën DS was the ultimate symbol of the design trend *first* set off by the Saab 92.001. The stylistic linkage is clear in terms of sculpture, scaling, angle, and domed form. Ursaab opened the gates for the more famous subsequent shapes that followed,

Saab Heroes: Sixten Sason

Who was the designer who created a new fashion in a small-medium sector car that looked like an expensive UFO of a coupé?

Karl Sixten Andersson was born in Skovde, Sweden in 1912 and it was not until the 1930s that as an emerging designer and stylist, he altered his last name to 'Sason', alluding to 'spice' and less common than the ubiquitous Andersson. But Sason was no flamboyant artist as he was also an engineer, a calm thinker who could work with men like Ljungström and Mellde. Ljungström said of him, 'A genius; an engineer with the talents of an artist, or an artist with the temperament of an engineer...the ideal partner to work with.'

Tall, handsome, a debonair and charming Swede with a taste for Italian style, Sason was a pilot and a technical thinker. His 1930s ideas for a micro-car predated the post-war German designs by over a decade and his designs included a people carrier and an aerodynamic, low slung, steam-powered limousine. UrSaab was novel yet timeless, certainly not a quickly-dating fashion. The Saab 92 was an amalgamation of ideas and themes that manifested not as a retro-pastiche, but as something genuinely new. But the 92 was not Sason's only defining work. From an early fascination with flying, he trained as a pilot in the Swedish Air Force, but in an aircraft crash his chest was penetrated by a wing strut, he lost a lung and was struck down by infection, remaining in hospital for months, yet within a few short years he had re-invented himself as an illustrator and then as an industrial designer. He also studied silver-smithing and that passion may explain some of the exquisite detailing in his designs, be they cars, cookers or cameras. By 1939, he had started to work in the illustration department of the rapidly expanding aircraft maker that was Svenska Aeroplan Aktiebolaget – the SAAB as Swedes termed it. Initially, he specialised in producing x-ray type see-through structural drawings of Saab aircraft and their components.

He also designed the Husqvarna Silver Arrow motorcycle in 1955, the Hasselblad camera of 1948 and the company's later 1600F series. Sason shaped the first 1940s Electrolux Z70 vacuum cleaner, the Monark moped, and not only a Husqvarna chain saw, but also that manufacturer's waffle cooker – a stunning device that looked just like a spaceship or UFO beamed in to Area 51, or Hangar 18 at Wright Patterson's secret air force base, the place where in the war years Alex Tremulis sketched and styled flying saucer shaped devices for the U.S. Military, before he designed the Tucker.

Sason also came up with a defining shape of the electric iron – one copied even today. He designed the 'Zig-Zag' sewing machine, and his drawing board and studio were packed with sketches for boats as well as elliptically shaped flying machines of great futurism. He also designed a proposal for a curved-buttress supported suspension bridge at Oresund. All this work was product design and industrial design with a scale of function and perfection without excess.

In a sketch of 1941, Sason shaped a delta winged, all-wing or blended-wing shaped, short take-off and landing, rocket powered fighter that, over 70 years later still looks like an advanced stealth design. How much this 1941 design influence Saab's later Erik Bratt-designed Draken jet fighter, itself a design icon, is a long-argued point, but there are those, including Rolf Mellde, who have suggested some similarity so maybe some linkage is not as fantastical as some might argue.

Sason's archives, exhibited in the Vastergotland Museum in 2008, also show that in the 1930s he was designing micro-cars, pre-dating German micro cars by over a decade. He also drew a people-carrier MPV and shaped the 'Catherina' two-door styling proposal that introduced the targa-top roof design and had C-pillar rear buttresses. He was known for his long research trips around the design houses of Northern Italy where he was held in great affection. He died in April 1967, aged just 55, as his last car, the Saab 99 was about to be launched. By then, he had taken on the young Björn Envall and encouraged him to contribute to the 99 as his own health failed. Envall, himself the 'father' of 1970s-1980s Saab design, relayed to me that, 'Sason had a strong sense of humour, he was quite English in that sense … He was the best, a top industrial designer.'

Sason died tragically early from his lung problems, but left a legacy of elegant and functional industrial design, his Husqvarna motorcycle and his waffle cooker symbolising his sheer blend of style and functional elements at their best. But perhaps his flying saucer of a car, the Ursaab 92.001 and its production descendants leading to the 99, should qualify him as one of the unsung heroes of design of the twentieth century. Whatever the verdict, Sixten Sason was a forgotten hero of car design and, of a Hasselblad camera design that went to the moon. How many designers can say that?[Ref 2]

Saab Sonett

If you think the Saab Sonett is a late 1960s-to-1970s glass-fibre bodied coupé that embodies a for gotten, sportier side of Saab, you might be correct, however, the Sonett actually started life in 1954 as one of the most revolutionary and advanced examples of post-war car design. It was a uniquely constructed open-topped two-seater that looked like a cross between an MG and an Alfa Romeo.

Yet it was years before this wild child of a Scandinavian design group actually became the Saab Sonett. Unlike its 1950s contemporaries, the original Sonett did not have a tubular steel fabricated body nor a floppy monocoque with more shake than a jelly. Instead, the Sonett boasted a unique body made from a blend of aluminium sheets and plastic moulded panels weighing only 70kg, that were bonded together to form a stiff, aviation-style, stressed hull. It would be years later that Colin Chapman created the original Lotus Elite's glass-fibre unitary monocoque body, and decades before a car-maker made an aluminium car. The original Sonett 1 was dreamed up by Rolf Mellde, Saab's suspension and engineering genius. Along with Sason, the Saab team included Lars Olov Olsson and Olle Lindkvist and Gotta Svensson. With them, Mellde created an alternative Saab to the firm's teardrop-shaped 92-93 range. They cooked the car up in a barn at Asaka, half an hour's drive from Trollhattan, mostly in their own time. Saab management let the geniuses get on with it, without actually being officially involved. On seeing the Sonett, Saab whisked it off to become an official motor-show prototype of their new sports car: the ultra-light Sonett could do 130mph from 57bhp.

Despite various plans and projections and a great reception from press and public alike, including in America, Saab's exquisite little car never made it to production life: At one stage, Jensen were to build the bodies in the UK, but Saab faltered. Only six were made before the idea died. But in 1966, the idea of a sporty Saab coupé came to the fore again. By this time, Sason had designed another pretty Italianate coupé, the Catherina, showing the world a lift-out, stowable, targa-style roof for the first time. Saab decided to push a coupé into production, yet the Catherina design was not chosen; instead, the work of Bjorn Karlstrom of Swedish aircraft company Malmo Flygindustri was taken up by Saab's management. Karlstom's car was called the MFI 13; it became the Sonett II: Sergio Cogglia would shape the Sonett III.

Premiered at the 1966 Geneva motor show, the two-stroke-engined car had a steel chassis with conventional tubular reinforcements. Draped over the top was a delicate looking glass-fibre shell with an early use of a large, wraparound, glazed rear window. From 1966 through to 1970 the pert little Sonett II evolved with typical Saab product-development. In 1968, it gained the V4 engine from the Saab 96. But, by 1970 the car was looking odd, with scoops, engine bulges and stylistic fiddlings; only 4,000 were sold. So, Saab commissioned a revised Sonett. This Sonett III was a long-nosed coupé with overtones of Italian exotica as sketched by the Milanese designer Sergio Coggiola. Saab did however get its own in-house artist Gunnar Sjögren to style much of the new Sonett's plastic body-details. The Sonett III survived until 1974, with the final cars mostly being sold in racing colours; many remain in use and for sale at good prices today, notably in California. In the USA, Sonetts scooped up many sports-car racing wins in the 1980s, with Jack

URSAAB: The 92 prototypes were built in 1946-1947

Lawrence and his tuned V4 injection Sonett proving that it might not have rallied, but it could race.

Classic cars might come and go but the appeal of some remains constant. None more so than the Saab 900 – the last 'real' Saab – say some of the marque's devotees.

In the 1990s, General Motors owned Saab and bastardised the brand with ersatz Saabs, though thankfully only in America where a flat four-engined Subaru estate became a 'Saab-aru' and the ancient cast iron lump that was the Chevrolet Blazer off-roader had a Saab nip and tuck facelift. It was overseen by GM's head of development, car industry supremo Bob Lutz, a classic-car enthusiast and aviation fanatic who had revitalised BMW in the 1970s and went on to success at Ford and Chrysler, and therefore should have known better than to meddle with the beloved Saab.

Lutz maintained that this diversification was just a stop-gap measure. He said the 'brand dilution' was short-term and the justification behind it is that it gives the dealers more cars to sell as they may abandon the franchise otherwise, saying, 'We have to sacrifice brand purity for a while, till the next generation.' So, for the true Saab enthusiast, that only left the classic Saab 900 as the car to own. But there was a wider audience; more and more people caught on to the style and cool of the 'boat shaped' Saabs as the last pure Saab before GM grabbed the firm from under Fiat's nose.

Driving the Saab 900 is a world away from today's flat-screened greenhouses. You sit, deep, behind a unique curved windscreen with a dashboard that rolls away for acres. The windscreen is slot-like and your knees go under the fascia, not over it. It is more like sitting in a deep Victorian cast iron bath. There is a vintage feel to the gearbox too, which can best be described as notchy and at worst appalling. The seats are orthopaedic and the boot space is massive. The faster versions are great fun, with rocket ship-like boost; the slower versions can be asthmatic though. *Autosport* magazine spoke of the charm and fascination it had for this remarkable car, wondering if the 900T was just about the best motor car then made.

Saab's original 900 Turbo – probably one of the best driver's cars *ever* made.

10

Neckarsulm's Neophyte

NSU Ro80 and Rotary Magic

Just occasionally, there comes a moment when change is seen. It is either embraced or decried. The forces of convention and perceived wisdom usually win, smothering those who dare to challenge and question the status quo. But mavericks can simply just get on with the job and present their work. It takes confidence to do this. Time passes before such wisdom becomes acceptable. In a valley in southern Germany, a place of vineyards, rivers, hillsides, beauty and sunlight, the mid-1960s saw such a moment, a chapter of opportunity. Upon this event car design *could* have leapt into a radical future. But it was not to be. Ironically, decades later, the learning and the lessons of that moment, would be re-invented, recast and the new future claimed and marketed.

A similar thing had happened in aviation decades before, when the early monoplane and all-wing designs were cast aside in favour of the retardation of ability that was the biplane, only for the monoplane and all-wing to be latterly hailed as a new future. The same fate befell the NSU Ro80 of 1967 – for here was the moment, the opportunity for advancement. Yet it failed upon the headlines of risk and of the forces of torpor. Yet at Ro80's launch, even hardened motoring writers lauded it as 'Car of the decade'. Today, some of us see it as more important than that. Yet Ro80 remains shrouded in the mists of being a forgotten oddball – something it never was.

The Neckarsulmer Strickmaschinen Union (NSU) which became the Neckarsulm Fahrradwerke and then Motorweke AG, was originally established in southern Germany in 1905. They made bicycles and then motorcycles in the town of Neckarsulm and the first NSU car of 1905 was based on a Belgian car design, the second in 1906 was a Pfaender-designed car available as 1.4 and then 2.6 litre. In 1909, a 'voiturette' appeared. By 1913 the NSU car looked more like a Model-T Ford. Soon, a large, 3.3 litre engined NSU model arrived. Intriguingly, from the mid-1920s, the company was co-owned by Fiat as NSU-Fiat Automobili AG and, in the 1930s also employed a British designer named Walter Moore. NSU's motorcycles had a competition pedigree and became favourites with many riders; a tuned NSU moped took a speed record at Bonneville – 120mph from 50cc!

During the 1930s, NSU was commissioned to build three prototypes for the VW 'Peoples Car' by Porsche. In the Second World War, NSU produced military vehicles including a superb half-track, the 'Kettenrad'. From the 1950s, a re-born NSU turned out small cars – weird little things with two-cylinder engines that so many have likened to wheeled bathtubs and were named 'Prinz'. In several two- and four-cylinder variants, Prinz debuted as a small economy-type car, then grew into something more viable as a small family vehicle. This variant lasted in several iterations from 1960 to 1973; strangely styled and looking like a cross between a Corvair and the (latterly launched) Hillman Imp, the 1960s Prinz cars were competent, brilliant in snow and sold over one million examples in an era of pre-economic boom German austerity. The Prinz would lead to fast-backed version known as 'Sport Prinz'.

NSU developed the Wankel-type engine during the 1950s with its inventor and NSU came up with several variations of chamber design, rotor cycle and revised action – all stemming from Wankel's compressor designs for NSU motorcycles. NSU called their version the KKM – the 'Kreis Kolben Motor' or circular piston engine. NSU made the rotary compressor have a fixed external rotor, a static block and to limit the rotational action to the inner rotor and shaft.

By 1963, NSU shocked the big car makers and launched a rotary Wankel-engined coupé –the 'Spider' – a re-engined and topless version of the old Sport Prinz – as the world's first mass-produced use of this piston-less (single) rotary cycle and de facto 'orbital' engine of Dr Felix H. Wankel's design yet with many significant NSU-defined changes.

Not long afterwards, the twin-rotor Ro80 came and went. For a few short years, the Ro80's star shone over Europe. The problem however, was that the rotary engine failed regularly, resulting in massive warranty bills for NSU. Worn rotor tips, and poor fuel economy eclipsed the engine's smooth source of power. Other delights of design that became invisible included in-board brakes, superb handling and that rare early clutchless, semi-automatic transmission. Also eclipsed was the car's actual body design; its shape, aerodynamic excellence and also the under the skin engineering. Remember, when this car stunned the Frankfurt motor show in 1967, most cars had fins, chromed bulges, swages, and channels and gutters you could slice cheese on. Ro80 really was the future if you compared it even with the advanced Rover P6, never mind the agricultural delights of the Ford Zephyr, or just about any other 'normal' car.

You climb down into an Ro80 over a very wide and deep sill – far wider than anything found in a contemporary car of the era. The domed roof and high-arched windscreen still seem futuristic, the cabin is huge, the floor flat, the glass area massive yet the pillars reassuringly thick. The seats, Volvo-like in design comfort. Equipped with a velour trim, (preferably in blue) Ro80 had a luxury cabin and mostly eschewed the then fashion for 'fake' wood. Even today this feels like a modern car, a real spaceship of vehicle with a great sense of occasion. Back in the 1970s, such an impression, such surroundings were unheard of. If you thought that Ro80 looked futuristic with its low nose and chamfered lights amid the elegant, curved sweep of pillars and roof shapes, then getting on board only heightened that sense of the future. The cabin design, the dashboard, the 'lounge' effect – especially in the rear, the semi-automatic gearbox, a padded three-spoke steering wheel, the windscreen curving up into the roof, the whole package reeked of the 'new' and of having been consciously designed, but not for fashion.

All of which was complemented by the drive. Easing away, there was no piston-cycle vibration, no valve-chattered harshness. On start-up, there was no 'tick-over' idle, but instead a near-silent 'thrum' or mid-toned 'whirr'. Moving off in auto-drive, a phase of rotary-revved torque and somehow turbine-like sound and feel grew as the long wheel-based, stiff capsule proceeded. The rotary cycle is *not* of externally driven turbine effect, but it is perhaps of gas-flowed mechanism in having separate chambers for its orbiting or rotating piston-in-a-casing, combustion mechanism. The sound and the feel from under the bonnet was different. Once spooled up, the twin rotors hit about 3,000 revs and woke up to deliver a seamless wall of trochoidal torque. The feeling was akin to the difference between a propeller aircraft and a jet. The clutchless three-speed semi-auto with a manually microswitch-actuated vacuum function just aided and abetted the feel of making grand progress. Ro80 made the Citroën DS feel like the mechanically wheezing anachronism its engine was under the veneered aura of its stunning shape. If ever a car underlined the view that automatic transmission and well-tuned suspension allied to a smooth engine provided the ultimate saloon car answer, then Ro80 did. L.J.K. Setright, writer of motoring intelligence, held such a view and Ro80 surely proved his point. More recently, scribes like Stephen Bayley and Martin Buckley have championed the Ro80 for very sound reasons.

Ro80's aerodynamics were superior to the DS and so to was the Ro80's safety. There was one area where driving the Ro80 *did* remind you of the DS – for upon turning into a bend, Ro80 would initially roll and lean quite heavily, then to stop the roll and settle into a tight, understeered grip as the front-wheeled torque pulled you through the bend. Yet this was not a lurching affair and great security could be found, even if you pushed the limits; there was no throttle 'lift-off' drama or tail swing. Somehow, Ro80 never felt nose-heavy unless you really went into a tight bend too fast for sense. The steering, although fully powered, was full of feedback and accurate weighting – it was never left behind compared to what the front wheels were doing. In-board disc brakes kept the roll-centre and low c.g. and long travel suspension soaked up the ruts and bumps without ever making the car wallow. The suspension's rebound rate was well controlled too. We might argue that on back roads with bumps and humps, Ro80 rode better than a hydro-pneumatic DS. High-speed cruising in the Ro80 revealed a smooth, air-cleaving progress and limousine-like ride and cabin comfort. The wheelbase was long, and the wheels perhaps a touch small, but with the Wankel engine thrumming away, this long-legged cruiser offered an almost Jaguar-like sense of calm – until it broke down of course.

I loved driving the Ro80; it felt like an expensive German car yet one that was unique and not a deluxe boardroom on wheels. In Ro80 I felt completely connected to what the car was doing and what the road was saying. Some say Ro80's Wankel engine lacked torque, but at mid-range through the gears, I thought it had plenty of urge, as thrust not just rated power. Here was a large saloon car that was also of inspiring character, a rewarding drive and with that sense of being designed and built by people who cared about and understood cars. Scything along in the Ro80 on a wide, sweeping British A-road, this car was consummate. At 100mph, it was stable and strangely calm with barely a ruffle of aerodynamic disturbance; this was a serene drive in a car that just had to be a classic car jewel in the making.

I felt sure Porsche could or should have made this car or one like it, and that Saab would love to have produced something like the Ro80 too. Citroën ought to have matched it and not let the DS stagger on like a pensioner on a day pass with excuses made for bad habits and leaks. Just remember, when NSU were selling Ro80s circa 1970, Ford were offering the thin-skinned attractions of the flimsy Cortina; Austin were offering the stiffer-hulled but strange dinosaur-by-design of the 1800 and 2200 'land crab'; Volvo were selling unwieldy tanks, and even the Renault 16 was old underneath its contemporary styling. Rover's P6 2000 and 35000, however technically competent, were still of the old-school, made up with chrome flanges and thin, brittle plastic cabin appointments, fake wood and added vinyl; the giant Zodiacs of Ford and the Ventoras of Vauxhall were simply passing moments of cheaply framed, here today and gone tomorrow fashion. Across the Atlantic, large American saloon cars were still inefficient barges that boasted all the structural integrity of a garden shed, amidst the aerodynamics of a cow and the handling of a trawler at sea. Today, it might be argued that NSU's knowledge of engines, aerodynamics and structures, were a major yet hidden contribution to the advancement of the company that took NSU over – VW Audi itself.

The Ro80 may well represent that greatest lost opportunity of mainstream car design. After all, it was all-new, yet followed no fashion and set its own. The pace of aerodynamic, safety, and design developments might all well have been much quicker than they were if Ro80 had not imploded upon its rotary self. For if it had succeeded, other car makers would have *had* to have matched its advance. Seemingly out of the ether, NSU's design team, led by veteran chief engineer Ewald Praxl, and a bright young body designer named Claus Luthe, created an organic piece of modern architecture that happened to be a car with an engine that was different from the norm. Herbert Brockhaus and Rudolf Strobel were the chassis design team and framed the car's brilliant ride and handling characteristics, helped by that long wheelbase. When you see it in the flesh, the car's incredible scale and proportional balance are obvious; the scale of the rear doors, side window, sixth light and wheel arch, the arc of the roof line, the sweep of the waist, the sheer sculptural elegance of the thing, all are goldspot gems. Sadly, Luthe's idea for a grand interior with an instrument binnacle and a centre console, was dropped on cost grounds. So only Ro80s fascia disappoints, yet it *is* of almost Bauhaus simplicity. The unadorned architectural elegance was the uniqueness of Ro80 – for however much we love the Citroën DS, we cannot say the same of that car as an *entire* entity. Yet, like the rust that killed the Lancia Beta and tainted and obscured that marque's great history, people remember the Ro80 for its failed engine, not for its other transcendental brilliance of all-round design that was not just advanced, but was the gateway to a future only now so belatedly seen in the shapes and behaviours of today's cars, not least in recent VWs and Audis and just about every other high-tailed, curved 'aero-weapon' in the mainstream marketplace.

To prove the point, imagine an Ro80 with the steel bumpers and old-fashioned mirrors removed, re-imagine it with colour coded plastic front and rear aprons, modern alloys, and sleeker mirrors and new rear lamps; would it look not just completely contemporary, but still, advanced? 'The Future through Design' was the legend printed all over the adverts for a car that had a unique never-seen-before design with a high rear-tail deck, flush glazing, a low front, curved roof, tuned aerodynamics and a rotary-cycle engine. The car with all this quality design content was produced from 1967 to 1977 in just under 40,000 examples. Compared to other cars of 1967, it was as if Ro80 had arrived from Mars. Yet this car was industrial design taken to the exquisite. In its shape lay the roots of modern car design. That is no hollow boast or statement. It is a truth.

Ro80 was the first *saloon* car to 'chop' the tail, as well as to build it up high and,

The NSU RO80 was more then futuristic (VW/Audi)

allied to a very low front end, to massively reduce the drag over and behind the car, as researched by Dr Kamm. In the 1960s, there was no other car like it, and even today its shape is aped by all (even Jaguar) and still looks fresh. Ro80 set trends – the car had the first use of brushed stainless-steel trim on the smooth roof pillars, headlamp lenses that were chamfered into the body, there was a 'greenhouse' cabin with elegant rear quarter windows, and, above all that, a unique, high tail and low front (afforded by the Wankel engine's compact dimensions). The shape had a stunning-for-the-time C_D 0.355 drag figure and it kept its rear end clean in rain; likewise, the side windows. The car created a sensation in the motoring press and much debate, not least as to who designed it. Luthe gets the credit now, but NSU kept his name quiet at the time and it was his first big success. Latterly, his hand can be seen in the shape of the early, high-tailed 1990s BMWs – he was chief designer for BMW.

As for re-engined Ro80s? Plumbing in a Wankel device is one thing, adding a Mazda rotary engine is another, but installing a Ford V4 (as some owners did) was heresy and should remain so; genetic modification is very dangerous.

Quite correctly, Ro80, NSU's flagship, was European 'Car of the Year' in 1968.

It may well have been the most technically deserved winner of that sometimes-dubious title. Yet by 1977, Ro80 and its rotor-tipped engine failures and massive warranty costs, had killed NSU. All that was left was the Ro80's, NSU-designed, K70 sibling, a car designed by Georg Wenderoth that had been turned into a very competent saloon for NSU's new owner VW, yet one that was ignored by those tempted by the likes of the re-skinned dinosaurs that were the Cortina, Marina and Victor, their superficial gloss that covered up ancient underpinnings and deliberate, anti-design.

But there is another truth behind NSU's failure because, long before its Wankel engine costs and claims, NSU was dying as a motorcycle manufacturer and as the 1950s public switched from austerity and two-wheeled transport, to four-wheeled motoring, NSU had to search for funding and private investors, albeit propped up its Wankel engine research and development. So small was NSU, that few thought that it could or would develop a radical new engine and a radical new car. Desperate for cash, NSU started selling Wankel licences to big names like Curtiss-Wright, GM, Citroën and eventually Mercedes. Curiously, in light of Mazda's interest, NSU sold a licence to Nissan and, as late as 1970, Suzuki purchased an NSU Wankel licence. But the truth was that actual rights to the NSU-developed technology lay partly with Dr Wankel himself and his own private company and its investors. By 1960, NSU had spent a whopping $8million on developing Wankel's engine design and still the engine was not in production. Things got very messy indeed for NSU long before Ro80 warranty claims drove it under nearly a decade later.

Ro80 deserves a place in the motoring hall of fame. Few have realised it, but Ro80s are going to be worth a very great deal of money in the not too distant future. But there remains an unanswered question. Why and how, did a small company like NSU, one with no real history of advanced aerodynamic knowledge, and one surrounded by VW's and BMW's then very mediocre output of rear-engined contraptions and boring saloons respectively, suddenly create a car that was not just brilliant, but pushed the boundaries of the then standards of design and its application? Put alongside a mid-1960s VW or a BMW Neu Klasse saloon, Ro80 felt like it had landed from Mars.

Intriguingly, NSU and Citroën did work together from 1962 onwards, forming by 1964 a Societe d'Etude – a research company, and then a Compagine Européenne de Construction de Moteurs Automobiles Comotor S.A. – the Comotor Company – in 1967. Citroën and NSU were at the leading edge of Wankel engine developments, with Mazda and then General Motors paying vast sums in license fees to catch up. NSU supplied Citroën with Wankel engines for the Citroën Ami M35 rotary project.

But the deal went no further, with neither partner wishing to be subsumed into a greater entity, yet NSU would soon be swallowed up by Volkswagen who would benefit from the cheque for $50 million that GM would pay VW just one year later for Wankel design licences. But before that, NSU carried on with its grand saloon project. Strangely, Citroën's change to using copper around the vulnerable spark plug portal, was not seen in the NSU engine. Citroën also modified the rotor's tip seals – an area of much debate. [Ref 1]

What was it that made the men of NSU wake up one morning and decide to create a stunning car, one so futuristic in shape, construction and powerplant, that it had the ability to change everything? There were few genealogical clues in NSU's history, but the German industry and it its homeland, had been the scene of giant steps in engineering knowledge and aerodynamic design in the 1920s and 1930s. Stuttgart's nearby university housed a notable centre of early automotive knowledge about airflow. But NSU had no particular 'aero' history. Just over the border from NSU's Swabia, in Bavaria, BMW at this time was utterly conservative and very far from being the 'ultimate driving machine'. Further north, VW was, at best, mediocre and Beetle-reliant. But for NSU and its Ro80, the question remains why? Who took the decision to make Ro80? How did they *know* what to do? How did Claus Luthe defy perceived design wisdom circa 1965, surrounded as he was by the conventional and conservative?

We may never know how it happened, but there are clues – NSU's motorcycles were highly advanced and over-engineered. An NSU 6-cylinder racing car had won the 1925 German Grand Prix beating Mercedes and Bugatti and then taken all the podium places at the 1926 race. In 1932, NSU may also have had contact with Ferdinand Porsche, and associated Adler designs and the creations of Joseph Ganz, as well as observing Ledwinka's thoughts at Tatra. But no obvious aerodynamicism at NSU was obvious.

The little twin-cylinder NSU Prinz contained very clever engineering, even canting the engine block by 45° to put the engine's weight near the rear-axle line to reduce the potentially lethal rear-engined induced dynamic 'swing'. The NSU engine was air-cooled but highly unusually, configured in-line not horizontally opposed and its individual camshaft covers were an expensive solution for a cheap, small car. [Ref 2] So NSU as a motorcycle maker and then as a car maker *did* have a history of engine design excellence. After the Second World War, NSU's top director was an old Prussian aristocrat, Gerd Steiler von Heydekampf, who had spent the war guiding tank production for Hitler. Putting aside the dubious aspects of that, the excellent engineering tradition becomes obvious. But, quite where, when and how NSU got into aerodynamics for the Ro80 and so fervently, remains an unsolved riddle. Maybe the argument went something along the lines, of, 'what is the point of building an advanced twin-rotor Wankel engine and putting it in a box shaped car of prevailing fashion? Had we better not make the car's shape advanced too?'

One French motor-industry insider is adamant. He says that NSU had been talking to Citroën from 1962 onwards about an engine deal which led to their joint Comotor project from 1964. It is claimed that from such contact with Citroën, NSU 'got' aerodynamics and learned much which could be applied to the Ro80. Yet an old Audi man told me that NSU took its inspiration and knowledge from the aerodynamics expertise at Stuttgart University and the work of Wunibald Kamm and from Reinhard von Koening Fachsenfeld, a man who had streamlined DKW and NSU German motorcycles in the 1930s.

Knowledge of Felix Wankel's work led NSU to build its Spider, the world's first Wankel engined production car albeit single-rotor; a bigger version was a simple logical step, say the old-timers of Audi-DKW-Auto-Union-NSU lineage. Why follow the Wankel route? That riddle was more easily solved. Felix Wankel had been well known in 1930s Germany and in 1951, NSU called him in to solve a problem they had the rotary valves on a motorcycle engine. This set NSU thinking about Wankel's rotary-cycle engine and NSU began to discuss its future with Wankel. He also designed a rotary supercharger for NSU to deploy and gain world records as early as 1956. So, the small company had unique access to a new technology.

The benefits of Wankel's engine centred on being lighter, smaller, and having fewer moving parts and less vibration and harshness within its mechanical action,when compared to the traditional piston engine cycle. The Wankel's piston rotated or swivelled around a chambered casing and this then drove a geared transfer-output shaft. In the NSU version of the Wankel engine design, the chamber is static, only the rotary piston mobile, the fuel/air mixture function is valveless and the control of ignition timing was far simpler than even Wankel had envisaged when he had the idea of dumping the pistons and using rotors instead – an idea he patented as early as 1929. Interestingly, like Viktor Schauberger another pioneer of energy mechanics, Wankel was the son of a woodsman, a forest boy fascinated by nature who simply set up his own workshop and began to invent things.

By 1934, BMW had given Wankel a job and then came war and the interest of Goering and his research fantasies. But Wankel was, like many of his generation, a Hitler Youth member, yet one who and ended up under arrest by the Nazis. Soon, he was to come under Goering's protection and encouragement. So he went back to work and created the Wankel disc valve in a V-12 aero-engine made by Daimler-

Benz that would power German aircraft. As early as 1934, he had studied rotor tip-sealing issues and designed a 'packing body' around the tip, so he knew what the engine's main bugbear was, long before NSU got caught out. Putting aside his wartime role for the regime (as the Allies did with so many German experts that they scooped up post-May 1945), by 1950, Wankel was talking to NSU about new engine technology based on his rotary-cycle ideas and by 1958, he had created a four-stroke rotary engine. Walter Frorede and Georg Jungbluth worked on the rotary engine design, the former being NSU's leading engineer who guided the engine's development as NSU developed Wankel's ideas and his motorcycle compressor supercharger into an engine that incorporated NSU's own developments. Wankel's design was actually more complex, involving a rotating rotor and rotating housing. The NSU-modified version of the Wankel concept had been created by Froerde after he realised that a simpler approach could be invoked. Wankel is said to have belatedly admitted that Froerde's modifications were advantageous.

Aware of the Ro80s engine issues, NSU developed a new seal coating of nickel plate containing fine particles of silicone carbide (having previously created bronze springs behind the metal-surfaced tip seals to brace them against the chamber wall), whereas Mazda decided on thicker (and heavier) carbon-rich apex seals and the life of these seals was dramatically improved over the course of several years, yet the high forces (gas, friction and centrifugal) acting on the rotor seals would require 1980s developments in thin-walled ceramic coatings and improved lubrication technology before a tip seal-life of 100,000 miles could be claimed.

Mazda's developments of the Wankel engine *seemed* to have solved the seal issue, but not others of oil and fuel consumption. Mazda of course, claim that their 1966 110 S Cosmo, was the world's first twin-rotor in production, but NSU might contest that claim by their Wankel-licence holder, not least as Mazda only built one car per day! The RX7 and latter RX8 gave the Wankel engine commercial life, yet did not completely solve the issues of its high fuel consumption, even if it did build one million rotary engined cars by 1979.

Today Ro80s remain a left-field choice. Some still slowly rot, others have been rescued and restored, a few original examples still whirr about. A man named Simon Kremer who ran a company named RoTechniks, even shortened an Ro80 and turned it into a two-door soft-topped cabriolet. Ro80s enthusiasts insist that NSU was, in 1970, readying its own, sleeker two-door coupé version and we can only salivate at the thought of what might have been. Mercedes would not have known what had hit them. We may never know what 'eureka' moment made NSU and its chief engineer Praxl think such revolutionary, rotary-powered, front-wheel drive, aerodynamically-bodied thoughts for a car, but Ro80 itself remains an enigma, a paradox and a lost moment in automotive history. Ro80 has even been the subject of an article by Stephen Bayley who agrees that the car's proportions can only be described as flawless. [Ref 3] But Ro80 was more than that. If you agree that Ro80 was a car of the century and a defining act of engineering and design, then save one, or at least, drive one if you can. NSU and its Ro80 – another act of greatness lost upon the howlings of fate.

11

Michelotti: A Triumph of Design

Italian Style over British Austerity

Triumph's cars were quintessentially British, yet their body styles were latterly designed by a little-known Italian, Giovanni Michelotti. Suave, smoking, nattily attired, yet human and warm, not some ego-busting preacher of certainty, Michelotti was a nice man and his cars were so damned *cool*. He was a decent and kind chap whose sketches were wonderfully free and uninhibited. Guigario, Pininfarina, Bertone, these are the famous names of Italian automotive couture, yet beyond their influence, there was Michelotti, a lesser-known Italian car designer whose work touched the lives of the British more than the illustrious grand scions of design 'carrozzeria' for which Italy is famous. Michelotti, Spada, Scaglione, Brovarone, Martin, Cogglia; these are the almost publicly invisible heroes of Italian design. Perhaps Giovanni Michelotti was the man with the design CV that travelled furthest, via Japan and, the dark and damp British Midlands car making crucible.

Standard Triumph was a leading brand name of the British affair with the motor car in the post-war decades. From the pre-war Triumphs to the TR range of open sports cars to the middle-class manners of the Triumph Herald, and on to the smooth style of the Stag and the saloons of the 1970s, Triumphs encapsulated a certain something. Yet few of the motoring public knew that their cars, from Standard Vanguard Mk2, to the TR4-TR5, Herald, Dolomite, Stag, and 2000, were shaped by an Italian. His name never appeared as a badge on the flanks of these cars. As late as 1979, he was asked to re-work the TR7 into a coupé that would never be.

Giovanni Michelotti was one of the motor industry's greatest talents. He established his own design house, one that today continues as an industrial design specialist under his son Edgardo; Giovanni's daughter Daniela, influenced fashion design. Yet Giovanni's car designs lacked a badge saying 'Designo di Michelotti'.

He did not just design Triumphs, he shaped BMWs (from the diminutive 700 and 800 through to larger saloons), The Prince Skyline (Japan's first big two-door GT attempt and forerunner of the Nissan Skyline series), Maseratis, the original Renault Alpine, more than one Lancia and he was behind the shapes of many of the Japanese cars that came to dominate the European market in the 1970s – starting with the 1960s Prince Skyline and with the Hino Contessa. His disciple, Tateo Uchida, influenced Toyota design. Another student of Michelotti was the Swiss designer Dany Brawand who went on to be chief designer at Moretti. Giovanni Michelotti was also the designer who created the distinct imagery of the Scammell truck design. A sculptor, he insisted on a purity of line, avoiding the effects on design of what he likened to his view that 'a camel is a horse made by the designer, after a meeting of the board of directors'.

As the 1950s turned into the 1960s, Michelotti's designs dominated the halls of the motor show circuit. At one Turin motor show, more than forty car types bore his trademark sharp-yet-sleek styling, but *without* his name appearing upon them. In 1951, he designed a special Ferrari 212 GT for Ingrid Bergman. Up to the 1980s, Michelotti shaped vehicles for DAF, Volvo, and British Leyland – the P76 saloon and coupé, both for the Australian market. He shaped a one-off Morgan proposal and an Italia showcar.

He was born in 1921 and died aged just 58 in 1980. In the 1930s, he joined Batista 'Pinin' Farina's brother at Stablimenti Farina as a young styling apprentice, and by the late 1940s was working for Vignale, a leading Turin design house. Through such works, he was chosen to influence the shape of early Ferrari road cars, Lancias, and a range of Maseratis including the mid-1950s A6 GC, and 3500 coupes. His first post-war days were in a business he ran from his home, and few people know that he influenced Vignale's 1950s Ferrari body designs. He was however credited with the Ferrari 212(E). When Bertone designed a Bristol 404 body in the 1950s, the car's design consultant is reputed to have been Michelotti. He also created the shape of Renault that formed the basis of the first Alpine-Renault as the Alpine A106, then he styled the A110. DAF's 55 was Michelotti-styled and became a bizarre and short-lived badge-engineered Volvo 66. [Ref 1]

BMW's hallmark

Michelotti also drew the early BMW 'shark front' saloons including the 2000 and in doing so, set a BMW design motif of the lean-forwards or reverse-slope grille and front valance with framed headlamps. Legend says that a Herr Hofmeister created the famous BMW rear side window design motif 'kink', others attribute it to Guigario, but some say it was a Michelotti- idea. But it was for Triumph that the quiet Italian really carved a niche. Invited by Standard Triumph to restyle the Vanguard, Michelotti established a relationship with the company that gave its cars a unique style amid the blandness of slab-sided styling trends of the era. He ignored American trends for excess in design, yet did add some aspect of trans-Atlantic and

European glamour. He created an elegance of line. The 1960s 'look' of four round headlamps set at a rakish angle on a low fronted bonnet that had a chrome grille at its prow, was a Michelotti hallmark and, one copied by many.

For Triumph, his most emotional design must have been the dainty little Herald and later the Vitesse. This design stemmed from the oddly named 'Zobo' design proposal he had put to the Standard Motor Company. It turned into the Herald but with less curves as these were deemed too expensive to manufacture by the company.[Ref 2] The subsequent Spitfire and GT6 added to the Michelotti- aura. All these cars looked far more exotic and expensive than they were. Ordinary people could drive around in an Italian-styled jewel of a car. The Triumph Herald and its shape became a social statement and an icon to rival the Mini.

For the Triumph Spitfire, Michelotti crafted an elegant car with sculpted-in or embedded headlamps set into a frontal graphic of classical proportions. Michelotti did detail, but he also created complete, balanced whole bodyshells. Turning the Spitfire into the GT6 coupé was elegance made easy. His designs for the TR3 and TR4 sports cars remain timelessly elegant, devoid of excess styling. He also drew a low fronted, quad headlamp shape for a TR5 concept car named 'Ginevra' (Geneva) in 1967 and latterly the Toledo/Dolomite ranges. The Ginevra became a one-off design basis of the Triumph Stag and the restyling of the 2000 saloon as the 2500 PI. For the 1970s, Michelotti's Triumph saloons featured a hallmark design motif – a sharply cut off roof line with an inset rear windscreen; this offered significant aerodynamic advantages at a time when few used such techniques (by defining the critical separation point for the airflow off the rear roof section of the car).

The freelance consultant that was Michelotti worked in an interesting way. At his offices, he had a little room, off that was a studio where he would build up a styling buck over a chassis and add to it by hand with clay, wood and metal. He would paint the prototype by hand, often using coachbuilders enamel. He was as a quiet, elegant, sincere man devoid of celebrity ego, and used to take his staff out to football matches, staff who worked to create styling models to seemingly impossible deadlines. He was a major figure in industrial design and had a massive influence on British and global car design and on the social nuances of car buying suburbia. Michelotti's hand touched many emerging Japanese designs for major manufacturers, yet his name was so often obscured.

Perhaps no other car designer has blended tweed with a Turinese cut of cloth for the mass market, in such a triumph of international style. But Michelotti influenced not just British cars, but the global industry and the emerging world of industrial design. In his Triumph Stag, we see a superb capturing of an era. In his BMW shapes, we see an essence created without embellishment. Across the industry, there lay the quiet hand of a genius named Giovanni.

Triumph GT6

Was the Triumph GT6 that company's version of the Jaguar E-Type? To some it was, and remains a delight to drive and own, a fastbacked, straight-six engined, quintessentially British sportster with Italian style and that character that makes people yearn for 1960s Britain. Was it the style or the engine that made the car? Was it both? It was not the handling though; Triumph had to keep fiddling with the rear suspensions across various series of Spitfire and GT6, adding bigger rubber bushes to GT6 and only to finally remove from the last cars, the very tweak; reverse lower wishbones and rotoflex couplings between the half-shafts and the hubs that it had applied to the earlier Mk2 and the initial Mk3s. Later Mk3s went *back* to the cheaper transverse leaf spring swing axles set up. The cabins and seats, the trims, the bhp, all were changed, but through it all the basis of Michelotti's so expertly grafted-on tin top, turned the old Spitfire base model into something truly desirable. Throw in the restyle and smart new rear lamps, and here was an antiquated car, made in an antiquated way, that still sold and which today, forms the basis of a cult following. MGB and BGT owners were unlikely to switch allegiances and *vice versa* was true of Triumph owners, but here was a 1959-era car on a Triumph Herald basis, tweaked and stroked across two decades into a lovely little gem that had, with a straight six engine, the poke to be quite 'hairy'.

Things like rust resistance, crash safety, mpg, these were not really the GT6's remit, nor were they of many 1960s cars if truth be told. But thanks to that great influencing figure that was Harry Webster, Triumph had a sporty sales weapon that touched the world. The car had originally been code named 'Bomb'. After its launch in 1966, it did the opposite in sales terms. If Spitfire was spartan, GT6 was' GT' in every sense except perhaps girth, yet the two were build up from identical pressings; only changes to the rear floorpan, fuel tank location and that roof adding to the GT6's tooling up costs. The engine came not from the Herald's Vitesse iteration but from the larger Triumph 2.0litre saloon. Early GT6's had wire wheels – a benefit to the track due to their greater width ratio – thus reducing the swing-axles preponderance to slip, and skip towards flight. Tyres must also be crucial on GT6 and Spitfire.

What was it like to conduct? Well, you climbed down into the thin little cabin, fed your legs forward of the windscreen and did not think of the fact that just as in a Herald or the Spitfire, between you, your legs and a big frontal impact there was almost nothing – just a thin, hollow, one-piece clamshell bonnet devoid of any impact-catching structure. There were no wingliner wheelarches, no longerons, no crush cans, no flitch panels, nor steel linings, nothing to absorb and transfer energy down into the chassis, all there was under that bonnet's thin shell was air, tyres and your footwell. The first bit of steel wall *across* the car – between you and the crash was the scuttle and fascia box. What about the engine and chassis? Oh, they were there, but so low and so close to the car's centre line, that most impacts would slide over the top or around the side. Unless you hit a compatible object at the same height, fully 100 per cent head-on, GT6 offered little between the headlight and the A-post except that floppy bonnet pressing. That all this was legal reveals how far car safety has come and GT6 was not alone in such characteristics.

Never mind, in its time, GT6 was rorty, direct – if not point-and-shoot, then squat-and-go, and had near-100bhp – like an MGB. That pendulously suspended rear end needed caution, but above all this was the legend of six-cylinder motoring with a bulge in the bonnet, in a fastback form, yet at a price the average punter might afford. Now wonder they sold. GT6's E-Type fantasies were not such a bizarre metaphor after all – were they? Today, whichever version, 'pure' Mk1 or later cars, interest and values are rising for what was a true British character. Fit a Triumph 2.5 litre engine and the car turns into something that even an Allard enthusiast might approve of.

These lovely six-cylinder cars drove with verve, had style and were so damned characterful. Buy one now before prices go berserk. Standard Triumph's GT6 touched the lives of many young drivers and now, many older ones. We should look up and think, *thanks Harry, thanks Giovanni.*

12

Fiat's 'Fake' Ferrari

Driving the Dino: A Ferrari in All But Name

The sound of the thing was incredible. The alloyed quad-cam motor really did sing like a siren of the seas, the induction-roar and the holed exhaust only added to the moment. I was driving a rusty, 'oily rag' condition 1968 Fiat Dino 2000 coupé on Berkshire's back lanes. Left-hand drive was a big risk on roads that lacked adequate sight lines and had hedges obscuring what view ahead that there was. The seats were tatty, the silver paint flattened and patinated with rust and faded grandeur from too many sunny Italian days under acid blue skies; Cromodora alloys were pitted with alloy acne, wheelarches were scabbed, sills were blistered, seats were torn, oh and the number plates said the car was registered in Napoli – style! Despite its rough condition, this Fiat with a Ferrari engine, (belonging to Lancia fanatic, the late Hugh Ferdinando) was in rorty health, the timing was spot-on. The gearbox was direct and accurate: a new set of shock absorbers were housed under those faded wheelarches. I knocked the big coupé down into second, twirled the big plastic wheel and turned into a sharp left-hander, then just past the apex, pushed hard on the throttle. A roar emanated from in front of the bulkhead and the Ferrari engine gulped, then we shot forwards on a wave of torque amid that incredible sound that rose in pitch as third and then fourth were grabbed. Next up, adverse camber S-bends taken in third caused the rear end to seem slightly skittish. Hard acceleration never bit back with a big slide, although it might have done on an Italian Grand Col a couple of decades previously. In *The Italian Job*, it was the Lamborghini Muira that starred, but in the mountain-road confrontation scene, the Mafia boss and his acolytes were mounted in a fleet of shiny black Fiat Dino Coupés that must have hastened up from the valley to meet Michael Caine and his men in their soon to be demolished Aston Martin and E-Type steeds. This was a Fiat like no other and it told an intriguing story.

Launched in 1967 as Pininfarina-bodied convertible described as 'Spider' and as Bertone-styled coupé design that was actually tagged 'Coupé', the big Fiat cost £3,300 and £3,500 respectively in Britain. Dino was pitched into territory below the Aston Martin DB6, DBS and Ferrari 330 sales arenas, but above more prosaic

Red Devils: O-series 911s as atmospheric art by the author's hand

Ready to sing its flat-six-song: classic 911 at Goodwood Members Day

Alpine Moment: A110 in the correct colour - plastic fantastic. Michelotti's design and a range of Renault engines created Dieppe's delight that won the Monte Carlo Rally more than once, took the International Series title and the new, 1970s World Rally Championship in 1973. For many, A110 was truly the drive of your life and a stunning example of man and his mechanical interaction

Alpines old (A110) and less old (A310) but both are French classics. Seen at Alpine Club of France rally in Brittany

Early Bugatti Type 13 barrels up the hill at Prescott in a blur of blue brilliance

Bugatti magic. The Type 35 from the helm

Classic people: John and Thelma Huntley and Type 25 at Bicester Heritage Centre

GS genius captured in all its aerodynamically efficient elegance

Amphicar goes into the water at Loheac Museum, Brittany

Studebakers had style. Just look at the jet turbine intake inspired nose on this 1950 Champion

Asleep at Prescott – classic days out as Healey and Jaguar gems keep watch

Citroën SM as Chapron convertible – very rare and tres cher; one recently sold for over £150,000

SM's sheer style, with Opron's glazed frontal aspect making its mark during the European SM Club's annual rally

Allardiste, Dave Loveys at the helm of his Allard at speed on the Prescott hill. It's nostalgia on steroids

British classics day out. More superb Prescott action and access up close to automania

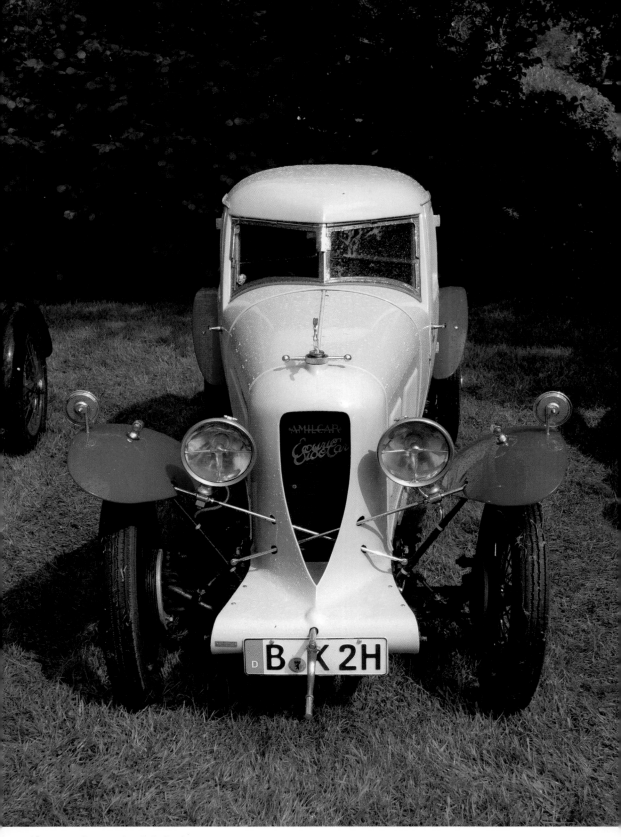

Amilcar and wonderful design

Classic people: Chris Partington – ex Saab GB and rally expert took his car to the Le Mans classic. Chris is the Saab 96 guru-to-go-to

Once, Volvo's were curved and low. 1800 ES setting the style at the UK's 'Swedish Day' event

A new take on the 2CV has been tried by many. This was the author's 1990s design idea – which was featured in the motoring press

Classic people: Former Concorde and VC10 pilot and Brooklands Museum volunteer Christopher Orlebar with his blue MGBGT – naturally

Mercedes heaven at Goodwood Members Day. One of the world's greatest classic days out

Classic Americana. Late-1960s Ford Thunderbird at speed with sheer style

Women like classic cars too! Female pilots in a BMW 328 at the Silverstone Classic

1956 Allard Palm Beach Mk2 restoration by the Allard family. Alan Allard at the wheel.
A golden moment that proves nostalgia is better than it used to be.

Austin of England and its Burzi-styled Baroque brilliance. Accessible supercars seen at the Cotswold steam and vintage extravaganza — another wonderful classic car day out

offerings from mainstream European car makers (think Capri! Ford not the island) yet it bore the badge of Fiat which, if not exactly humble, was hardly the stuff of legend yet in fact steeped in early motor racing that had seen it win fame across the early grand prix scene. An Edwardian-era 27 litre Fiat racer is now remembered as the 'Beast of Turin' but most 1960s car buyers were ignorant of Fiat's racing heritage – as they are today. In fact, a much 'newer' brand and its Jaguar E-Type fixed head 2+2 then retailed for £2,456, and had far more allure and *apparent* pedigree; the cost of the Fiat could have a bought a reasonable house at the time too. The one I was driving had just been bought for under £5,000 – the era was the late-eighties and orphans like the Fiat, were never completely swept up on the boom in classic car prices. The badge was the problem. But the car was not – once you found out how good they were.

Launched with the all-alloy V6 designed by Vittorio Jano and which was destined to power a Ferrari named for Enzo Ferrari's dead son Alfredino, Ferrari had to homologate a decent number of these engines (500) in order to flog them to the world of Formula 2 single-seat racing in Europe. Fiat agreed to help Ferrari which lacked the capacity to do so. This engine went into the Ferrari 206-246 range and a derivative found its way into the incredible Lancia Stratos. The engine was hemi-headed and had three twin-choke carburettors. It had a 65° V-angle, not 60° or the 90° as was more common. This was also the era of the development of (now common) multi-valved heads and much thought went into the valve operating efficiency of this engine. The valve (port) angles in the design were significant contributors to its efficiency of function and were studied in depth by Ferrari's engineers in 1965. The Formula 2 variant had Heron-Type bowl-in-piston cylinder heads and differing dimensions and volumetric capacities. There was much more to this engine design than has been told. A British engineer is reputed to have made significant contributions.

In being developed for a Fiat, the engine project gave life to Ferrari's 206/246 model – itself tagged 'Dino' having initially been denied an actual Ferrari badge. Yet it was Fiat that gave birth to the first car bearing Enzo Ferrari's son's name – Dino – the shortened form of Alfredino. Dino himself had died in 1956 – a decade prior to the latter car projects and strictly speaking, his name is applied to the Ferrari engine types of V12 – V6 – *not* the car, but that fact has become lost in the mists of memory. Just over a year after Fiat's Dino, came Ferrari's own 206 'Dino' varietal; the legend lay in the engine. Some degree of confusion in the observer is allowed.

More confusion was to become apparent because Fiat put the Ferrari-designed engine into a Fiat-built coupé body by Bertone and at the same time it also created the Pininfarina-built Dino convertible or spider-type which was decidedly different to the named Coupé. Pretty as the soft-top was with its curves and raised front wing line, it was the Bertone coupé shape which was so beautifully tailored and wonderfully scaled. Lithe and classy, it oozed glamour, until you read that badge. The early versions of both cars had about 160 bhp (DIN) and topped out at around 125mph with a following wind. The 0-60mph dash came up in under nine seconds. The rev limit was a howling 8,000rpm.

Sales went well, but Fiat had done that strange thing of launching the Dino two-seater convertible version *first* – with the completely different, Pininfarina-styled body that used some proprietary Fiat 124 parts-bin items. This included some internal steelwork and the 124's windscreen and frame somehow made to look wider. The soft-top car was a curved Pininfarina sculpture that was, as the Aussies say, a 'bitsa' – bits of this and bits of that. Still, it boasted Ferrari engine, and a quality item gearbox (fitted with a dedicated extra oil pump), even if the front suspension of wishbones and tubes looked like a stock Fiat saloon item; the rear suspension seemed rather crude with lengthy a single leaf spring each side, tied down by single longitudinal links mounted above the solid rear axle's line. But the Pininfarina car and the Bertone coupé did *not* share the same suspension. Costs mounted. The Coupé had more time before it reached the market and benefited from twin-leaf rear springs and revised damper rates, better longitudinal dynamics, a longer wheelbase and an especially developed Pirelli tyre. [Ref 1] So the Coupé was the 'purer' car in engineering terms, especially if you favoured the lighter, 2.0 -litre alloy-engined Mk1 of 1967-1969. Both cars in early models however shared a rigid rear axle and Fiat claimed that it would attend to this and in time it did, the Fiat 130's coil-sprung system being grafted in. Claims of a transaxle being fitted in the *original* Fiat Dinos are inaccurate however.

The Coupé alone also benefited from its own, new, front seat design; huge Volvo-style armchairs of supreme comfort. The rear seats were large enough for adult occupation and also folded flat at the same time as opening up cabin access to the boot. An advanced cabin ventilation system was also installed. The coupé used fewer Fiat plastic trim items in the cabin and fascia and looked classier for it.

Post-1969, both the Fiat Dinos were then given more power, up to 182bhp which, on the face of it, sounded like a good idea. Except that this meant the sweet alloy engine was modified to iron-block casting and seemed less revvy. However, the handling was improved by that new coil spring rear suspension from the 130.

The convertibles, by dint of soft-top style as opposed to fixed head elegance, have always been worth more money and are now heading towards five figures for a perfect example. But it is the Coupé that was the more cohesive design and a better drive. Today, the Coupés still linger in the £20-40,000 sector, which seems like an incredible bargain for a Ferrari-engined true sports GT that, in its Mk2 iteration, was actually built in the Ferrari factory. Regretfully, the badge 'thing' still weighs heavily upon the clouded perceptions of car snobs.

Intriguingly, the two Fiat Dinos, Coupé and Spider, *do* drive differently and feel as abstract as they look. Indeed, Fiat stuffed a large number of existing components into its design for the Dino under the direction of chief engineer Sgnr Montabone and design development man Dr Zandona. Ferrari's engine was essentially a re-working of an earlier design idea and it too saved cash and Fiat helped with the development to what was then an independent Ferrari. This was the first joint project between the two companies; by 1969 Fiat had purchased shares in Ferrari.

This then was a story of one car model with two differing body options and differing underpinnings yet which delivered Ferrari performance and Ferrari ability for much less money. Most of the Dinos (under 6,500 built), notably the Coupés, rusted away in the 1980s as you might expect from anything made from Italian steel of the previous decades. Yet enough remain from warmer climes to leave today's classic car buyer with the intriguing temptation of the Ferrari that wasn't. L.J.K. Setright thought the Dino, specifically in Coupé guise was a superb car, something really accomplished. We might in hindsight, underline his sentiments and express regret that Fiat's achievement with this car went largely unrecognised.

To the Dino a Daughter

There was a very curious riddle in the story of the Fiat Dino. Most motoring writers jump straight from Dino to Fiat 130 in a plot of big Fiats that they say failed. Few people, writers or readers, are aware of Dino's baby – a daughter named Samantha! The coupé market in the late-1960s was expanding. Even redoubtable Audi would come up with a lovely, sexy coupé that bore a remarkable resemblance to the Dino Coupé itself – courtesy of Italian styling ideas. Fiat was also producing the 124 and 125 models and you could buy a cheap, rear-engined fastback variant of delightful style and ability. Bizarrely, in late 1967, the big-wigs at Fiat decided that a shrunken version of the new Dino was called for; Italy's market for small sportsters was strong and what could be better than a fastbacked, 'it shrunk-in-wash' poco Dino Coupé based on pre-existing Fiat 125 bits? The economies were obvious.

So arrived the strange story of a Fiat named Samantha. This curious yet very pretty device was an Alfredo Vignale-styled coupe that in fact was touched by Michelotti as Vignale's consultant. It used various 125, Dino and propriety Fiat parts-bin panels, components and trims and was therefore, a new car that was

realised very cheaply for Fiat from paid-for toolings and parts. Fiat threw a 1.6-litre stock four-cylinder twin-cam engine under the bonnet and a five-speed gearbox added lustre and fuel economy. The car had a smooth, sculpted nose and no front grille; it boasted two laid-back round headlamps that hinted at the Lamborghini Muira's style. Cromodoras, sports trims and real style of shrunken-Dino elegance punctuated this coupé on the cheap. Quite why it was called the Fiat 125 Samantha remains unclear. Fiat even built a few right-hand drive versions from stock 125 parts. Yet approximately only 100 or so were built before someone in power took the duff decision in 1970 to kill off the little gem. Samantha handled with joy, went with verve and rusted away with elegance. A few remain, notably in southern Italy. Values are rising for Fiat's rarity and only two have reached the classic car auction market in the last two years. As such, the Dino's daughter is rarer than its antecedent.

Not only did the Fiat Dino project beget the Ferrari 206/246 and the acquisition of Ferrari by Fiat, and the latter, 125 Samantha, it also spurred Fiat on to make the wonderful 130 saloon and the range-topping 130 – another big Fiat and a coupé in all but profile. Big Fiats seemed destined to a sad fate, even the wonderful Ardita of 1935, the badge being the issue as always, rarely the car itself. Indeed, the 130 coupé of 1971 is a gem and packed 3,235cc. Much of the learning that created the Fiat Dinos (including the suspension and the seats) went into the 130 – notably the coupé with boot. Aspects of the car were world-class – enough to rival BMW, Mercedes and Jaguar. Fiat built only 4,491 up to 1978. If only they had used better quality steel and applied proper rust proofing, then more would remain. As it is, the 130 coupé is also a bargain classic, yet one fraught with huge restoration costs. Like the Fiat Dino, it too encapsulates an era, a feel, a sheer sense of style unencumbered by health and safety or political correctness and EU directives.

For the originator of the 130, the Dino remains an astounding effort. The sound of the Fiat's Ferrari-designed engine lingers long after you have turned off the ignition and let the motor cool. In a way, we might equate the Fiat Dino's accomplishment to it being Fiat's Porsche 911 'moment'. Heresy? Perhaps not.

But the question of that first big, flash, modern era Fiat that was the Dino remains today as it was in 1967 or 1969. Coupé or Spider? 2.0litre or 2.4 litre? Purist or polished? It is a matter of personal preference and it is unlikely that these cars will reach truly stratospheric prices, but on the up they are. Personally, I would buy the early Dino coupé and preserve it as fine example of a driver's car from a clever era of Fiat engineering – woeful rust resistance ignored. Here was a car where the drive, the act of man and machine interacting, was the thing. The Italians always understood that.

13

Citroën GS

Of Spaceships That Rust in Peace

After decades in the design doldrums, Citroën has, with its new models, returned to daring to be different – on the surface. The C4 Cactus is great, but does it flatter to deceive? Let's hope not. But the new Citroëns have parts-bin underpinnings and coil springs, unlike the Car of the Year 1971 that was the characterful Citroën GS – which was new in every respect and a true hydro-pneumatically 'sprung', air-cooled, lobed Citroën hailing from the old stables of the company's Bureau des Etudes, Rue du Théatre, Paris. Whilst the limelight always falls on the Citroën DS as the 'goddess' of Citroën design, it is the GS that kept Citroën alive into the 1980s. But because we *expected* a Citroën to be bold, the shock of the new GS in 1971 failed to make the impact on the public's perception that it might have done. Yet the GS was the world's first small car with 'active' inter-linked, constantly self-levelling hydro-pneumatic suspension, a chopped 'Kamm' tail and teardrop aerodynamics that were years ahead of the opposition. It also had a large cabin, superb ride and handling and was a modern design that stood out from the usual fare of the time of Vivas, Cortinas, and associated 'three-box' car designs. Perhaps only the Rudloph Hruska-engineered Alfasud came close to the GS in technical terms with both cars sharing a horizontally opposed flat-four boxer engine design, fwd, Kamm tail, and other traits. And the GS had not just all round disc brakes, but in-board brakes – taken from racing car design to improve handling. Its wishbones and liquid mineral suspension also gave it the ride of a Rolls Royce too. The air-cooled, alloyed engine was almost unburstable and for Citroën was all-new and developed at great cost. Only a lack of power would sap at GS's legend, yet did not a Wankel-engined version beckon?

The GS started out as 'Project C' and 'Project F' as 1960s Citroën prototypes for a new smaller, family car. 'Project F' is shrouded in legend, for it looked very much like the later Renault 16, itself a milestone car in design terms. Had there been industrial espionage involved? Such were the rumours. Designed by Robert Opron under the influence of the past works of Flaminio Bertoni at Autmobiles André Citroën, the GS was expertly styled; it needed no rear wiper and kept its flanks clean through tuned airflow control. It looked right from every angle and as with all Opron designs, captured the light beautifully. It even survived being stretched into the long tailed GSA hatchback in 1979 with its grafted-on plastic bumpers. The GS estate – a flat-floored favourite with French farmers and British families – carried on almost unchanged.

Special editions such as the sporty 'X1', the black painted, red-striped 'Basalte' and the strangely named GS 'Cottage' made the most of the 1015cc, 1220cc and 1130cc engines that the car was offered with over the years (a 1301cc engine was made to beat Italian tax laws). The ultimate GS had to be the rare twin rotor, Wankel-engined, 'Birotor'. In 1974, through a tie up with NSU, the GS became a powerful, automatic-only, smooth cruiser and the only rotary car with hydro-pneumatic suspension and brakes. As such GS Birotor contained expensive engineering; the rotors were hollowed out with oil transfer trenches inside them and advanced seals and valves were deployed. Birotor was so much more than GS with a Wankel engine shoe-horned in under the bonnet; in fact it was a recast idea, an act of bravery. Often painted a rich antique gold and with Pallas trim, 847 Birotors were sold. Citroën bought them all back as they were troublesome, and too thirsty as the 1970s fuel crisis raged; in their brief lives the Birotors wowed France, they were equally at home swishing through a rainy Paris, or storming down the Autoroute. GS Birotor was and remains an amazing car, a missed opportunity and a forgotten act of genius – GS genius.

GS was Citroën's first totally new-from-the ground-up car for years, its development costs were large, but so were its sales. GS's success turned Citroën from a massive loss maker into a profitable concern, albeit briefly. GS was exported and was also built at factories in Australia, Bulgaria, Chile, Indonesia, Slovenia, Thailand, Spain, South Africa, and Zimbabwe. In total, Citroën sold 2,466,757 of the GS and GSA.

In the end, as so often with 1970s cars, it was rust that did for the GS and the GSA, just as it did for that only other car at the time to offer advanced design, the AlfaSud (or Awful Sod as they became known). The GS had a strong hull with thick doors; good in a crash, yet when water got under the 'Tectyl' undersealing, they rusted away from the inside out. Rumour has that at Citroën's Rennes factory, they got the anode-cathode-effect paint dip bath for the bodies wired up in reverse for several months – so paint was repelled not attracted to the GS bodies during manufacture! That might explain the early cars rust! How true is the apocryphal tale? It was told to me by my neighbour in Brittany, who had worked at the factory in the early 1970s.

The suspension was never as complicated or as troublesome as some suggest;

my local village garage mended my GS's hydraulics with a re-sleeved pipe for £20 whereas the Citroën dealer wanted £500. My GSA (strangely rust free) stormed up the M4 to London every day for years, its boxer engine burbling away as the airflow cleaved over the car in silence. An *Autocar* technical editor (Michael Scarlett) once told me that he thought the GS was one of the best cars ever designed. I seem to remember Andrew Frankl agreeing. Compared to a Ford Escort, a Triumph Dolomite or a Vauxhall Viva, compared to Fiat 128 or an Austin Maxi, GS was a true spaceship from another dimension – it offered so much more in terms of engineering, design and its advancement. Here was a small car that cheated the air like a Jaguar coupé, rode like a Rolls-Royce, and yet remained a family hold-all.

The men behind the GS included: Alain Roche as project manager with Robert Opron as design leader with a team that included Michel Harmand who designed the interior; Henri Dargent; Jean Giret; Regis Gromik; with Jacques Charreton and Monsieur Albertus as body designers. Engine design came from Andre de Bladis as leader with the Monsieurs Cordier, Dupin, and Hondet. Paul Mages' hydro-pneumatic suspension design was used. Other design/engineering team members include Messrs Maillou, Nozati and Quinn. [Ref 1]

Beside the GS, only the Alfasud came close to offering the customer and the driver the brave new world of truly 'new' design. In the mid-1970s, most other car makers simply regurgitated old ideas and old practices. GS (and AlfaSud), delivered something new.

What of the VW Golf? Well, brilliant though it was, it was not an advance in terms of offering the average car buyer something completely new in engineering terms. Instead, it was simply a collection of well-engineered ideas that eclipsed the by then outdated and utterly awful range of rear-engined Volkswagens that were the low benchmark against which the new Golf was principally measured. Golf was indeed great to drive and to own, but underneath, it was simply an admission that the industry had been in a torpor, and that it had failed to give car buyers of the 1970s what it knew it could. In delivering the Golf, VW threw away an out-of-date product range and presented the state-of-the-possible as something new in the art – which it was not, but compared to a VW Beetle or a rear-engined jalopy like the VW 412, it *looked* like revolution.

In the Citroën GS, the real future *was* delivered, yet in a flawed execution which doomed it. As so often, a problem tainted the halo. Poor build quality eclipsed brilliant design. Golf *was* better made, if ultimately less of an advance as an engineering package. But GS did give VW, GM, Fiat and BL a shock, it made them pull their socks up as the motoring public realised that there was much more that they could and should have been given by the big car manufacturers' back-room boys. For example, as GS was offering what it did to the family car buyer, Ford's Escort was serving up antiquated engines, traditional suspension, metal and vinyl lined-cabins, seats that were no different from the 1930s metal framed perches, all wrapped up in 'three-box' booted, chrome laden, coke-bottle shaped flimsy bodyshell with a drag coefficient far worse than the Citroën's.

As the lozenge-shaped front-wheel drive GS delivered its lightweight engine, all-round powered disc brakes, low drag (best C_D of 0.318 for GSX3 and average range C_D of 0.355), advanced suspension and fully trimmed comfortable cabin, most car makers were churning out offerings of cast iron-engines, drum brakes, tin-plate interiors, leaf-springs and live axles amid anti-design that gave car buyers what they were *told* they wanted. Car makers delivered the least that they could and deliberately avoided delivering what they knew they should achieve in terms of safety, comfort, handling an aerodynamics. They tempted the public with motor show 'concepts' and 'design specials' that showed a future not *allowed* to be delivered. And then Citroën made a futuristic design a sales reality in the GS. Meanwhile, other car makers just repeated old practices, old designs, that were wrapped up in a re-skin of a 'fake' modernism.

In 1970 British Leyland was turning out square rigged galleons of cars – like the Triumph Toledo and Dolomite ranges – as dinosaurs of design and build. Yet Leyland had an early opportunity to view and purchase the design rights of Pinin Farina's 'Aerodinamica' studies for a large and medium sized car range that were based on BL's existing cars of 'ADO16' and 'ADO17' underpinnings. Scared of the 'new' that such design represented, BL continued on its conservative path to disaster. However, others would share Carrozzeria Pinin Farina's thoughts – the ones that BL refused to countenance

There was something magical about driving the GS and GSA. However underpowered, provided you drove it properly GS rewarded. Just as with the little old two-stroke Saabs, you had to keep GS revved up and 'on the cam'. Punting along through the gears, feeling the 'active' hydro-pneumatic suspension pumping away, getting the road's messages through the front wheels and the steering, the little GS somehow delivered a true driving experience. This car 'talked' to you – just like an old Saab, an old Porsche or an old MG. Long journeys in the GS were easy, the seats comfortable, the cabin peaceful, the self-levelling ride of limousine quality. GS could be hustled into corners, turned in and powered out. Get it right, use the gears not the brakes and GS could be conducted with aplomb, just like an old Saab two-stroke – no wonder they made surprisingly good little rally cars. Formula 1 Grand Prix driver Patrick Depailler found that rallying the GS on snow in the 1972 Chamnoix Rally revealed that the car had very good traction.

Long journeys in the GS had a sense of occasion and were not tiring unless it was very hot when the car's ventilation proved weak. But here was a cheapish, small-to-medium sized car that delivered superb comfort and ability as a driving tool and a passengers' carriage. The larger-engined GS variants found more favour, but whether of 1.2, 1.1 or 1.0 litres, the sound of the air cooled flat-four boxer engine was characterful and evocative. In the cabin, only that poor ventilation might have marred things; GS could be stuffy in the summer. The single-spoke steering wheel and ellipsoid shapes and fittings all added to the 'true' Citroën feel. Safer than a 2CV or Ami, more nimble than the later CX, GS was a hugely advanced 1970s car. GS was not just Car of the Year, it gained the *Style Auto* design award. We might cite it, and the NSU Ro80 as great cars eclipsed by circumstance and perceived opinions. But make no mistake, GS and its GSA variation, was and remains a real classic of a car and, of real driving.

Graham H. Wilson is a serial GS and GSA owner who really 'gets' the point of the GS. So too does David Evans at *Classic and Sports Car* magazine, another man who adores his GSA Spécial and runs it as a daily driver, recently fully restoring the car in a major fettling designed to ensure its longevity. 'I can drive it five hundred miles in a day and get out feeling fine and having enjoyed the drive. It's such an accomplished car.' said David when we compared GSA ownership notes at Martin Port's Thatcham Classic show..

Graham Wilson is certain. 'My GS is better to drive than my new Golf TSI. You just don't want to stop driving the GS because it is so comfortable, has great visibility and has low noise levels – much lower road and tyre noise than in a modern car. GSA has better heating and ventilation than GS, but the pair were a technological marvel when new and even today – self-levelling, aerodynamic and so many advanced features in a family car. If you enjoy driving, try a GS or GSA.' Ref 2

Surviving GS can still be seen in Eastern Europe, Asia and across South Africa. So GS *was* a success and in warmer climes, lasted longer. But in the end, rust and the public's resistance to change did for the GS, even if it morphed into a mild update as the GSA and took its advanced origins into a new era where not all the competition had caught up. The fact that over twenty years *after* GS's heyday, Ford should turn out the Focus – a car that so blatantly echoed GS design motifs tends to prove the point that GS was advanced in 1971 and that the mainstream industry refused to embrace or deliver such advance for years.

Today, a small number of GSs can be seen pottering about Britain; some even survive in Canada and a few made it to California. Britain has a GS 'guru', Rob Moss, who runs Chevronics. There, today's GS and GSA enthusiasts can get their 'fix'. The French still love the GS and GSA, but they are thin on the ground except in dryer southern climes. After 2.5 million GS/GSAs came out of the factory, the car died in 1986, but was quietly reincarnated via production in Yugoslavia and Indonesia. Many rest up in Africa's heat.

Citroën was once great by design, deliberately different, anarchic and confident. GS was much more important than you might realise, for it opened our eyes to what we could expect and demand. GS really was a car of French philosophy, GS Birotor was something even more. So this was the GS's story; brilliance was wasted for want of that elusive factor of quality.

Sadly, Citroën, having excelled with the new Cactus C4, has just ruined the double chevron dream – dumping hydro-pneumatics and hiving of the 'DS' line into a new and completely separate company as a 'DS Automobiles' marketing platform. And yes you've guessed it, the original Citroën DS is missing from the new brand's history because that DS was not a DS in the sense Citroën now wish you to perceive their DS marketing trick. So we have a new 'DS' legend yet one which bears no relation, nor any bloodline to the 'real' DS that started the affair of advanced design in the first place! Citroën is re-writing history and the brand is defining the product – not the other way round – which experience suggests might be preferable. Meanwhile, Honda has turned out a brilliant new Mk10 Civic, a car that looks like the aero-weapon offspring of a Citroën GS and Saab 900, leaving the 'DS' offerings to their badge-engineered bluster.

Was the C6 truly the last Citroën on the road oblivion? You might wonder. Oh Citroën what have you done?

14

Mazda Cosmo

Tripping the Light Fantastic

There is something different about Mazdas, even though the new ones share a legacy of past Ford, and General Motors input. Originally, Mazda was a bit alternative, rather like Saab in some ways; engines and aerodynamics and their arbiters of efficiency played large in the development of the Mazda story, yet it seems Honda took similar plaudits.

Today, there is a growing Mazda fan base, notably for the older cars – up to the RX7 and perhaps even the RX8 incarnations of a very Mazda way of doing things. Classic Mazdas seem to have character and presence, they communicate. Strangely it all began with cork – grown from a tree and with a reference to light and light bulbs. The word Mazda is based in a reference to ancient religion a god of light. It also happens to be the case that the founding family of what became branded as Mazda, in the late eighteenth century, were named Matsuda. Just like many a nascent car maker, Jujiro Matsuda went to work as a blacksmith. From there stemmed interest and experience in all things metal. By a convoluted series of events, he ended up as a director of post-First World War company that had its roots in the production of cork – a vital substance in many industries. That company was soon to be named the Toyo Kogyo Kaisha and, just as with Fuji Heavy Industries and its Subaru offshoot, the Toyo Kogyo diversified into steel making. From there it was an obvious step to become a manufacturer of cars by way of motorcycles and small trucks – a very familiar process.

By 1940, the company had designed its first car and only the Second World War stopped its progress. Significantly, the Toyo Kogyo had designed its own car and not simply licence-built a European or American existing design. In the 1950s, Japan's 'K' or ' Kei' taxation class for small cars with tiny engines of under 500cc soon led to a boom for home-produced light cars. Mazda became a brand and as early as 1959, Tsuneji Matsuda, son of Jujiro, had become fascinated by the rotary cycle engine which had been publicised in the American market by Curtiss Wright who had purchased a licence from NSU in Germany; holders of the Wankel rotary patents.

Shocked by NSU's slow progress and very keen to develop the rotary engine as fast as was possible, Mazda was prepared to throw money at Wankel engine development and appointed its long-standing engineering guru, Kenichi Yamamoto, to the role of not just developing the engine, but solving the issues of fuel and oil consumption and rotor tip sealing, that had led even NSU itself to contemplate walking away from the rotary concept.

As NSU and its licence holders abandoned the Wankel unit, Mazda persevered, an act for which we should be very grateful indeed, because sometime in the mid-1960s, some very clever men spent a great deal of Mazda money coming up with a series of cars that were very special. Mazda made notable variations to the Wankel design, changing the engine's porting to improve torque, achieving this by placing the inlet ports within the rotor casing. The alloy Mazda rotary was a water-cooled, tandem twin-rotor not dissimilar to the NSU KKM-612 design in configuration. The Cosmo 110S' engine weighs a mere 225 lbs and was only 20in long, 21in high and 23in wide.[Ref 1]

Indeed, Mazda beat NSU to actual sales of a twin-rotor-engined car.

The 1960s styling is exotic, clean, and for its time, very futuristic. This car looked more like a GM motor show concept car than a production vehicle. Throw in some 1960s Ford Thunderbird design themes, a touch of Michelotti and maybe a touch of Panhard, and you get the idea. Strangely, it all comes together to form a unique and distinct style that not only works, it has an identity. Given that it was drawn up in 1963, before the Toyota 2000GT, Cosmo becomes Japan's first real sports car and one of super car context. Cosmo had a very long, low front, a deep and stylish angled windscreen, then swept back into a long-tailed aerodynamically tuned rear-end. There were faired-in headlamps, exotic wing vents and the rotary equivalent of two-litre power capacity under the bonnet. With its twin-rotor power, cleaner breathing engine of nearly 130bhp and very low drag, the Cosmo could glide to 115mph and nearly125mph/201kph with ease in its post-1967 B-spec version with five-speed gearbox. The suspension saw a Dion axle, semi-elliptic leaf spring and trailing arm link to the rear and expensive wishbones at the front, powerful disc brakes (front) and latterly a five-speed gearbox ensured a good ride, handling and dynamic package, although the short-travel suspension and dampers created a firm ride. But this *was* a high-performance sports car designed to take on the Porsche 911, Jaguar E-Type and other western exotica, notably Ford and GM V8 coupés.

Approaching the Cosmo, you can spot its lack of then fashionable 'coke-bottle' curves. Instead, a straight-lined, clean-limbed look is punctuated by a dominant, side swage line running into a semi-shrouded rear wing and wheel arch motif. The cabin turret is curved and smooth and very Ford-esque, the rear end decidedly GM

Americana in its lamp shapes and detailing. As with much early Japanese design, the purity of the underlying shape is a touch marred by over exaggerated detailing of the gargoyle school of design. However, Cosmo was one of the cleanest-lined Japanese efforts and did create its own style, being far less of a cut and shut style than might be found in later Lexus designs which looked for all the world like a BMW and Mercedes-Benz cut half and welded together. Seen in the flesh, this Cosmo has shades of an aircraft without wings to it. The fuselage-like body somehow like a fuselage of a 1960s design fantasy.

The gear change was short-throw and notchy, in fact delightful, the wall of rotary torque, smooth and vibration free but leading to a high pitched rotary throb-cum-scream. A dark wood, cherry-hued steering wheel rim with drilled spokes, set amid a black cockpit effect fascia with a plethora of dials gave the Cosmo a real sports car feel at the driver's command post. The performance and the handling also delivered a taut, rear-wheel drive experience. The steering was light, direct and communicative. That long rear overhang might involve some tail wagging in extremis, but Cosmo could be hastened along with aplomb and rotary thrust through the gears.

There is indeed a touch of the personal jet fighter about the Cosmo, a smell of that GM concept car styling special prototype era, yet Cosmo was real, even if Mazda did only produce 1,176 examples of this defining machine. Strapping yourself in, Cosmo comes alive, the cabin a tight fitting but cockpit affair of Cosmo of 1966-1972 laid down the roots of later Cosmos and a range of rotary-powered Mazdas. In the end, the last Cosmo was a sleek, elegant, two-door GT of somewhat Pininfarina-like appearance.

Here in the Cosmo was a sports car with a sense of occasion, a true moment. It then gave rise to the Mazda R-100 (a re-engined conventionally powered model), the RX-130, the front-drive RX-2, the RX-3, Luce coupés, and the very elegant, Michelotti-influenced R-130 coupé with its BMW-crossed-with-Lancia looks. That Mazda's rotaries went onwards to RX-7 and RX-8 should really come as no surprise to anyone. All these Mazdas are now cult cars in Japan, Australia, New Zealand and America. That they remain lower profile in Europe is intriguing and perhaps a reflection of how good they were and how Europe refused to believe it. We should not forget that three Mazda-entered R-100s took part in the 1969 twenty-four-hour endurance race at Spa Francorchamps These rotary cars lasted the race and came home fifth and sixth overall (one crashed) despite being up against best works-supported race teams in the world. Mazda, and its version of the Wankel engine, had well and truly arrived. Even Italian racing driver Constantino Magistri of Abarth fame, converted to racing rotary Mazdas. And a Mazda rotary-powered Chevron competed at Le Mans in 1970 but retired; however the same car finished second in class at the Nurburgring.

If only the 1970's fuel crisis had not focused minds on the rotary's high fuel consumption. Many observers feel that the Cosmo 110S and its siblings and offshoots, notably the RX-7, signify a mark on the map of automotive history that should be better appreciated and higher valued. Was a Porsche 924 really so much better than a first edition RX-7? After all, Mazda sold more RX-7s in North America alone (378,000) than Porsche sold in total (151,000). And was a Porsche 944 really 'purer' and better designed than the third generation1990s RX-7 FD Twin Turbo? Was a Nissan Skyline GTR really more preferable to a tuned up rotary Mazda RX-8 [Ref 2] Should we have forgotten that the Mazda R-110 of 1968 was the world's first volume production Wankel rotary-powered car?

A not insignificant technical achievement.

There is just one Cosmo 110S on British roads – ABW 136F – owned by Wankel fanatic Phil Blake, who also runs an RX-7, RX-8, Eunos Cosmo, and fifteen NSU Ro80s. Clearly a man of taste and intellect! Mazda, purveyors of interesting and characterful motor cars that led not followed the herd; buy now before they become rarer.

15

Leyland's Antipodean Efforts

P 76

The British Motor Corporation and its BLMC and post-1968 'BL' corollary and its ex-colonial-inspired worldwide export empire produced some heroic failures. Yet BLMC's so evocatively named P76 was once Australia's Car of the Year. Most Brits had never heard of it. In the early 1970s, the by now British Leyland as 'BL' became synonymous with dated design and thrown-together cars. Worst of all was the company's habit of 'badge engineering', the system where it would take a body shell and produce Austin, MG, Morris, Riley and Wolseley variants of the same thing. But, beyond these shores, Leyland did things that few Leyland-buying Brits ever saw in an age before mass travel. In India, a five-door hatchback version of the Triumph Herald was sold, while in Africa and Australia, hatch-backed versions of the Austin 1100 were locally made. In Australia, Citroën had tried to flog the Slough-built Traction Avant as a British Citroën! But that was not as bad as when a big Austin got Bruced up and given a girl's name. Someone must have had a kangaroo or two lose in the top paddock.

The best of the worst of all such colonial Leylands – was a car named 'Kimberley' that the late comedian Victoria Wood would have adored if she had known about it. Built in Australia by the antipodean offshoot, the Kimberley was the centre section of the Austin/Morris 1800/2200 'land crab' model, which then had a boxy boot tacked on to the rear and an aircraft carrier-style bonnet stuck on the front, under which lurked an enlarged engine that ran hot and needed more than bush tucker servicing. It was an attempt to sell to the typical Australian market, which meant that it was doomed from the start. Any Aussie could have predicted such a fate. A lesser version, badged as the 'Tasman' was also made. Aussies knew that these modified cars really did have a face like a smashed crab, or as some said, 'a car with a face like the northbound end of a southbound cow'.

Not long afterwards, a tweaked down-under version of the Morris Marina heralded the PR puff of 'Leyland Australia' as a brand on the up. Aussie Marinas were all right around town, but show them an outback road and it all went wrong very quickly indeed. It was an act of farnarkling – Australian for an activity which creates an appearance of productivity but which has no substance to it. The trouble was, the Australians of the 1970s loved the Holden FX and big rear-drive V-8 or V-6-engined cars with large boots, tough bodies and easily repairable mechanicals. Bench seats, decent heavy duty suspension and big wheels were de rigueur before the heady 1980s days of 'poncey' Japanese coupés, as outback red necks called them. Aussies liked 'utes' – pick-up truck, open-backed car-van versions that included a V6 Ford Cortina ute. 'Beaut-utes' with shiny parts polished paint – or 'duco' as it is called in Australia, were also popular.

So, faced with such realities, Leyland Australia came up with the land crab derivative – the Kimberley. Realising its failure, it then came up with a 'proper' Australian car known as the P76 of which even the best-informed classic car enthusiasts tend to be unaware. In 1969, Leyland Australia was given the go-ahead to build a new car for Australia. With very little money to put into the project – A\$20m – the Aussies got a new car. Triumph's Harry Webster commissioned Giovanni Michelotti to style the new car – the P76. The cars could be had with either a 2.6-litre in-line Leyland engine or a 4.4-litre V8 unit that was a legacy of the still-born Rover P8 saloon, for the Rover 3.5-litre ex-Buick V8 was in the parts bin.

The bigger-engined version had nearly 200bhp and more than 280lb/ft of torque and Aussie farmers reckoned you could tow a plough with that. The handling was sorted by an ex-MG Abingdon man, a Mr Brocklehurst, who developed the car at the MIRA test-track in Warwickshire.

The styling was superb, and was only dated by the 1970s fashion for chromed grilles and ornate trim. The lines were clean and elegant, helped by minimal use of panel pressings and boasted features such as hidden windscreen wipers. The shape was a modern high-tailed wedge with presence; Michelotti had produced a truly international shape that, with only a bit of minor tidying, could well have lasted into the 1980s. Launched in 1973, the car was a sensation for Leyland and was voted Australia's 'Car of the Year'. There were Deluxe, Super and Executive versions, and a sporty Targa Florio model with alloys and side stripes. The P76 had a massive interior, excellent handling, and a 36cuft boot. It was also advanced in safety terms; every door contained a wide steel crash barrier plate to ward off intrusion in an accident (BL's British built cars did not boast such devices). The P76s were built in Leyland's plant at Zetland, near Sydney. The orders poured in. Yet, as so often with Leyland's history, issues with parts supplies and the small matter of a strike took their toll. Within two years, the wheels began to fall off the P76 project, even though it was also built in New Zealand and the British motoring press were given UK-spec cars to drive in London. The thought of potential British sales rose on the good write-ups the car received in Britain but, as so often with BL, it all fell apart.

By 1975, Leyland Australia's losses were mounting further and the P76 lost its way as BL closed its last Commonwealth outpost. Unsupported in comparison to home-grown Holdens and Fords, and then the Datsun invasion of the Australian market, the P76 wasted away and died quietly after less than three years in the market. Only 12,525 cars were sold. An estate version, intended as a mainstay of the Australian market, was made but never marketed. But before the P76 died, there was a sting in the tail of the story, a sting that to many observers, including car designers, represents one of the greatest and most typically British losses of the era. The P76's twist was that it had spawned a coupé version.

Labelled bizarrely as the 'Force 7', the P76 coupé was tooled up and produced in low numbers; less than 100 were made before the factory was closed. The styling was European, aping the Audi Coupé of the time and the Renault 17. A huge glass hatchback framed a fastback rear with muscle-car extractor vents. The side windows had pillarless construction and Michelotti gave the grille an Italian supercar style. It looked sleek in side profile, and wide from any angle, but it *was* stylish. Both these P76 designs are now rare. Only two P76s are known to be in the UK and a few of the coupés still exist in Australia.

This is yet another tale that encapsulates the story of British Leyland 'BL' or 'Bloody 'ell', itself a disastrous experiment by politicians of Left and Right and by management good and bad, of workforce willing and unwilling, a story that frames a peculiar period in British industrial and social history. Yet hidden in the entrails of Australian motoring, utterly overshadowed by Holden and Ford, there lies an amazing tale – that of the 1934 Southern Cross saloon. This was entirely Australian designed and built with British influence, a car that looked like a futuristic re-working of the Riley Kestrel Mk1. Backed by aviation pioneer Sir Charles Kingsford Smith, the Southern Cross was noteworthy in being a very early attempt at a big, tough, wooden-constructed plywood monocoque – years before de Havilland's did the same thing in an aeroplane in the Mosquito. The Southern Cross had an Australian-made and unusual flat-four engine giving a very healthy 55bhp, the provenance of which was and remains very hard to define. Deemed a fire risk in the outback, the wooden monocoque had to be sheathed in light steel to allay such fears under the sun, adding to its weight. But here was a potentially successful, true Australian car. Sadly, only eleven were reputedly built before Kingsford Smith was killed in an air crash while attempting the England-Australia record; so ended the Southern Cross.

Leyland Australia would come along decades later and itself crash and burn.

Today, Aussies, even outback Aussies, drive Hondas, Kias, Hyundias, Nissans, Toyotas and thankfully, the last remnants of Holden and Ford, but as for the Kimberleys, Tasmans, and stumbling ossified Marinas? They are gone, back to the rust and the red dust of a time best forgotten. Aussie classic cars still rule and Rovers and Alfas still have a place in the heart of Australian motoring memories. Leyland's P76 is long gone from the consciousness however, a shame as they were so very good.

16

Volvo-Itis

What is it about old Volvos? Why do people love them or hate them? Apart from the big bumpers on a late model 140 or a 240 series, there is little to offend, provided you get beyond the conservatism. It is often assumed that Saabists hate Volvos. This is not true and like many Saab owners, I have owned Volvos. In fact, I have owned more Volvos than I have Saabs and, with one exception, the Volvos have been utterly trouble free and racked up huge mileages with nothing more than basic servicing and an occasional small part. The Volvo secret has always been build quality – well almost always. There *is* a quality of Volvos – quality to the steel, the structure, the engines, the orthopaedic seats (from 1965) as surely the best car seats ever, and quality to the way they were put together. True the early P1800s rusted, but I know of no other rust-prone real Volvo. You may disagree, but all I can say is that from 121 to 240 to V70, my Volvos have never rusted, never gone wrong and they just oozed that vital build quality. My recent early-2000s V70 had massive quality, the parts were durable, the car never, ever broke. Sadly, the same could not be said of the appalling quality of my General Motors Saab 9-3, a car which failed to match the standards of my classic 900 GLE, a car truly built to bomb-proof quality.

Volvos have been thick skinned and heavy for decades. Whether that will continue is a moot point, but if you a running a 120, a 140 or 160, or even a later 200 series, one thing is for sure – the damned things last. But do people still think Volvos are unwieldy tanks with poor handling and boring 'three-box' designs? No. Latterly, the Volvo styling revolution gave us the likes of the C70, and another era of big shouldered cars, but back in Volvo's classic decades, some Volvos were curved and were great rally cars, notably the 120-series. 1950s Volvos such as PV444 and 544 may have aped American styling themes but they did not mimic American thin steel or single-skinned construction. In 1956, Volvo built the P1900 Volvo's one and only experiment in glass-fibre; sixty eight of the US, 'jet age' styling effect two-door soft top were built. Today they are all but invisible, but they were curvaceous.

The ubiquitous 1950s stylist Mr Loewey did not design the 120 series, although it looked like he might have done. 120 was in fact the work a young chap named

Jan Wilsgaard who had little experience but a huge talent for creating space, scale and delightful yet simple detail. His idea beat the design proposal of Volvo's existing design consultant H. Petterson. But were there shades of Italian elegance in the Wilsgaard shape? Whatever the influences, the design 'worked' in that it was clean, timeless, international and unlikely to date too quickly. Volvo's Board chose it to take the firm into a new age and a new marketing territory. The interior was the work of another Swede, a Mr Lange who had also proposed a body design for the new car.

As the 1950s closed and the new 120 series (latterly branded 'Amazon' in Sweden but not elsewhere due to copyright issues) debuted around the world, Volvo had set its brand markers and proved its promises with strong, tough, durable cars. As early as 1960, Volvos had great big seats with extra support, seatbelts, headrests, armour-plated doors and thick roofs. But at 1.6-litres they were never over-powered, a factor soon rectified by 1.8 and 2.0 litre versions which, with the right carburettors, tuning and technique could be hustled along quite nicely thank you. The 122S model was in fact 1.8 litres, but the engine had massive torque and was unburstable, having its origins in a boat engine design.

These 120s had the look of Americana about them – especially to the snout and tail – yet were cleaner, less adorned. With wishbone suspension up front and proper multi-link type axle location at the rear, with plenty of depth to the suspension travel, the big cars rode well and were not 'lurchers'. Rear-wheel drive they may have been, but they handled. The original three-speed gearbox was quickly supplanted by a four-speeder. By 1963, Volvo was building 120s in Canada for the North American market.

Soon there was a 123GT two-door with a stiffer body and 110mph top speed. In 1962 there came an estate car that created the market for big box-backed wagons that could take a family and save its life. Volvo's next iteration of its up-market theme was the equally tough, equally unburstable 140 series – which, like its home-grown rival the Saab 99/900, stayed in production for too long and had a new nose grafted on. But the original 120 series were even longer in life, being produced from August 1956 to July 1970.

Italian designer Pietro Frua's influence was said to be seen in the curves of the Volvo P1800 coupé – in which Petterson was a lead stylist. Today, Volvo has been re-born with curves and better handling, so newer Volvos have a wider audience. Volvo is now Chinese-owned and, so far, has retained its integrity and design language. But the roots of our perceptions of Volvo are in those quintessential Jan Wilsgaard styled, 100 and 200 series from the 1960s and 1970s. These cars were dubbed 'tanks', possibly the safest cars made – so safe that when car safety took off in the US, the authorities used the 240 as its crash-test benchmark. Pillars and sills were not just thick, they had reinforcing fillets and seam welding. The doors were deep, rigid and reinforced by a proper steel tube not some tin strip. The steel in this car was superior.

The 140 saloon and its estate model the 145, which sold more in Britain than anywhere else, *made* Volvo. Farmers, horsey types and the middle-class suburban set took to these cars in their millions. The 140s had a heavy old 2.0-litre engine, a lump that reflected Volvo's truck, boat and aviation engine work. A 'posh' version of the 140, with a 1950s-style upright radiator grille and a six-cylinder engine, came out; the 164, '6' for six cylinders (with 175bhp) and '4' for four doors. There were even rare 165 estates. Even today these classy gems with equal build to 1970s Mercedes, still languish as cheap classics amid an ownership cult that extends from London to Lousiana.

The Volvos had, in the opinion of many, the best car seats ever made. The estates had acres of space. The entire range was made from thick, top-quality British steel; in fact, the car had a high percentage of British-sourced components, including the wonderfully named Laycock de Normanville overdrive unit, a 1950s device last used by Humber. The Volvo body design stood the test of time. In the 1970s, these Volvos passed the now fashionable offset frontal crash test which is far harder to engineer for than the full frontal head-on- into-a-wall test. In the US, Volvo's boast was that, for years, the fatality rate in its 240 models was the lowest of any car. Volvo's safety reflected the work of engineer Nils Bohlin at the advanced Volvo Safety Centre. Bohlin invented the three-point safety belt and pioneered reinforced 'safety cell' design, padded cabins and one-piece roof panels. Volvo gave the three-point belt to the world for free to save lives.

When the 240 came along in 1975, Volvo made the nose and tail softer to absorb crash forces better; the roof was still a roll-over-proof cage, though. The doors were still armour-plated and when you compared them to the thin, single-skinned door panels on other cars, you knew where the money had gone. The passive safety was high, but it was active safety that let the cars down. Rear-wheel drive, long overhangs and slow steering meant that the Volvos were not agile; they had less chance of avoiding or steering around danger. New suspension and steering improved things on the 240 range, through which Volvo truly went for the big-bumper look by hanging acres of what most thought was angle iron – actually aluminium – off the car. So was born the most obvious aspect of the 'tank' or 'Swedish brick' image. In the end, the 700-series cars replaced the old chariots. But they refused to die, they rarely rusted, the engines, especially the four-cylinder version, were indestructible. Only time has thinned the ranks.

Volvo 120s, 140s and 240s, are all cheap to buy in Britain and beyond. These old Swedish tanks just keep on rolling, whistling along with all the aplomb and serenity of a car that you know that if it encounters a modern hatchback, will simply shrug off the assault and bound on, Labrador-like, to its destination, leaving the mangled remains of its opponent quivering beside the road. Can we say the same about the 850 or V70? Almost, and yet good as they are, notably the 850T5 and V70R, they were built to a different, more modern incarnation. They last, but old Swedish battleships they are not.

Having been re-invented by Peter Horbury's pen that evolved Volvo into a new age via the elegant and timeless C70 (surely a modern classic in the making), Swedish 'bricks' are no more. Instead of laughing at Volvos, you might want to try one – they really are proper cars for adults.

17

Rover's Revenge

SD1: Bache's Brilliant Bruiser

In what feels like a moment of recent time, yet which is four decades old,Rover
– or, rather, British Leyland's legacy – produced one of the best British cars ever
designed. Sadly, this car was also one of the worst British cars ever made; the sense
of having been thrown together with all the aplomb that BL, its sometimes inept
management, and an often defeatist workforce, could manage. The Rover 3500
hatchback or the SD1, as it was better known, was an icon of industrial design
and a car with immense character. It was a product of BL's Specialist Division
(hence SD1) of Rover-Triumph. For the want of build quality, this car could have
become the definitive 1980s executive car. Instead, BMW grabbed the glittering
prizes (and, in the end, Rover itself). Sadly, the rest is a typical example of recent
British history. Rover's great heritage reached a modernist peak in the SD1. If you
parked a 1976 SD1 next to a 1938 Rover streamliner fast-backed saloon, youmight
see a lineage. Rover's 1960s P6 had also been modern if somewhat 'British' in its
chrome work and gargoyles, but it had boasted a V8 and advanced technicalities
under the skin and in its suspension and handling. Rover had a proud engineering
and design heritage; Rover's P5s had been favoured by HM Queen Elizabeth II and
a host of British Prime Ministers, even Labour ones. Who could have predicted that
the once proud Rover's final output would be soft, re-badged Hondas as 800, 600
200, or the execrable 100, the 'City Rover' and, a bastard by design, named '75'?

The SD1 was fast and very safe; it passed the now fashionable offset crash test
in 1975. It handled well and, of course, it had the venerable ex-Buick light-weight
alloy 155bhp V8 that had found its way into Rovers from the 1960s. Above all,
the SD1 had style. Faced with an aborted Rover P8 and a Giovanni Michelotti-
designed half-Rover, half-Triumph 1970s saloon proposal, Rover let the designer
David Bache loose. Bache turned in a car that shocked Rover traditionalists
from the torpor of their square-rigged certainties; SD1 was a curvy, hatchbacked
behemoth, yet one that was also lithe and elegant, and sold in an odd range of
brave colours; mustard, puce, slime and abattoir hues. A colour called Triton Green
really spiced up the super-car looks, though; Rover's design team drove Triton

SD1s. The car also looked very fine in 'Richlieu' a dark imperialist marron. Set alongside square-rigged saloons, SD1 looked like the future. Only the Citroën CX and Lancia Gamma aped its style, yet soon many more would follow SD1s lead.

Legend has it that the Ferrari 365 Daytona inspired Bache and overtones of it are clearly visible in his styling – yet there were hints of Pininfarina's 1960s aerodynamic show cars, too, especially in the rear-end design. But Bache's car was *not* a copy; it was a hallmark. Lancia's Gamma and the Citroën CX sought similar answers to the same problems, but Bache's design had real cohesion. Unlike the more recent 1990s Rover 75, the SD1 wasn't a galleon of a car, sporting more shiny jewellery than a retro-pastiche time-warp could carry, it was a low-drag hatchback of its own fashion.

The interior was also a significant step forwards in car interior design and the single piece instrument 'pod' looked modern and permitted easy and cheap conversion to left hand drive. There was no traditional Rover wood, be it real or fake. The massive fascia moulding was a sculpture in its own right and also provided excellent impact absorbing qualities. The seats were brilliant – up to Volvo standards of comfort. Only the Citroënesque steering wheel with its lack of traditional 'arms' or spokes presented a question. Here was not just design modernity inside a car, but also a trend or fashion setting moment that left rivals' interiors (think BMW, Mercedes-Benz, Volvo) behind in another age. SD1, so often discussed for its exterior design, actually created a major stepping stone in interior design. Meanwhile, back on the outside, one of Bache's key SD1 hallmarks was the shape and 'emotion' of the front windscreen and A-pillar design. With its sharp top corners, raked angle and curved lower corners, the windscreen and pillar shape bestowed a look upon the car that was subtle yet vitally important in terms of its graphics. It seems, from the glass to the wheels, to the indented flute along the flanks, set beside the headlamp slits, the overall profile and the rear aspect, that every aspect of this car had been thought about, considered and honed. It clearly was *not* a Ferrari 'copy'.

The SD1 pulled together all sorts of themes and made them work; photographed parked under the nose of Concorde when the SD1 was Car of the Year 1976, this Rover really was a captain's carriage. Mrs Thatcher's ministers fought for them, as did the police. But, in typically British fashion of the era, it all went wrong. SD1 buyers soon noticed that bits fell off. The new factory's problems meant that the paint flaked, the electrics went awry and the hull leaked. Then Rover had a brain wave; lumber the car with some wheezy 2.0, 2.3, and 2.6 litre engines as economy specials with thinner wheels, delete the Dunlop Denovo run-flat tyres, and, according to Rover's adverts, 'success' would 'breed success'. And pigs might fly.

Needless to say, 'success' didn't. However, once sorted, the 2.6 did provide a natural middle ground for Rover owners and sold well to companies. The next Solihull-inspired piece of IQ was to move production to Oxford and lard up the car with a wood-trimmed facelift in 1981. They did, however, source an Italian diesel engine for a version that came along before the diesel fashion took hold. Two examples of an SD1 estate were built (one of which can be seen at the British Motor Museum in Gaydon). But Volvo was safe, as Leyland binned them and missed the estate-car boom.

However, all was not lost. Enter the Rover SD1 Vitesse. Pumped up with 190bhp, plus, via some tweaked 'twin plenum' induction, and superb rear-drive handling, the big Rover saw off everything in sight with its low-tech charms. It did the same thing on the racing circuit, where the SD1 had run rampant over the European Touring Cars series in the early 1980s. A 200bhp, leather-and wood-lined luxo-barge version of the SD1, sporting the Vanden Plas name, staggered around the 1985 market for a while. Mine was navy blue with massive alloys, and I just resisted fitting a 1980s body kit. Naturally, it broke down a lot and drank fuel, but it had style and grunt. But by 1986, the SD1 was a dinosaur on limited time. It was soon replaced by the front-drive Honda-derived Rover 800, which like so many Honda-Rovers of the era, was a different animal; the rest of the debacle is history.

However, the SD1 was to live on – in India. Rover shipped 12,000 SD1 kits to Madras, and there, the old SD1 was put back together, but incredibly, with a 40-year-old 1991cc Standard-designed engine, as found in India's ancient Ambassador taxi fleet. This asthmatic old engine and changes to the SD1's suspension finally did for the Rover, as did a Nissan diesel-powered version! There were more than a quarter of a million SD1s made. Just few thousand remain worldwide, and only 300 or so are registered with Britain's licensing authority. SD1s remain rotting in the undergrowth where the SD1 owners club now goes to rescue them. The club is based in Swindon, home to Rover's ex-owner Honda and where Rover had its last industrial stand with a body-pressing plant once of Pressed Steel Ltd. The club does a marvellous job saving Rover's and Bache's elegant but flawed devices – be it the American-spec SD1 (looking even more like an early Ferrari Daytona with its four-round headlamps), the 2000, 2300, 2600, or VM-Motori-engined diesel variants. SD1 made a mark, but sadly, often for the wrong reasons.

SD1 was fast, but suffered from roll and a touch of wallow when cornered quickly. It was revisions to the suspension (not least to 'improve' police-spec SD1s) that led to the SD1's race-car specification and consequent, race-dominating Touring Car Championship success driven by Steve Soper and Peter Lovett. The superb Vitesse model with its 'mini-Aston Martin' feel took such SD1 delights to the public. The lightweight ex-Buick engine was a dream and once properly, stroked,a , SD1 became the classic rear-wheel drive V8 weapon: a mini-Aston Martin. On wide A-roads, an SD1 Vitesse could see off supercars of exotic badges and vast expense. Yet it could seat four, swallow luggage and cheat the air. Here was a grand tourer. A V8-S version born from the North American market SD1 specification proved very popular and boasted some exquisite alloy wheels finished in gold (unless you ordered a silver SD1). Yet, as with so much of BL's output, the quality was lacking and that manifested in a less than wonderful ownership experience. But the fact remains that SD1 was (arguably) the last, mainstream, great British car of the 1970s and 1980s – a last wave of the flag that gave you the Avro Vulcan, the Vickers VC10, the BAC Concorde, the Aston Martin V8 Vantage, and the Ford Capri; SD1 was the last output of a tradition of British engineering and enthusiasm. SD1 was indeed special, a real car. A last of the line hero.

SD1 was originally to be replaced by a BL SD2 as that unwise amalgam of Rover and Triumph themes, but in reality, as Rover commercially peeled off from the great BL dinosaur, SD1 was replaced via a BL-Honda link-up that had begun with the unfortunate process of replacing the fifteen-year old Triumph Dolomite with a re-badged Honda Ballade, the result being a banal vision, often in beige. Soon afterwards, with SD2 and a so-called BL 'LC10' prototype abandoned, Rover became Honda-infused and the next 'Rover' was the SD1's replacement – the 800 series – based on the beautifully finished but softer, Honda Legend and its own floorpan and structure, one that heralded a low-fronted, big-windscreen, front-wheel drive executive car market contender amid slush-moulded plastic, an admittedly creamy Honda 2.7 litre screamer of an engine (the 2.5 being too wheezy) and a lack of depth as a badge-engineered product. In Rover's new Honda-based iteration of Englishness, branded as 800, 825, 827, 'Vitesse', and bizarrely as 'Sterling', the interior plastics faded into varying colours under the sun, the door and wing panels' swage lines rarely lined up, the gearboxes needed care, the plastic spoilers wilted, and the electrics threw fits of mood and Pirellis lasted not long at all. The 800 just felt, *thin*. Not a Rover at all old boy. Still, it drove quite nicely, notably in later 827 Vitesse form. Mine was gold and screamed along with its amazing Honda motor – the best bit of the car!

Rovers – real Rovers – of old had been heavy-gauge built and tough and SD1 ended the last of the true Rover lineage, to be replaced not just by that shock of the new, but by the beginning of the end. Let's not mention the Rover 75, except in KV6 or Ford V8 engined guises – real muscle cars on the quiet.

Wrapped up in the flag of 'British' patriotism, SD1 was a brilliant idea, badly made, poorly presented, and left to wither. Rover was eventually to be sold off to a foreign buyer as part of the apparent deliberate denuding of the British engineering base seemingly amid some ideological paradox of giant construction yet one wrapped up in the waving of the Union Jack. So, RIP Rover, but let's not forget the classic, brilliant-but-flawed SD1, the car that was Thatcherism's tainted wheels. This truly was the old world's last stand. If they had got the SD1 right, Rover would still exist, Britain would be richer and the Midlands would still make mass-market cars by the millions.[Ref 1]

18

Unsung Heroes

Classic Car Designers

The great designers have tailored many of the greatest cars in history – the cars that are now our classics. They were sculptors in steel who knew about three-dimensional design and appreciated a car from all angles and in all lighting conditions – indeed, the way light falls upon a car body design remains one of the essential ingredients in the act of design demonstrated by classic cars; such sculptural scales and tensions seem missing from many of today's new computer aided, lines-on-a-map school of car body designs where on-screen CAD designs of repeated regurgitation often become definitive before the modelling phase. Is *this* the real reason modern some cars look the same – *not* the effect of safety and other legislation, but the effect of cars being designed on a CAD screen by people who have been taught to fly-by-wire rather than hand and eye co-ordination?

Good car design must be the resolution of conflicting demands and ideas by a three-dimensional process; how can these issues of tension, scale, stance and light, be resolved digitally and from set menus and modes? Some top designers say that they can be, and easily. Others, fundamentally disagree. In the old days, certain designers worked very quickly, going from brain to hand-carved sculpture with an urgency that avoided hours of styling rendering drawings. From this came expression and movement. Today's young car designers must find other ways to achieve such results. It is a conflict of and in design, one that causes many arguments. If you are wondering why all cars now look the same, there are many answers, but fashion, celebrity, marketing, and the paradox of the limitations of computer aided design are some of the influencing factors. Yet does the carrozzeria 'school' still exist? Can the old ways of design reinvent themselves for a new future that, nonetheless, avoids the rash of copy-cat 'me too' styling that means the front of an Audi looks like the front of a Hyundai, or a Nissan SUV mirrors someone else's, or a Lexus resembles the bastard offspring of Benz and BMW after a night on the bratwurst?

Carrozzeria Pininfarina

Can any design house equal the Farina elegance? Others have chapters of genius, but it is the consistency of Pininfarina excellence, of line and balance, the setting of a scale that yet is never a fashion, which demands our attention. Sculpture in steel – Pininfarina genius – past, today and thankfully, tomorrow; learning from the past but never recycling it. Of Battista, Sergio, Andrea, and Paulo Farina, of Renzo Carli, Leonardo Fiorvanti, Aldo Brovarone, and Paulo Martin, we can only stand in awe and cast our eyes upon the canon of their works. Renzo Carli often gets forgotten but it was Carli who was a pilot and student of aerodynamics. Carli brought much knowledge to the 'new' Pininfarina and its expansion at the wind-tunnel equipped Grugliasco facility. And what was it that Sergio Pininfarina and Renzo Carli said in April 1980 at the launch of their book *Pininfarina Cinqantanni*? Something about, the young broadening their knowledge of the past they did not experience and, of the old having a reminder of feelings which must still be alive in their souls. [Ref 1]

Classic stuff for classic car enthusiasts.

I was lucky enough to meet Sergio Pininfarina, the visionary. He oozed brilliance but not in an arrogant way, just in an embodiment of quiet class. Sergio has gone now, as has his elder son Andrea, so today another son, Paolo, makes sure Pininfarina is looking ahead, not back to the retro past as some designers are doing in search for 'heritage'. Chief Designer for Pininfarina is the veteran, Fabio Filippini, the creator of the 2015 Ferrari 'Sergio' and its perfect lines. Leonardo Fioravanti has moved on to his own design bureau.

Pininfarina has created about 700 car designs or contributions, yet while Battista Farina and his son Sergio's works remain exalted, the designs of Franco Scaglione, Giorgetto Guigario and Marcello Gandini, do occupy a significant place upon the world's stage through their influence upon so many marques. We should recall that Paulo Martin, Giovanni Michelotti, Pietro Frua, Dante Giacosa, Aflredo Vignale, Felice Mario Boano, and Ercole Spada, have *all* touched global car design and branding. And would Alfa be what it is without Carrozzeria Touring?

Bertone, a great carrozzeria reaching back before 1920, shaped so many cars, yet is now gone, shut down and sold off, a tragic fate for the company that splattered lines and colour across the decades of car design. From Giovanni Bertone to his son Nuccio, Bertone's tutelage and opportunity, there came dozens of cars for many manufacturers. From Citroën BX, Fiat X19, to Lamborghini Muira and far beyond, Bertone (and the name of designer Gandini) is writ large upon the design landscape. Marcello Gandini at Bertone gave us so much, from Countach, Stratos, BX, Polo, concept cars, the GS-based Camargue, the XM, and the Renaults he latterly shaped; what of the Muira story? What of Gandini – we know so little about the man other than his genius. Of the earlier Bertone concept cars, the Scaglione-designed Alfa Romeo BAT series, the Marazal (that begat the Lamborghini Espada), the Delfino, the Sibilo, and the Slalom, all rank as stunningly designed and executed acts of car couture. If only Lancia had been able to produce Bertone's Kayak coupé.

Some say that Guigario's early years were his best, but if we look not just at his VW Golf, his Alfas, but also at his 1980s concept cars, we see true vision. The Megagamma invented the MPV, the Medusa was large yet slippery and classically architectural, the Etna was a Lotus. Aztec, Aspid and Asgard were defining sculptures of Ital Design. If only Renault had been brave enough in the 1980s to produced Guigairo's Renault prototype, the Gabbiano, the renaissance of Renault might have started earlier. Italian design excellence, the blend of couture and technicality started early – Alfa Romeo's own attempt at a pre-aerodyne came along as early as 1913. It was designed by Guiseppi Merosi and was not just teardrop-shaped, it had a curved windscreen and an alloy body.

One of the unanswered questions in classic car conversations is, how did French car design become what it did? What was the journey behind French styling and of focus – specifically Citroën design and its language? All too often, the expertise of Panhard and Bonier, Bonnet and Deutsch, goes unmentioned in the story, subsumed as Panhard was by Citroën. But is it possible to better understand the process of French design? These are valid question for the classic car enthusiast even if he or she is not particularly focused on French cars, not least because the roots of French car design and French car designers have touched other marques across the global car industry. An early streamlining movement started in France but *not* via the outrageous 'styling' of the 1930s Baroque carrossiers as is so often erroneously suggested. Frenchman, Austro-Hungarians, Germans and the British have all led design development, yet it is too easy to forget 1920s and 1930s American design and airflow pioneers. There are many men whose names and works remain obscured.

Throughout car design there are lesser-known names behind the headlines. I relish discovering more about designers such as Roy Axe, Dan Ambramson, Art Blakeslee, Peter Cambridge, Wayne Cherry, Gerry Coker, Bjorn Envall, Rex Fleming, Roy Haynes, Don Hayter, Ron Hickman, Graham Hull, Dudley Hume, Alan Jackson, Tom Karen, Colin Neale, Peter Stevens, or Harris Mann, Geoff Matthews, Gerald Palmer, Irv Rybick, Dawson Sellar, Martin Smith, William Towns, Satoru Nozaki, to cite some names known inside the industry or to the *cognoscenti* but not necessarily beyond its shores.

British designer Frank Feeley was the man who had trained at Lagonda and from the later-1940s shaped Aston Martin's new cars. Neither should we ignore Dr Tom Karen, Ogle Design, and the world's first sports coupe-estate design hybrid that was Karen's elegant Reliant Scimitar. Despite being constrained by parts-bin borrowed items, Karen turned out one of the most elegant examples of sculpture on wheels. Like so many designers, he had an aviation background – having studied at Loughborough College (as had Malcolm Sayer), and was also a man who understood sculpture, scale, light and thinking in three dimensions; such issues being major points of discussion amid the tutoring of today's, CAD, on-screen designers in a two dimensional, digital setting. Scimitar by the way, was the only glassfibre-bodied car of its day that incorporated steel reinforcements into its shell, so Scimitar was stronger than certain other plastic-moulded cars.

Steve Harper is the little-known name who under Harris Mann's tutelage at BL, worked on Solihull's stlying and then the MGF, before touching various Ford and Volvo designs. Harper also worked with the leading independent of MGA design and there, penned the Bentley Turbo R. Few have heard of Harper, but you may have owned one his cars. He is still sketching – from the rather curious car design base of Paignton, Devon.

Perhaps can we now agree that Martin Smith's Audi Quattro design – the one that wrapped Jörg Bensinger's engineering idea in pure style in a project overseen by Ferdinand Piech – is perhaps the most intriguing modern classic in terms of its engineering design effect upon the then and the now.

What of Oliver Winterbottom? He is the Brit who trained at Jaguar (suggesting new concepts for the 1970s), shaped TVR and Lotus glass-fibre cars, and has contributed to the emergence of the Chinese car industry. Still with Lotus, we cannot ignore the styling contributions of Ron Hickman, Peter Kirwan-Taylor and John Frayling to the original Elite and of Hickman to its offspring as the Elan. The name of International Automotive Design (IAD) is now obscured by time, but under John Shute and his men such as Brian Angliss, Les Lawson and Alan Jackson, this great British design house shaped and influenced car design across a decade.

Roy Haynes, ex-Ford then BMC, is the man who was given the unenviable tasks of smartening up the Maxi and tailoring the Marina. Gordon Sked assisted with , as did ex-Triumph designer David Kippax.

Of the French, Jacques Gerin, Gaston Juchet, Jacques Ne, Phillippe Charbonneaux, André Jouan, Rene Ducassou-Pehau, Louis Bioner Henri Dargent, Michel Harmand, Regis Gromik, Olivier Mourgue, Robert Opron, there is more to be told, or of Swedes, Jan Wilsgaard, Per Peterson, or the lesser known names of great Italian carrozzeria – men such as Aldo Brovarone, Aldo Castagno and Pierro Castagnero, Sergio Coggiola Franco Scaglione, Ercole Spada, Carlo Anderloni. All these names and others, were the pens *behind* the styling legends we revere as our cars.

For fans of 1960s and 1970s classic cars, the names of Bruno Sacco and Paul Bracq frame the delights of Mercedes design. Bracq went on to BMW, and Peugeot design. Sacco gave us the supreme 1980s S-Class saloons and coupés. These men's names are known by the enthusiasts, the cognoscenti, but like so many car designers, they remain obscured by wider society – even if it did (or still does) drive their cars. Bracq almost stumbled into his first job at Mercedes Benz during a visit to the factory and never looked back. The Mercedes Model W113 SL – the 'Pagoda' – can only be described as coachwork perfection, not just a design or a style. The main mover in sculpting its form was the Frenchman Bracq with leadership from Bruno Sacco. Bracq also worked on the 220 coupé, the 600 and other Mercs. Then he worked for a French design consultancy, which is how he styled the emotional frontal aspect of the Train à Grande Vitesse TGV, then came items for Matra. He soon moved to BMW where he co-created not just elegant car bodies (early 3, 5, 6, series), he sculpted their wonderful interiors and fascia and control panels that defined an era of BMW design. Bracq took those skills to Peugeot as its interiors expert, then retired to his painting career based from a home near Bordeaux. Today, his original artworks sell for large sums. [Ref 2]

These are the men that created so many of our cars, our classic cars. And there are still forgotten secrets of design awaiting higher profile – Tom Tjaarda's stunning 'Sinthesis' Italian coupé being a perfect example. If it had a name like Guigario or Pininfarina written on the side of it, it would have by now become world famous as one of *the* greatest carrozzeria creations, but it did not. Yet Sinthesis was as good as anything any 'name' might have turned out. Only one was built. Tjaarda was a leading light of the Ghia styling house and went on to fame at Ford, Tjaarda's concept cars being radical yet rational highlights of 1970s and 1980s design that rival the best. It was Ghia that gave the young Callum brothers their first profile with the 1988 Zig and Zag concept studies (also co-designed by Ian Wilkie and Sally Wilson).

How can we ignore such seminal moments as the essential, defining correctness of F.A. 'Butzi' Porsche and his shape for original 901 – the 911? Put aside the fact that he had the opportunity because of his name and location and just look at its form and its details. There lies a defining fastback form of German (if not downright Bohemian) perfection that reeks of place, function and pure and utter integrated design that flows from one panel to another without jerk or break. We might have said the same about the Ferry Porsche/Erwin Kommenda body design

The author's 1990s design proposal for a new 2CV

of the Porsche 356 series that set a new style in 1949 alongside Sixten Sason's Saab 92.

F.A. 'Butzi' Porsche also drew the often forgotten Carrera GTS904/6 as a lithe, low, mid-engined competition race car for 1964. It was an equally stunning, whole, organic 'one-man' single design that many rate as the best looking-Porsche you might never have heard of.

What of Trevor Frost – Trevor Fiore – shaper of TVR and Trident? Seemingly, it is now forgotten that he headed Citroën design in the 1980s at one of its most difficult times, yet created outstanding concepts of futurism as the British man who was chief of style for the double chevron. Frost as Fiore emerged in the late 1960s. He had designed household items for a new age – Pyrex kitchenware was one of Fiore's, but cars were his thing. By 1968, he had identified the use of a clean, delicate line around a car to give its shape action, shaping the TVR as a Trident (it then became two separate items); prior to that he had created the lovely little Elva-BMW shape, a car whose design, notably the upswept front wings and cabin turret, might, say some, have influenced others' thinking. Fiore then moved on to new themes and ended up in Paris and at finally at Citroën. Fiore's pyramid of car, the Citroën Karin, must rank as one of the best, most original concept or ideas cars of all time (Michel Harmand's interior for Karin was equally stunning) yet Fiore insisted that it could be real, it could have been made with very minor alterations. Then came the Xenia and other pointers to the future. When I spoke to Fiore, he was black leather-coated and looking more French than British, stating that a car's details should be fine honed and finished, that each design should be fresh and not a re-hash of the designer's back catalogue of ideas to be re-amalgamated. Fiore seemed to have become very Mediterranean, and why not. It cannot have been easy emerging from the British austerity society as an 'industrial designer' – whatever that was.

Dawson Sellar was a Scots master of style, an industrial designer who worked for Porsche, BMW and beyond the car industry, notably for Linn. Of often ignored significance, he was, with the designer Peter Stevens, a founding figure of the Royal College of Art's car design course. He helped many people and young designers listened to his words of wisdom and humorous recollections of life on the designer circuit. I was fortunate enough to have met and listened to Sellar and benefited from his clarity and passion for pure, unadulterated design devoid of excess and bling.

Sellar was without any doubt a very a gifted designer who died long before his ideas were exhausted. His work not only touched the hallowed ground of Porsche car design, but also helped lay the foundations for a car design teaching at the Royal College of Art – that has provided some of the most influential designers in the motor industry. Sellar also worked for BMW – designing motorcycles and latterly set up his own design studio in Scotland. The Jaguar design chief Ian Callum, himself a graduate of the Royal College's car design course, recently cited Sellar's Porsche design work as inspiration for aspects of the new Jaguar coupé's interior design. Meanwhile Ian's brother Moray, heads Ford design and the superb new Mustang must rank as a major achievement. My mate a has yellow one (with the intriguing 2.5 litre engine) and it stops the traffic in rural Britain.

The other day I 'discovered' another British designer, Cavendish Morton – a name that seems as if it leapt from Alistair Maclean or Jack Higgins novel, but in reality Mr Morton designed car bodies, notably for the Tojero marque. Morton had worked as a technical illustrator for the British aviation company of Saunders Roe from 1939 and had married the sister of John Britten, who, with Desmond Norman designed the famous Britten-Norman Islander aircraft. Britten had a wind tunnel in a shed at the end of his garden – which helped. Morton drew up and crafted scale test models of his body designs which were tested, not least in university wind tunnel with expert mathematicians on hand to help with the figures. Morton was also Chairman of the Snetterton Motor Racing Club. Like so many classic car men, he was a total motoring man, yet few know his name.

We might say the same of a man named Peter Cambridge who designed the interior of the original, beautifully sculpted Lotus Elite and then went on to teach design at the Central School of Art and Design. What of Ford's top 1950s designer Colin Neale, the bow-tied stylist who set the Zephyr, Zodiac and Anglia upon their ways before he moved to Chrysler? Intriguingly, Neale's brother Eric was also a car designer and shaped the early Jensens – 541 and CV8. He resigned from Jensen's when the Vignale design for the Interceptor was framed amid reputed management goings-on. Kevin Beattie was the talented engineer who made the Interceptor reality with chassis man Mike Jones – these are the forgotten events of a great classic car and its design and engineering story. Have you heard of Graham Hull – Rolls-Royce/Bentley designer? His work at Crewe was preceded by that of John Blatchley, whose career began at Gurney Nutting Ltd in 1935 and ended via Mulliner Park Ward with the shaping the Silver Shadow. As with other early British car designers, he had an aviation background. What of David Jones, Leo Prunneau and Wayne Cherry at GM and in Britain at Vauxhall? These men made huge marks on our motoring consciousness and the often ignored early 1970s pioneering mass market aerodynamic styling themes at Vauxhall. From Firenza, 'droop snoot', Cavalier Sports Hatch, XVR, SVR and Equs, Cherry and his team deserve wider recognition for making Vauxhalls 'designed' cars that we desired.

We might think similarly of Roy Axe at Rootes and BLMC. It was Axe who styled the crisp elegance of the coupé version of the Rootes Arrow series – the sublimely scaled Sunbeam Rapier – a car that looked like a piece of Italian design fresh from Lancia, yet blended into a British coupé with American overtones. With its shallow-angled fastback, clever window graphics, and pillarless cabin section, here was design with a golden spot. The trims, the lights, the chrome and vinyl details were however pure-late 1960s and did not age as well as the Ford Capri design as the 'Seventies unrolled. Rootes (soon to be Chrysler) made 46,200 Rapiers, yet less than 100 are known to survive.

Other forgotten names of car design include Walter Belgrove who shaped the Triumph Mayflower and TR2; Leslie Moore of Standard Vanguard fame; and the curious tale of Riccardo Burzi who left Italy to work for Austin and created the Baroque forms of the likes of the A35 and Cambridge. At Crewe, the hidden talents of Martin Bourne and William Allen quietly contributed to Rolls-Royce and Bentley output.

These men (and others) are the now obscured names of the great 'classic' years of car design.

Spada or Frua: Belt or Braces

Ercole Spada was chief designer at Zagato, he styled an Aston Martin DB4 and the Fuliva Sport Zagato of Lancia. He shaped the Lamborghini 3500 GTZ and several Alfas – including the Guiletta SZ, Guila and Junior Z. Spada coined a hallmark – a curved, glazed cabin turret that he applied to many of his designs. Drag-reduction and wind tunnel development were an early Spada passion, yet he left Italy and went to work at Ford; the forgotten GT70 design (last seen in South Africa) was a seminal Spada sculpture. He also worked for BMW and then the Italian design institute I.D.E.A..

Pietro Frua occupied an earlier space in Italian carrozzeria design, yet his hand touched many marques from Renault and Ford, to Volvo. The beautifully balanced Maserati *Berlina Due Posti* – or the Mistral as it was quickly named – was a Frua work of excellence; did the Frua style somehow influence the Jensen Interceptor of Alfredo Vignale's pen? Park an Interceptor next to a Mistral and the brush strokes seem related. Mistral begat the AC 428. That Carrozerra Michelotti would construct the Mistral convertibles only added to the allure and the confusion over who designed what. Intriguingly, Frua had trained at Stablimenti Farina. After the Second World War, he was a consultant to Ghia and then across the Italian industry via his own freelance studio. Design contributions to Glas (the Glas coupé and the saloon that became a BMW Cheetah in Africa), Volvo, Fiat, Ford, Rolls-Royce, were complemented by his concept suggestions to Citroën, Renault, De Tomaso, and Jaguar. The Rolls-Royce Phantom VI was Frua's elegant (and last) design, but real honour must go to his special one-off four-door Quattorporte chassis ordered by the Aga Khan IV. This low-line, thin-roofed, six-window body had shades of Jaguar and of Lancia to its grand expression of coutured carriage. The elegance, the cleanliness, the facets of it do truly invoke exclamation when you see it. Like all big Masers should be, it is dark blue with a light tan interior. Was it a precursor to the Frua-influenced style of large saloons from Monteverdi or Bitter? Pietro Frua, wearer of trousers with braces, grand old man of Italian styling died in 1983. Today he remains an often-forgotten hand in the history of classic car coachwork – a true carrozzeria.[Ref 3]

We might say that early American designers are also all too easily ignored. What of William Stout and his pre-1920 aerodynamic 'Scarab' car-wagon derived from his aviation skills? It was a hugely advanced mono-pod that took nearly two decades to reach reality. Another American, Norman Bel Geddes is also too easily forgotten, yet his was a defining and pioneering influence that touched production cars even though he did not achieve series or volume sales of a design of his own. Influenced by art, architecture and advertising design and a major road trip around France in the late 1920s (surely informed by the effects of the design defining *Exposition Internationale des Arts Decoratifs et Industriels Moderne* exhibition in Paris in 1925), Bel Geddes took to designing elliptical, lobed, one-piece and cab-forwards designs for cars, buses and people carriers in America in the early 1930s. His shapes were aerodynamic or perhaps hydrodynamic in their mammalian forms. He was a founding father of America's new age of industrial design and the Graham-Paige concern adopted his ideas. Bel Geddes also worked for General Motors and trained Henry Dreyfuss. As early as 1930-1932, Bel Geddes was producing ideas under the title of 'Streamlined Motor Car'. They bore some resemblance to Gerin's Aerodyne yet were not copies, possessing their own style and detailed advances. These were pioneering ideas and far in advance of his earlier 1928 sketches for a smoothed-over open-topped roadster for the Graham-Piage concern. Chrysler used Bel Geddes as a consultant during the development of its radical Airflow streamliner saloon by Carl Breer and General Motors hired him to style a futuristic design event 'Futurama' at the 1939 World's Fair in New York. He designed other products but it is in his 1930s visions that so much potential was spotlighted and seen by others. [Ref 4] We might offer the same viewpoint upon the works of Buckminster Fuller (boat builder, architectural thinker, inventor) whose 1933-1934 iterations of an ellipsoid Dynmaxion also kicked at the doors of convention's perceived wisdoms.

How far ahead was Bel Geddes in the 1930s? Take a look at the Pininfarina X – an aerodynamic design study dated 1960 with a C_D 0.23. Shaped by Alberto Morelli of Turin Polytechnic using its wind tunnel, this weird device of teardrop, cab-forwards sculpting echoes his less scientific body works, yet also gave us a bizarre four-wheel layout configuration – one at each side and one front and one rear.

Tributes to great design can surely be transposed across the Atlantic and applied to Bill Mitchell for his Chevrolet Corvette Stingray. Many would say the same of Ford's Mustang styling guru, George W. Walker and his team that included Alex Tremulis, Roy Brown, Eugene Bordinat, Robert Maguire, John Najjar, and Elwood Engel (latterly a lead designer at Chrysler). Other lead Ford stylists included William Burnett, William Boyer and Franklin Hershey. Chrysler's Virgil Exner and his team made massive early marks upon post-war American car design, notably at Pontiac and at Chrysler. Cars like the Firearrrow and d'Elegance signalled huge stylistic intent as moving sculptures. Such effort, such energy in design stemmed from pre-war days of streamliners of cars, trains and planes. Harley Earl had a lot to answer for. The legacy of that era included names of great designers like Norman Bel Geddes, Howard Darrin (a leading independent stylist of his day), Raymond Loewy, Richard Teague, and Brook Stevens. [Ref 5]

All these men and more were part of a process that then manifested as the design-fest of the Ford-GM-Chrysler 'Big Three' style wars and the 'Dream Car' era that raged across American car design from the 1950s to the 1970s. Today, their work, their *cars* are the essence of American classic car passions, just as the names of Europe's designers are so responsible across that continent's marques. Without these men and women and their car designs, our world of classic cars would be a void.

Just as French 1930s design influenced emerging American trends, we can see that, post-1945, America's new design language influenced European design. Colour and detailing such as painted dashboards and matching trims, first seen on American cars, found their way into European cars, even basic, austere cheap runabouts. The Americans however, remained enthralled to Milanese and Turinese car couture – buying their way into Italian carrozzeria and in the case of Ford, buying Ghia itself. One of the most amazing showcar specials was the Lincoln Indianapolis of 1955 which Ford commissioned from Carrozezria Boano, F.M. Boano's son Gian Paolo creating the sheer style of a blend of American jet-age motifs tailored down with Turinese grace.

Yet such ideas, came after the effect of Pinin Farina's 1948 Cistalia 202 – the car that in Battista Farina's own words, 'broke the rules' thus creating a new look and a new school of designer followers. Pinin Farina (yet to become Pininfarina S.p.A.) then did the same thing again with the architecturally perfect lines of the more angular Lancia Florida II of 1959. From such 'moments' stemmed the cars that today are our classics. Such optimistic designs, such powerful shapes lie behind why we now like them so much. The lesson was obvious: focusing on function and getting all Bauhaus about it is one thing, but surely style as design, as emotion, was (and is) needed.

For the classic car fanatic, the old design school of the classic car years has a catalogue of genius to offer. Looking back was never so good.

Innes Ireland

Thoughtful Courage, Whisky Galore

'Ah, well done laddie, Scottish wine!'

Those were the first words Innes Ireland greeted me with as I got out of my pale blue twin-cylinder Citroën Visa one lunch time in the early spring of 1983. Ireland shook my hand and grabbed the bottle I was carrying, with the other.

'What is that funny little French thing like.' asked the retired racing driver.

'Incredible,' I replied. 'It steers brilliantly, rides well, handles far better than you might imagine and it's like an old Saab – you have to keep its motor wound up. It is huge fun.'

'Flimsy though,' said Ireland. 'Fancy a bit of chassis and metal around me.'

'Yes. It's typically French.'

Innes Ireland drank Scottish wine – whisky; he did so neat and just about approved of the bottle of Glen Morangie I gave him. Once we had drunk that, he introduced me to more booze from Speyside and then to Laphroaig the Islay peat-watered whisky. I drank that neat too. I did not dare argue. Afterwards, I had to leave the car at his house and hitch a lift home as I was paralytically drunk. Innes meanwhile appeared to be utterly sober; the man had lived, he had even survived the fragility of the early Lotuses that he competed in. Graham Hill did the same but, sensibly, moved on to BRM.

I doubt that Innes ever forgave Colin Chapman for dropping him from the Lotus team just after he had scored that team's (and Chapman's) first-ever Formula One points-with-payment victories. In 1960, he had finished fourth in the FIA Formula One World Championship and would have done better if the Lotus had not been so wretchedly fragile (Chapman's obsession). In 1961, Innes had two Formula One victories (in racing allowed outside the Championship as then was the fashion). He then won the United States Grand Prix at Watkins Glen and thus scored actual Championship points – his and Chapman's first. Less than two weeks later, Innes had been dropped. The winning Lotus 21 was Coventry Climax-engined and was the last 4-cylinder car ever to win a Grand Prix. But Watkins Glen was used to the Brits by this time; Allards had long made their mark.

When I met Innes in 1983, he was still prepared to swear about Chapman. I did not probe further, not least as I was not and am not a fan of Chapman's priorities however much I might respect his talent. To me, there is an essential paradox in building a car to win, yet which cannot, because it is so frail that it will break before it wins. However, Chapman may not have been the sole mover in the event. Innes knew that one of Lotus's major sponsors (Esso) had been unhappy at his opinions regarding events after the fatal crash at Monza when Wolfgang von Tripps and fourteen spectators had been killed after a collision also involving Jim Clark's car. Innes had apparently suggested that the rival Walker team (containing Stirling Moss) and their blue-hued cars might 'borrow' a car from Lotus – or so say those in the know. This happened – with Stirling Moss driving the repainted Lotus and Innes inheriting the previous year's Lotus 18/21 modificato. Ireland struggled with the car and retired it in the next race with a cracked chassis (a 'normal' Lotus issue apparently). But Stirling's borrowed Lotus 21 *also* expired.

Were Esso (who had not been consulted about the game of musical cars) unhappy? Did Esso pressure Chapman to dump Ireland? So allege the runes of racing. [Ref 1] Money and personality might have played a role too; was Chapman looking for an excuse to rid himself of Innes Ireland? Given the respective personality constructs of the pair, that outcome would have been likely. Behind the bonhomie, Chapman was ruthless, Innes less so. Paradoxically, only one of them had been in the Parachute Regiment – Innes.

One thing is for sure, Lotus would have been in trouble without its sponsors' money and as Esso was the biggest, they had to be kept on side. Chapman may have been between a rock and hard place, but he *was* the boss. Perhaps we will never know the full story. It was a mess and a sad chapter. They were tough times full of risk. The reader might not know that in the 1960 Spa-Francorchamps Belgian Formula One race, two drivers died and two others suffered serious injuries in practice. Stirling Moss crashed heavily when his Lotus' rear axle failed in the practice session, Moss broke both legs. The Formula One debut of Michael Taylor was marred when he suffered a steering failure in his Lotus and crashed into trees; he never raced at again. Chris Bristow would die in the race when his BRP Cooper went out of control and he was thrown from car. Alan Stacey died when he was hit in the face by a bird and his Lotus crashed. Such was one weekend in Belgium. It all hit Innes hard and he was unhappy at the prospect of Le Mans in a fragile Lotus.

At the 1960 Le Mans, Chapman had entered a suitably tuned-up Lotus – in fact the cars were entered as Lotus 2-litre Coventry climax-engined 'LX' Elite-derived types. The Border- Reiver team also entered similar Elite-based cars. The little plastic cars flew along at well over 140mph and many observers were astounded.

Yet Chapman's entry never competed in that year's race. It suffered a deflating tyre in practice and say some, as the tyre changed shape in the wheel arch, it destroyed the thin glass-fibre bodywork on that corner of the rear of the car and urgent hand-laid repairs with resin and strips of glass-fibre are said to have been necessary. Many people deny this story. Innes Ireland is always cited in the tale as the 'visibly shaken' Lotus driver who then refused to drive the car in the race. The respected racing driver and motoring writer Tony Dron, attempted to solve the mystery in *Octane*, [Ref 2] yet a definitive account of those 1960 events *is* hard to frame. All I know is what the car's co-driver Innes Ireland (the other driver was a young Sir John Whitmore) told me in 1983. 'Bloody Lotus, fragile things. I had one disintegrate on me at Le Mans, 1960 it was. The thing started to peel apart.'

A decade later, grand prix drivers were still dying, notably another of my other heroes, Jochen Rindt. He was another man who died in a fragile Lotus. With the likes of Piers Courage and Bruce McLaren so recently dead in 1970, Rindt had real fears about Chapman's car. At Silverstone in 1969, Rindt was set to win the British Grand Prix at his first attempt in a Lotus. The rear wing failed and he lost a certain victory but at the least the car did not flip and crash. Chapman is reputed to have complained at his advice to make the cars stronger, which meant heavier – an anathema to Chapman. Rindt was still concerned about the engineering standards of the Lotus, but he drove it, and he died in it via an alleged car failure, not a driver error. His car control was superlative and he thought you should be able to drive a grand prix car hard, as designed, not have to treat it with kid gloves and be constrained by that need. Innes Ireland told me that Rindt was a nice chap and his wife Nina, 'a lovely woman and a gorgeous smasher – real class'.

For Innes, championship points were lost when the Lotus failed. The same fate befell Jim Clark; he lost the 1962 and 1964 World Championships because the Lotus failed repeatedly to finish due to mechanical failures. Jim Clark died in a Lotus too, but it seems a tyre failure not a metal failure, was responsible.

Getting drunk with Innes Ireland was a highlight for me and, all these years later, remains so. I was twenty at the time and working as a junior styling apprentice in a car design company, but had developed an interest in writing, notably about design and racing. I was in awe of Innes' reputation. Lawrence Cummins, the editor of my local newspaper (the *Newbury Weekly News*) was a near neighbour and offered me a helping hand. He introduced me to Ireland, who happened to live a couple of miles up the road in an old cottage set in a small bowl on a wooded hillside where the rooks made a lot of noise and the rain dripped relentlessly from the overhanging trees; a reminder of Scotland perhaps.I do not know how or why, but I hit it off with Innes: maybe it was because I am part Scots, maybe it was just because, as an 'outback'-raised boy, I laughed at his humour and direct, straight talking, expletive-ridden style. Maybe it was because I loved Saabs and Innes had recently competed in a twenty-four-hour endurance event in a Saab Turbo. Maybe it was because I knew he had become a writer and I had read his articles in car magazines such as *Road and Track,* an exotic American title of which I was lucky enough to get my hands on each month courtesy of pilot friend who brought the latest issues back from America and passed them on to me in my rural backwater.

After meeting Innes, I wrote up my 'interview' with him and along with another article, it won the 1983 Sir William Lyons Award for young motoring writers via the Guild of Motoring Writers. The Lyons Award committee – daunting men in ties sat around a large table at the RAC Club in Pall Mall – asked me how I had found Innes to interview? I told them he had got me drunk on more than one bottle of whisky; they all laughed. It was apparently, 'typical Innes'. For me, a new life opened up as a writer and here I am, thirty years later, still peddling my own rubbish.

Meanwhile back with the whisky, the cars and the amazing man, all those years ago.

I recall that Innes had laughter and pain in his eyes, here was a life lived to the full. They (the arbiters of history) say that Innes was a 'hell-raiser'. These days, that is politically incorrect and we must realise that a drink, a dirty joke or the crime of a hand on a shoulder (let alone a bottom) of a consenting female is a major and imprisonable offence. Way back in the when of before I and maybe even you, were born, or still in nappies, or shorts, such behaviours were socially acceptable. So, Innes drank whisky rather well, went out with more than one woman, and attended some interesting parties. In a different 1960s world, many people, be they famous Formula One drivers, or suburban accountants, did so.

Innes had seen a bit of the good life, not least in Europe and America, but he was also a practical Scotsman who, faced with the end of his competition driving career, would turn to fishing and then to writing. Tragedy also struck his family life and in the end, Innes died of the wretched and ubiquitous cancer that is taking so many men of the 1950s and 1960s. Fags and booze come with a price. The physical injuries he suffered on the race track and the ingress of oil into his body could hardly have helped.

Perceived history has it that Jim Clark and Jackie Stewart were Scotland's 'golden twins' of motor racing, but the factual reality was that it was *Innes* who was Scotland's first grand prix-winning driver, a fact seemingly smothered by time. Innes also repeatedly out-qualified Clark at Lotus in Clark's first season; given that Clark is revered by many as the perhaps greatest driver of that era or any era, Innes abilities might now be better considered.

Before all that, my hero, our hero, was born with three names, Robert MacGregor Innes and was the son a Scots vet who lived in West Yorkshire (Herriot country) and latterly moved to the low hills and vast estuarine skies of the Solway Firth and Kircudbrightshire, now part of Dumfries and Galloway. Like Saab's Erik Carlsson (who married Stirling Moss' sister Pat), Ireland learned his craft of control on a motorcycle in his teens (a Rudge 500 and then an Ariel 500).

He had to do military national service and did so in the Parachute Regiment amid the mess that was Britain's Suez Crisis. Being Innes, he was made an officer in a Scottish regiment, but he had also had struck lucky before this experience. He had in his early teens, met a Bentley-owing elderly lady via his hanging around the local garage that serviced her cars. In fact, he said he was ten when he first saw the black 3-litre Bentley two-seater that made such a mark on the man as a child. He spent the next few years sniffing around this and other Bentleys – all owned by the same person. That early mechanical fixation led him to a Rolls-Royce engineering apprenticeship in Glasgow (where he said he blew up a supercharged Merlin engine). But he had had the chance to drive one of the good lady's Bentley's in a club race; it is said that he had inherited one of the old girl's Bentley's. A 'Red Label' model is the reputed item. So began a nascent *ad hoc* driving competition driving profile.

While still in the Army, Innes had purchased a 1940 Packard V8 that he managed to sell to his father for more than he had paid for it! Innes' father was at that time driving a Rolls-Royce 20hp 'doctors' coupé'. Selling the Packard gave Innes gave the funds to buy a French Blue Riley Nine Brooklands, two-seat roadster registration number KV 5392. Why was it bright blue? It seems the Riley had originally gone to France and had competed in the 1933 Le Mans with a French driver. It was in this car that Innes entered his BRDC class events including the June 1955Goodwood meet – which he won. Prior to leaving the army, Innes had been Motor Transport Officer for his regiment, very helpful for fettling the Riley! He said he loved the Riley and the only reason he reluctantly sold it was to fund the shared-ownership of a new Lotus 11 – his entry to the grid and the front row of the early events that made his name. Of the Riley, Innes told me that its greatest factor was the direct, 'live' steering the feedback and precision car control it created.

'Always rate a car by its steering laddie,' said Innes. 'You can tell a car's ability and the talent of the men behind it by the quality of the steering. Duff steering – duff car'.

This was advice I took to my road test and writing work and I noted that it was an opinion also held and expressed by none other than Leonard Setright himself – although the thought of Innes getting on with Setright was unlikely.

On leaving the Paras, Innes set up Innes Ireland Ltd from his Surrey base and with Major Rupert Robinson as co-investor, purchased that new Lotus 11. Apart from the fact that Innes bent it on its first outing, it was the watershed moment that launched his career and profile. Using other peoples' cars, Innes privately competed in more racing events. He drove at Brooklands and other circuits.

Driving the Lotus, Innes had an early victory against the Ferraris in the 1958 'Trophee d'Auvergne' at Clermont Ferrand where he evicted Maurice Trintignant from a podium chance. Innes drove for several small teams and in a variety of privately owned cars. He was not a rich playboy with access to vast reserves of cash, as some have so erroneously suggested.

After honing his skills and raising his profile, 1957 was the year he got the break he needed. He drove sportscars at Goodwood, he won the Brooklands Memorial Trophy and the United States Trophy driving for Tommy Sopwith's team. He drove officially for Team Lotus in the Swedish (sportscar class) Grand Prix. September 1957 saw him competing in his first Formula race – the International Trophy at Silverstone in a Cooper. Peter Collins would soon dead, Jim Clark was not yet a household name, Innes Ireland was all over the press. By 1959, after private-entry drives, Colin Chapman had offered Innes a team Lotus 'works' drive – where a young man named Graham Hill was the rising star and Jim Clark would soon arrive. Innes also got behind the wheel (in 1958) of a blue and Saltire-striped, Ecurie Ecosse Jaguar D-type and made Malcolm Sayer's ellipsoid dream really fly.

Ireland had his Formula One debut at Zandvoort for the 1959 Dutch Grand Prix; he drove the Lotus 16 at a 'safe' pace to finish fourth. The Lotuses proved fragile that year and he was denied several finishes by failures in Chapman's cars. He raced alongside the emerging Jim Clark at Lotus in the last front-engined Lotus Formula One car, and always said that he was at his most competitive at this time – not least at a German race held on the road circuit at Solitude where he trounced the Porsches of Bonnier and Gurney to deny the German team a 'home' victory.

Ireland and Clark would experience harsh words and sad regrets.

At the end the 1960 Formula One Drivers' Championship, he was fourth and in 1961 Formula One Drivers Championship (won by Phil Hill) he was placed sixth, Jim Clark was seventh, Bruce McLaren ninth, John Surtees tenth and Graham Hill was sixteenth. Clearly then, he was no back-of-the-grid hopeful.

As the 1960s dawned, Ireland seemed to be on the cusp of major Formula One status and he was part of the pack – which also included private teams doing deals with manufacturers who supplied cars but not drivers. He would latterly drive for a team formed by the Moss concern and its then manager Ken Gregory as the British Racing Partnership (BRP).

Other drives came and went in those, perhaps, the greatest days of the Formula One lifestyle. It was a different world and should not be castigated by those who today, know nothing of it or its time, or its rules and behaviours; actions freely and consentingly entered into by adult men and women in age when warning signs and 'health and safety' were less common, but common sense was more current.

Ireland drove against, drank with, and knew, the likes of Clark, Hill, Moss, Gurney, Surtees, Brabham, McLaren, the great names of the early 1960s scene. Turfed out by Chapman, he drove Aston Martins and Ferraris (notably the GTO) and carried on a competitive driving career across various classes. BRM (with Graham Hill incumbent) offered Ireland a drive but he turned it down out of loyalty to the Ken Gregory/Alfred Moss British Racing Partnership/UDT team he had agreed to race for on his old *ad hoc* basis.

Sir Stirling Moss always rated Ireland; Stirling was beaten by Innes at the 1960 Goodwood Easter meeting. Ireland was on the up, so much so that he purchased himself a new Jaguar E-Type – registration number 200 FNP.

He nearly bled to death after being thrown from his car at the 1961 Monaco Grand Prix, but he had his biggest accident in 1963 at Seattle in the North West Grand Prix. A collision with another car left him trapped in his Ferrari GTO and fully conscious as they cut him out without pain relief – with a thigh bone pushed far out of place. In 1965, now recovered, he drove a Ferrari 330(P) with Graham Hill in a co-driven endurance race – the 1000K Nurburgring event. A fuel leak scuppered their chances of victory. The following year, he drove a Ford GT40 but to no success. He drove in several races in 1965 for the Parnell Lotus team, the Mexican Grand Prix of 1966 being the last Formula 1 race of his racing career. An unsuccessful drive at the 1967 Nascar 500 vied for his closing chapter status. Soon afterwards, he became Grand Prix Editor at the world's oldest car magazine *Autocar*, but he also drove in the 1968 London-Sydney Rally and had a fling with Lancia, tried the World Cup Rally in 1974, and as late as 1985, entered the Playboy Endurance Series with his old mate Stirling Moss as co-driver.

He had to make a living, but a desk job at *Autocar* did not really suit him. At one stage, he was back in Scotland running a fishing business that also gave him time to explore the Western Isles in depth, a region that he came to adore. For the late 1970s, he would live in Radnorshire, Wales and then in England. He must have liked rain and mood-swing skies. In the 1980s, he lived in a country cottage between Newbury and Hungerford – Kiln Cottage at Wickham, Berkshire. When we met, I noticed he had a new high-powered Ford on the drive. He also had a good collection of classic cars that were rising in value.

'I have an Aston in the garage, do you want to see it?' asked Ireland when I met him for the first time.

'Is the sky blue.' replied the nobody – me.

We walked off around the back of the house to a small barn. The double-doors creaked open and inside was a collection of classic car metal that today, would be worth millions.

'What is that oddity,' I asked, staring at what looked like an Aston Martin estate car.

Innes smiled: 'Oh that. I had it specially done – an Aston DB 6 shooting brake. Gun racks in the back and room for fishing tackle and dogs.'

As you do...

Innes loved Astons and had driven a DB4 in the 1960 1000km of Paris GT race with Roy Salvadori and they came sixth. He would have a long association with the marque and the factory. In his garage was BJD 136H – his 1970 Aston Martin DB6 Mk2 Vantage, and YPP 798F – the DB6 shooting brake conversion by FLM Panelcraft (one of two). I did not see the very rare Bertone-bodied Aston Martin roadster that he ordered, but did spot a Ferrari, blurting out: 'That's a Ferrari with a Kamm-back!'

'Yes, rather liked those.' said Innes with utter modesty in his English accent that had only the slightest whiff of the north. The GTO was his favourite and in early 1962 he had gone to Maranello to drive a green GTO (chassis number 3505) home for the by UDT-Laystall team – for whom he had driven a BRM-powered single-seater and soon, the green GTO. He drove home in company with a dark blue GTO (chassis number 3589) purchased at the same time by Tommy Sopwith's 'Equipe Endeavour' and Colonel Ronnie Hoare of Maranello Concessionaires in the UK.

Chassis number 3589 would be sold to Rosebud Racing of Victoria, Texas, USA and he would drive her competitively in 1962-'63. After over a decade rotting in an American field, that very GTO was restored by owner Englebert Stieger in 1990 through the efforts of Fritz Leirer at his 'Sport Garage' in Stein. In 1990, thanks to Ferrari enthusiast Colin Bach, Ireland was re-united with the car prior to his illness. All the cars in the garage had stories, a bit like their owner it seems.

We sniffed around the cars. There was a Maserati in there too. Innes told me had had bought the Hon Patrick Lindsay's 250F in 1970. Then it was back to a fireside and more bloody whisky – neat.

Water in whisky? 'Don't do it old boy.'

The Glen Morangie was empty.

'Ever tried an Islay, a peat whisky, laddie?' asked my hero.

'No Sir.'

A brown smoky liquid tumbled into a glass. Laphroaig? Lagavulin? By the time the second bottle was gone, I could not have known the difference. Innes remained apparently dead cold sober.

How?

We got to talk about writing and Innes showed me the books he had written. I chipped in that I had read some of his articles, notably those in *Autocar* and the more exotic *Road and Track.* It was at about this time that he would also begin to write for *Classic Cars* and on occasion, *The Times*.

'Can you write lad?' asked our hero.

Could I?

I did not know what to say: 'I am going to try. I like it and I find it easy.'

'Best do it then, but try not to get it too complicated.' said Innes.

I wish I had listened to that advice. It took me years to de-construct my over-written style. You may think I have failed.

'Who is your favourite writer, lad?'

'Ernest Gann. He wrote *Fate is the Hunter.*'

'Not bad, not bad, laddie. I know it.'

Ireland told me that he had in fact begun writing long before his later words for *Autocar* in the late-1960s. He had apparently, written a big piece for the *Daily Telegraph* in the 1960s and his first motor racing article was published in 1958. I asked him some questions about his life and driving in the late 'Fifties era. I took notes and had enough for my entry into the Sir William Lyons young writers award. I must have been so naïve.

Before I left Kiln Cottage, Innes told me more. He reacted to the commercialisation of Formula One, and the early era's safety lobby within the sport annoyed him in some sense, although he was not anti-safety. He also praised four-wheel-drive. It was also clear that driving, risk, informed consent to danger, adult thinking was what he thought appropriate. In describing and explaining his views, he was forthright and expletives flew. Here was a man speaking as he found and thought. I asked him about the bravery of driving in the old days when a racing driver death was a monthly, sometimes weekly, event.

'Bravery! Courage! Rubbish. *Thinking* kept me alive. You had to think. To *concentrate*. Those that did it best, won,' Innes was activated now. 'Situational awareness – fighter pilot style. That's the best advice I can give anyone – you too. Don't just look *around* you, look a long way up the road. Swivel your head and have an eagle's vision.'

It was advice that I took away with me and always remembered.

Innes had been concerned about Formula One's death toll, but it was clear he felt that something was lost in the great safety campaign. In fact, he had been badly injured more than once – notably being violently ejected from a Grand Prix car at high speed when driving a Lotus 21 at the 1961 Monaco Grand Prix. Innes had had a gearbox problem – either that or he had, 'Selected the wrong ******* gear.' to use his own words. The Lotus had started to swerve and spin and, unbelted as was the fashion then, Ireland was thrown with high g-forces from the car inside the tunnel – lucky not be squashed by following cars as they flashed from daylight into darkness and their drivers' vision was negated.

'That was the year I came out of the tunnel without the ******* car!' he said.

He played down his injuries, but the truth is that he nearly died from a broken leg and a cut artery as he sat by the harbour. A nearby nurse applied a tourniquet and quietly saved his life.

He clearly disliked the corporate big wigs and it was corporate-speak and PR bullshit that he really hated, and Formula One was soon to be full of it. He admired James Hunt who I think he perceived as the last iteration of the old good old days of 'bad boys' days of having fun; he read Kipling at Hunt's funeral. To me, after several whiskies, Innes described some other Formula One drivers as, 'Utterly calculating – ******* machines.'

I mentioned that my grandfather had known Graham Hill, so Innes went on to tell me that tale of how he had stood on a table in a kilt after a race and Graham Hill stuffed a pot-plant – a cactus, up the kilt as far as he could get it! Oh, and hadn't Innes been arrested in the south of France whilst driving, wearing nothing more than a pair of budgie smugglers?

The lawyers won't let me write here what he told me about certain other Formula One luminaries ...

Innes and I talked more as the afternoon faded.

I was unfit to drive after my time with Innes. I had to leave the car behind and get collected.'Don't be a stranger. Let me know how you go.' shouted Innes from the doorstep as I left, the light fading and birds singing after an afternoon never to be forgotten.

I spoke to him several times afterwards. He was very pleased for me when I told him I had won the Lyons Award. He told me to use it, not waste it. To my regret and some shame, I did not keep up the contact as much as I should have, perhaps in awe of him and we spoke less frequently. Then there was the tragedy of his son Jamie's death that affected him and his wife so much. Then came the damned cancer that killed him in a year. Had grief unlocked the latent cancer in his body?

His son had completed racing driver training at Donnington and debuted at a circuit event in 1990.

Innes was a crack shot and a competitive clay pigeon shooter with Jackie Stewart. Innes liked Fords and loved his Ford Sierra XR4x4. The last time I saw him he was driving a tuned-up Ford Scorpio-Granada 2.8 Cosworth jobby. We met at a local petrol station. He looked haunted, as if he knew that he was very ill.

Innes Ireland might be said by some, to have been a hedonist. I am not qualified to comment as I was not there. He however admitted as much to those who knew and interviewed him. He said to me that he had lived life as he found it and wanted it, somewhat selfishly by his own admission. 'I live as I want to do, as events portray.' said the ageing racing driver to me as a twenty-year-old novice. In fact, he had opened our meeting with a comment about whether I had heard things about him – good or bad. I told him that I had been forearmed with the knowledge that I would not be bored and to turn up with a bottle of something decent. He quite liked that.

But did he gild the lily? Did he revel in the stories about him, as if contributing to the myth? Perhaps; he must have had an ego, we all do. But perhaps this was a feint, a cover for the hurt that came his way. All I know was that he was a gentleman, a human being of the most interesting construct, and one of those people you either like or loathe. The great Enzo Ferrari 'Il Commendatore' – himself an uncompromising man and some say, a bit of a dictator – said that he thought that Ireland was a 'reckless genius' and that he could have gone much further had he wanted to do so. Maybe Ireland *had* wanted to do just that, but life and events intervened. Did he throw it all away as some say? Of course not. Was he a lesser talent? No, but just because he was not a multiple world champion does not make him an also-ran. In fact, many think that Innes was near top-rate in terms of his ability to drive, but that he lacked the obsessive, singular self-regard or the self-discipline that champions of the later days of Formula One required to win. He also lacked luck. The fragility of points-losing Lotus did not help either, even if Ireland was not, as some argue, perhaps of the calibre of Moss or Clark.

I cannot now help thinking that he was a man placed by fate just slightly out of his time in an age of heroes soon to be swamped by an age and by men of a different construction. Others agree. If he had been born a decade and a bit earlier, he would have ended up flying Spitfires or Hurricanes, or driving a tank, or perhaps commanding a naval corvette off the west coast of Britain under sullen skies in a rough sea swell whilst standing on the bridge sipping hot coco laced with whisky; Jack Hawkins would have had nothing on Cap'n Ireland.

There was pause and outside the rooks chattered and a cold, silver blue sky brought its chill to the hillside. The fire crackled and the whisky tainted the air in the room with its own smoky aura. Innes told me that he was, 'Probably not consistent enough.' That was a very self-aware admission. Then, I knew not of its significance. Now, I do.

He wrote three books: *Motor Racing Today, All Arms and Elbows, Marathon in the Dust* – also known as *Sideways to Sydney*. He wrote dozens of feature articles in major motoring magazines from the 1970s to 1990s. He drove a Porsche 924 at Daytona and, in 1984, drove a large Lincoln in the Cannonball lap of America. Innes liked the Porsche 924 and then drove across a section of America via the original Route 66 in Porsche 944 – not just any stock-944, but one prepared by Brumos Racing, a race team from Jacksonville, Florida. The article 'Free-Spiriting Across America' was published in *Road and Track* in September 1985. During this drive, Ireland had received a speeding ticket whilst hurtling along in the back end of California beside the Colorado River – the ticket issued by what he somehow happened to note was a very attractive policewoman! But he had then failed to pay the fine. Back in Britain, and keen to do so and avoid interrogation or worse on his next entry into the USA, the magazine's esteemed editor Dennis Simanaitis coughed up a personal cheque to the Court and further trouble was avoided. [Ref 3]

Free-spiriting indeed.

Ireland also used *Road and Track* to tell a tale of a tour in Scotland in a Mercedes G-Wagen. Reminiscences of old races and lost friends were also written about. In 1987, he drove the Benetton-BMW B186 Formula One car in a track test as one of his last flings at the wheel on a circuit. On another occasion, he totally wrecked a very expensive Mercedes Press fleet car that the company had asked him to demonstrate on a circuit (Ian Botham did the same to a Saab 900 Turbo). He emerged mostly unscathed from the multiply-rolled Merc and went back to retrieve his black Labrador and his guns! [Ref 4]

Innes liked women and courted several of them (some F1 stars do) and had been thrice married and had three children. His son Jamie died. Around the same time, in 1992, Ireland was elected President of the British Racing Drivers Club, yet the ravages of time, of life and grief manifested in the cancer that would so quickly kill him. Not everyone loved Innes and he had his detractors; some people couldn't stand his pranks and attitudes. All I know that he was a real man in the best sense of that phrase. He was humorous, a raconteur, a joker, a writer and observer, a good shot, a superb driver and, very loyal to his friends. Loyalty means much to some. Above all he was a thinker, yet one who kept that part of his nature shielded. He wrote poetry too. Not many people knew that – then or now: Innes Ireland the philosopher was a hidden trait. [Ref 5]

In hindsight, I suggest that he was far more complex than we have realised, a man driven by many things. Was he a Cavalier at a party taken over by the

Roundheads? Possibly, but it would be massive mistake to label him as an also-ran or second-rate, or indeed, as having a cavalier attitude. There was much more to Innes than was obvious then, or has been told since. A few observers have realised that and written so. The context of the now should not be a basis for a judgement of the then – when Innes was at the wheel.

Now that I too am an old sod, I add my name to the list of those who admired a soul that held its head above high water.

There is a memorial plaque to Innes Ireland, but it is not in a city or town. Instead it is in the middle of nowhere in Wester Ross (Taobh Siar Rois) in a remote part of Scotland way up past Mallaig where Innes used to run his trawler. In the Western isles, a ten mile drive from Gairloch on the A387, on the way to the Rubha Reid lighthouse, you have to leave your car and walk a cliff path to a field and there a small plaque stands on a memorial stone. Here can be found Innes Ireland's last place of scattering upon this earth. Somehow it is a fitting paradox for the man born in 1930, amid an age soon to be shattered. Innes Ireland died in 1993 in a era when so much had changed, not all of it for the better in his opinion. If you look at the photographs of the man, you will see a wry smile, mischievous eyes and the potential of deep thought going on behind the scenes. Above all, Innes Ireland loved cars and loved life. He had a great time, but there was a reckoning, an accounting for good times with bad. There often is.

'Life's an adventure laddie, an adventure!' So said Innes the last time I spoke to him.

Time to pour a single malt Islay whisky and think of times and people past and, of going back to where we began.

The Last Chance Saloon

(WARNING! Contains Opinion: Deactivate Airbag Before Proceeding)

Chrome trimmed, multiply air bagged, electronically throttled, steered, and geared, rubberoid textured inside and with, it seems, the ubiquitous gawping great 'mouth' grille and an aggressive stare between bejewelled headlamps slashed back into the front wings, modern cars are more alike than cars ever have been. True, they are much safer and much more reliable, and who can argue with that. But telling them apart from the outside, or in, is becoming ever more difficult in a 'me too' world of design. The driving experience is also now an expected amalgam of the anodyne and the low-profiled rumble of fashion. Regulations, copying, anti-design and more are all responsible for something being missing in modern cars – which may be why so many of us are turning and looking back at the cars of old and the motoring dreams of our youth, or of our fathers' choices, analogue cars from the day when the driver was actually connected to the device beneath him or her. Brands like Hyundai and Kia, once former purveyors of lightweight, velour-lined devices, now provide us with very good, very safe, very well designed cars that frankly, are beyond serious criticism as consumer items. They have taken on the establishment and beaten it. Honda remains an evocation of philosophy and the new NSX is a leader of supercar thinking in a new age.

Meanwhile, the 'lemons' of the 1970s – from BL's Austin to Fiat and onwards to Zastava – all have vanished as the automotive lessons of history. But with them went character and a deliberately designed identity – which is why post-war and modern classics are on the up. The fact is that our new cars, our new consumer-durable products, sometimes serve to deceive. They perform a function, but they are a veneer; safe, sound, reliable, nicely painted, and fully foamed and plasticised inside, such cars achieve a common denominator, they seem to have no soul, no spirit and, few foibles. They are characterless. This is the *new* age of the car. The difference between a car of 2017 and a car of 1990, is massive – far bigger than the difference between car of 1989 and 1969.

As a car-obsessed teenager, sometime in about 1976, I can remember comparing the bodies and build quality of the several cars, notably the Ford Cortina Mk III, Volvo 244, Saab 99, Morris Marina, Renault 12, MG1300, Toyota Crown, and a Fiat 132 – all were new and parked beside each other in my school's teachers' car park. The differences in design and quality between these cars were obvious and quite startling to a young enthusiast. Build quality was the thing, and it remains a vital factor in cars old and new. Even listening to these cars doors being shut revealed a story – from the flimsy to the over-engineered. The Marina in basic trim felt like a wartime ration book of a car. The Cortina shone and sweated in a romp of vinyl and gloss. The Renault reeked of brown velour and the flash of Dior-clad tanned cleavage on a hot afternoon in France. The Fiat had a rash of little black rubber plugs festooned around its metallic gold body and these looked silly. Yet they were the plugs for an after-market rust-proofing process named 'Ziebart' which stopped the Fiat rusting away and gave it near-Swedish levels of sealing. Ziebart saved many a 1970s car for a classic afterlife. But we might now ask why some penny-pinching car makers utterly failed to protect their new cars in such manner on the production line.

Beyond such thoughts, back then, as an innocent, I would simply sit and stare at the metallic silver-blue Lancia Beta 2000ie that a relative owned. Sod the rust issue, this was Italian style and verve presented in a car that drove wonderfully and looked and sounded even better. It had class, a sense of occasion – that signal of a great car design. Consequently, I owned a Lancia Gamma a few years later. It was a car that inspired the soul, a car that you simply adored driving and, showing off to others so like-minded. Gamma remains addictive to those of us who suffer from its infection – one that has crossed the blood-brain barrier and lodged in our souls. There is no cure.

What of the works of the Bugatti family, father and son? How could you not enthuse at their passion for utterly exquisite and intuitive design. Perhaps it is the old Jaguars, especially XJ13, which simply capture my senses as I gaze at the design genius of Malcolm Sayer's work and Sir William Lyons achievements on a shoestring. How did Lyons become not just a motor industry magnate, but a designer/stylist, motor sport genius, and the man who went from side-cars to specially-built Austin 7 Swallows, thence on to Le Mans and latterly cars so great that they ranked alongside Ferrari and Rolls-Royce? Maybe it was because he was a polymath, a natural sculptor and a man who surrounded himself with the right people in an age when anything was possible and the thought police had less power. We should cite Soichiro Honda as a notable, a pioneer of design and exquisite engineering. A self-made man as a designer, pilot, hang glider, biker, engineer, maverick polymath – what a man and what achievement his legacy and his brand has become. From humble moped to Type R, and NSX, Honda's story makes it and its most of its cars, truly classic – albeit with one or two blander moments en route across its history on the road to automania.

Great things were achieved by the Jowett Company and once again Gerald Palmer's name is writ large in the marque's design language. Most know of his Javelin saloon, but fewer know of the Jupiter dating from 1949, which had engineering of Austrian influence courtesy of chassis design by Prof E. von Eberhorst and a body styled not by Palmer but by Jowett's chief designer, Reg Korner. A Jupiter competed in the 1950s Le Mans, but the Jupiter and its lighter derivative the R4, were Jowett's last cars and by 1954 the proud British marque was gone, yet another example of daring design – flat-four engines, torsion bar springing and aerodynamic bodies (all very European) – done for by circumstance and larger volume marque competition.

Like many, I love the cars of the 1970s era of BMW boss von Kuenheim and his 'bahnstormers, and am still moved at the site of the original, shark-snouted 5 and 6 series – semi-trailing rear suspensions twitchery notwithstanding; but might we suggest that more recent BMWs are a case of the brand defining the product rather than the previous and more desirable case of the product defining the brand? All I know is that the recent BMWs I have lusted over have, upon inspection, suffered from orange-peeled paint finishes and scratchy plastic appliqué cabin garnishes. Horrid. Yet they still boast sonorous straight-sixes, wonderful yet evolutionary styling and they drive superbly. How about a 4-series coupé with M-pack bits? Maybe, but what about a 1980s 5-series Alpina! Now *there* was joy through driving. Alpina retains its class and exclusivity and talking of class, was not the 635CSi, much classier than the ruched and blinged-up 850?

The current crop of new mainstream market cars make a very good family car choice. But they are not *drivers* cars (Golf R, Civic Type R, Focus RS, and a few others excused). New cars do not talk to you in the way that once, inanimate lumps of metal with wheels, did. No longer do normal cars communicate through the seat-of-the-pants, the steering wheel, the pedals, the chassis, and the very structure. The old link to what the car was doing and what the road was doing under it, seems in the main, to have gone. Driving has changed in the last few years because cars have changed. Technology has taken over in a sort of Airbus fly-by-wire kind of way. Good old fashioned skills of hand, foot, and eye co-ordination have been cast out and electrical and digital devices have taken over. Turn off the ESC anti-skid control and watch the young' uns flee for safety.

Nissan's wonderful new GTR is a fantastic car yet one soullessly devoid of 'feel'.

Some say driving it is like having virtual sex (apparently, that really is very popular in Japan). Is not a manual Lotus Evora the perfect antidote to such flappy-paddle electronics and utterly synthesised grunt? Evora steers like a Supermarine Spitfire and goes like an English Electric Lightning; Evora is a hidden joy of depreciating fibres, it retains a classic allure. Chapman for all his faults, lives on it seems.

Yet beyond such gems as Evora, Focus ST or Megane RS, NSX, or 911R, degrees of separation seem to be being built in under the bonnet and behind the wheel of many of our new cars. Now we even have a Bentley Benataga 'SUV' and even a Jaguar iteration of the truck-as-car idea. Thankfully, the Jaguar, like Porsche's Macan, makes the jump without becoming a dumper truck fit only for the pavement grand prix.

Old BMC or BLMC and British Leyland 'BL' cars like the Maxi and the Allegro now seem to represent a purity of engineering, an evocation of a post-Issigonis era of weird austerity genius. Yet the new Mini is, to me, a soulless pastiche upon an original car, one that was great to drive but in reality was an unfinished and unreliable rust bucket that was so very 'unsafe'. But such things seemed to matter less back then. Rovers, P5 and P6 still grab my attention as they do other people's. There really is something about the P5 and P6 and while the V8 versions are fun, lower-powered models still offer a very special recipe indeed. Rover P6, in 2000 and 3500 V8 guises, had so much pure engineering in them; structure, suspension, cranked dampers up front and de Dion at the rear – they looked so smart then and utterly 'cool' now. No wonder the P6 was tagged the 'Solihull Citroën'. Americans love them (David La Chance the Editor of *Sports and Exotic Car*, drives a P6) and I can see why. It's hard to accept that the last Rover was the Honda-derived, BMW-modified 75. What on earth *happened?*

Episodes in my own classic car travels, evidence the breadth of the great classic car conversation. I once drove around Tasmania in a classic Saab (as you do) and urge you to visit that paradise island and attend the classic gathering at Salamanca market where Tasmania's classic car fans gather. And the Targa Tasmania is one of the best classic and motor sport events in the southern hemisphere and runs every April. It is billed as the world's biggest, toughest and longest tarmac traversing rally and held over 1,250 miles of stunning scenery; it is a 'must see' event. Oh, and there is a bi-annual wooden boat festival every other March as well – not on any account to be missed, and you can stay on for the Targa. So, it seems that Tasmania has it all – classic cars, classic boats, classic food, world class scenery and some very friendly locals, it is a truly classic place. Go before everyone else does.

A few years ago, I found myself in a small rural village in Bali, Indonesia. There, I was dumbstruck to see a 1966 Ford Mustang in rust-free original condition being used by a local. Then a Citroën GS and an Alfa Romeo Guiletta chugged past me. I saw a Morris Minor 1000 convertible on someone's driveway and a lovely dark blue 1960s Mercedes saloon parked outside the shops. I talked to several of the owners. One of them asked me if I had seen the Citroën DS in the rice paddies, owned, apparently by a Dutchman who was restoring a Citroën Maserati SM on the island. I soon saw that SM, basking like a sleepy shark, hunkered down on its stops, a patina of tropical sweat seeping from it in the fuji-coloured greens of Bali. An SM in the rice paddies! To me, it was a bizarre yet delightful classic car moment.

I know a small town in Zimbabwe where a Citroën DS Pallas, a Jowett Javelin and a Lotus Cortina all sit, seething in the dry heat awaiting the turn of time and tide. They are rot-free but sun-faded.

Tropical climes harbour many classic car 'finds'. According to Jaguar's records, D-Type chassis number 521 was sold new to Cuba. I like to think of it fulminating in the undergrowth, but it has I am told, been recovered to the USA. The recent discovery of a clutch of Porsche 356s also secreted away in Cuba yet eagerly driven by their passionate owners, offers a tantalising glimpse of the reach and the touch of classic car enthusiasm. Autofarm the Porsche people have just secured the last-made RHD 911Careera RS 2.7 after its rescue from two decades under a tin shack in Trinidad. It is purple and somewhat modified, but seethes with promise – once the sun-dried parts are rejuvenated. Africa also boasts caches of hidden Porsches just waiting to be discovered; I know a barn in Zimbabwe where a very early 356 rests – as it has for forty five years...

Some car makers do still invoke 'feel' and feedback into their cars and such behaviours are not solely the preserve of the rich. And yet it seems that even a brand new Porsche 911, however desirable, has lost its *soul* – because now you cannot buy a non-turbocharged new, mainstream, 911. So the engine is super smooth rather than a howling banshee; no longer the song of the siren calling you to adventure and possible death. Add in good but lifeless electric steering, and the brilliant but utterly detached Porsche PDK gearbox with its electro-mechanical double clutched, paddle-shifted gearing, and it is clear that having robbed the driver of *direct* physical-mechanical intercourse with the act of driving, is why of course, Porsche have very quickly turned out the new revised, raw, 911R in attempt to redress some 'spirit' – point proven then. But you cannot readily procure one.

Does anyone remember the 1.5 litre Porsche 356 beating its more powerful (and heavier) rivals? What of the perhaps ultimate, chuckable Porsche, the little four-cam 135bhp 1.5-litre 550A of 1957? They only built thirty-seven, but was this not the ultimate iteration of Porsche DNA – as driven by Sir Stirling Moss and Wolfgang von Tripps to Targa Floria, Nurburgring, etcetera in the era? What of Porsche's Works 904/6, it is another forgotten Porsche moment of lithe and light. *Can* Porsche still do lithe?

Of Patination?

What of over-restoration? Perhaps certain car collectors, notably American ones, ought to ask themselves about this practice. Should millions be spent turning out cars that are not just 'better' than they were when newly-built, but actually different? Patination, is it important to you? I suggest it should be. Patina, that growth of layers of substances laid down over time, is what makes something old and characterful. Over-restoring, ridding a car of its patina, can actually *reduce* the car's value, so why do people insist in replacing the old or even lightly patinated, with 'new'? But if a car has become beyond saving, only 'new' can prevent its death. And what if previous restoration works have undermined originality anyway? So you can make an argument for rebuilding and restoring a classic, but I fear that it can be an excuse for bad taste.

Through patination comes a sign or a clue to the psychometry of time and events; to denude a car of its patination, is to remove its history and those of its owners and of their driving, *their* story. If that is what you want, so be it, you are free to make your old car new. But if the memories of time as laid down upon and within the hull of an old car, cry out to you in their authenticity, then you must leave them in place.

Occasionally I stop creating my dream garage, filled as it is with Citroën SM, and GS, Peugeot 304 coupé, Lancia Gamma, Rover SD1, Alpine A310, NSU Ro80, Porsche 911 2.7RS, Corvette Stingray, Jaguar XJ13, Ferrari 275 GTB, Bristol 404 SC, Allard J2X, Tatra T70, Bugatti 57SC, Voisin C27 coupé, Amilcar and Bedelia, only to give in to materialism and go out for a classic car fix at a posh dealership. The nearest one to my home is Dick Lovett's Ferrari, Porsche, and posh classics emporium. It is a multi-million pound job – big enough to hold a motor show in and is all glass, tiles, men in suits and women in expensive skirts. The latest Ferraris are arrayed in front of you as you walk in. Next door on the next 'hall' can be found previously enjoyed exotic cars and supercars. Upstairs, on tier two, we find oh, five or six probably million quids worth of rarer classic car metal.

You get 'vetted' on the way in just to make sure you're not a scratch and sniff tosser, then they give you freedom to lust. They know me now and they know I cannot afford to buy a wheel, yet alone a car. On my last visit, there were three Porsche 997 GT3 RS 4.0 litres, a Riviera Blue 993 GT RS, a blueberry coloured

964 RS, a classic 1970s 911S, half a dozen newer 997s, and two of the recent Careera GTS – at six hundred thousand apiece. But they were not my target. What I wanted was to see the lovely, bottle green, two-door, fastbacked 1956 Bristol 404 SC – registered 337 YUE with a scant 51,000 miles showing; for sale for a mere £144,000 of anyone's pounds (it was £3,542 new), Edward Lovett had kindly cleared me to inspect the car and sit in it.

Just looking at the Bristol evoked memories of an England I am too young to have known, but to wish I had. This was the shorter wheelbase fastback with two vestigal rear fins and a jet intake nose. Apparently, the prototype had had three rear fins – one central spine – Tatra-like. A Dudley Hobbs and James Lane design no less, one free of Italian or German influence. Hobbs, like Lunjgstrom at Saab, was a former wing designer and it shows. Underneath the bonnet or inspection hatch, there lay the 1971cc straight-six engine that was the unburstable Bristol rock. The car was built like a rock too – solid, wide sills, heavy gauge in chassis but alloy skinned for aviation lightness. Climbing in really was like getting into the cockpit and constrained cabin of some great post-war prop job. The car was original, unrestored, reeked of its stories and was all the better and more valuable for it. It was not perfect and I was so glad of that. So I just sat there and took in all the design details, the thought, the craftsmanship, the labours of love that men put into creating this vehicle.

My notebook of impressions, made as I sat there in the cockpit of car, remind me of its design brilliance. My notes read: Hobbs line Hull. Chamfered form. Aerodynamics. Rear fins for stability and low drag. Clamshell hatch as hood or bonnet. Lozenge-shaped cabin turret canopy. Swept rear pillars lead to tail cone. Cockpit command post. Alloy over wood and steel. Wheels fill the arches. Patina. Leather. Original. Aura. Wonderful. Keep it this way, it talks!

Just up the road from Lovett's emporium of excellence, lies the home of European Classic Cars – snuggled under the foot of the Wiltshire Downs and the location of a regular supply of wonderful old Lancias and Maserotica. On my last visit they also had a 1956 Porsche diesel for sale – in bright red with yellow wheels – a Porsche tractor! But this was trumped by a 1974 Zagato Zele electric car. A few miles north, Ashton Keynes Vintage Restorations are nice enough to let visitors in too – just don't touch anything!

Meanwhile, men in sheds all over the world, have many treasures to yield up.

Posh Days Out

The lawns of Villa d'Este, Syon Park, Goodwood, Carmel, the Quail, and Pebble

Beach, do look very nice with the random scattering of exquisite, high-value aristocratic metal amid the beautiful people. But amongst the cheaper world of cars of 'nuts and bolts', restorations, and more recent 'modern classics', a different strain of the classic car movement can be found. At the Amelia Island Concours, restored cars rule, but now, original cars *are* also being shown with preserved originality and rewarded with prizes. Bill Warner, the classic car enthusiast, photographer and Maserati Ghibli Spider owner who created the Amelia Island event, has realised that patination can be perfect.

The Hon. Sir Michael Kadoorie – the classic car man behind 'The Quail Lodge' classic event at the Carmel location of his hotel of the same name, sensibly sent his Portout-bodied Talbot 150C SS to Ashton Keynes Vintage Restoration and it came back properly restored but still 'real' and in a paint that was blinding in its blue brilliance. But when you also own a Rolls-Royce Phantom II, a Bugatti Type 57, a Lamborghini Muira and a Vanvooren-bodied Hispano Suiza, losing one car for a bit, is not a body blow. Can we persuade Sir Michael to go 'oily rag'? Imagine that at Carmel.

I confess that I attend Goodwood Members' Day and it remains probably the world's greatest classic car action 'fix'. It is hard to beat. Conversely, I have given up on the once superb but now so-cramped-you cannot-see-anything event that is the Festival of Speed – too crowded, too celebrity, too damned 'see and be seen' where the aftershave of choice seems to be eau du ego and cars cannot be seen because so many people want to do the same. A brilliant but now flawed event seems to have got out of hand; action needs to be taken. The Revival event must not be allowed to go the same way.

Malta hosts a stunning annual classic car show in October, while Germany's big annual classic car 'do' is at the Schloss Dyck and it manages to be both 'posh' and also open to, and for, all, with a huge, eclectic range of classics to saviour, not to mention the beer; you do *not* have to be thin or rich to be seen on the lawn either. You can get a 'fix' in dingy Düsseldorf at 'Classic Remise', the new concept in classic car storage and exhibition. Yet for me, classic car days at Brooklands Museum are a true 'fix'. Much fun can be had at the Morris Minor Owners Club too. My event of the year however, remains 'La Vie en Bleu' at Prescott, where veteran, vintage and classic cars all meet in a small, intimate setting and the entry ticket is cheap. But this is an entirely subjective and personal opinion – and a contradictory one, because despite that cheap entry fee, a lot of 'money' turns up, but I rarely encounter a classic car snob at Prescott on 'Blue' days or on August VSCC days. It is pure joy and any 'Don't you know who I am' characters can have their pomposity wonderfully crushed. The French have a saying: 'Il pete plus haut

Should 'design' begin with a sketch or a computer graphic?

que son cul' which translates as, he farts higher than his bottom. Only rarely do people of such behaviour transgress the grass at Prescott or other more expensive 'posh' events. Prescott rewards with blue (and other coloured) Bugattis, and the Bugatti Trust itself – another addiction in the great adventure.

Thank goodness we have the Brooklands Museum where it is still the right crowd and no crowding and, we have days at the Beaulieu Autojumble and assorted gatherings of Prescott events, Cholmondley weekends, the Silverstone Classic, and lots of local classic car shows where everyone, regardless of income or class, *can* access real cars; try the Essex-based Warren Classic, or Martin Port's October 'Gathering on the Green' at Thatcham, to really feel the classic car magic up close – with free entry! Alternatively, try the annual summer high of the Gloucestershire Vintage and Country Extravaganza, which has become a three-day, stay-over event. And if you really are a modern classics nerd, the Festival of the Unexceptional does, as it says on its advertising, celebrate 'the threatened and endangered pieces of orange, beige, and plaid automotive history'. Oh, to turn up at that in an orange Renault 14 GTL, now *that* would give the Allegroists something to think about.

To France Mon Ami: Loheac to Chateau de Savigny-les-Beaune

Like many classic car people, I regularly need an old car or classic car 'fix' and once a year I wander off to rural France on the incomparable Brittany Ferries from Portsmouth to St Malo or Caen. In more than twenty-five trips on the *Bretagne* or the *Pont Aven*, the experience has always been five star, the crew brilliant and the late night wining and dining with fellow classic car people has been superb. They talk cars and drink, while down below on the car decks, assorted Bugattis, Morgans, Jaguars, Cobras, and more, sleep easy as the ferry churns onwards through the night while cars and owners dream of empty French roads and the delights of France. I don't mind paying the high, summer ferry fares for myself and a car, it truly is case of you get what you pay for and, it *is* brilliant, a highlight of the year and the perfect reason not to fly or take the tunnel funnel. Why can't these people be allowed to run our railways?

After an early breakfast at 0600, then to disembark and drive, or better if you are on foot, to catch a cheap train from St Malo southwards, to the rural depths of France. There is no excuse for not attending an event such as the Manoir d'Loheac automotive museum's annual auto-jumble and gathering. So good is it at Loheac, that I and others will camp out or sleep under a tree just to spend a weekend there. I once spent a cold night under a bush in a St Malo park with rabbits for company, simply in order to get an early train and bus to Loheac and its wonderful inter-tribal assembly. Loheac is packed with French classics from the dawn of motoring right up to 1980s cars; this museum is worth a visit at any time of year but the annual Loheac autobrocante show in October always rewards whatever that year's automotive theme. A trip down the road to Redon and its chestnut festival is an added highlight. Here at Loheac and in Redon is the proof that French really do know how to live. It may be a British perspective, but many of our classic car clubs have discovered the delights of driving a classic through Normandy, Brittany and the Loire. Numerous classic car hostelries cater for owners clubs en route through France. One of the finest is the Châteaux des Briottieres near Angers where the wonderfully named Hedwige de Craecker-Valbray provides classic car wining and dining of excellence.

Up the road near Orleans, there is the museum of the L'Espace Automobiles Matra in Romoratin-Lanthenay. There nearly every exhibit is blue and a gripping tale of Matracide is told. It is worth the trip just to stare at the blue Matra-BRM.

Across the other side of France in wonderful Burgundy, if cars and aircraft (and wine, and mustard) are your things, then there is only one place to go, the Château de Savigny-les-Beaune (exit 24 off Autoroute A6). Owned by Michel Pont, there you will find a squadron of ex-air force fighter jets mouldering away in alloy rot disease. Oh, and there are Hunters, Lightnings and other brilliant British machines too. Inside the barns, an unexpected collection of Abarths and a fine motorcycle collation complement French car marques and a tribute to a Frenchman named Jean Pierre Wimille who was a racing driver and Resistance leader. The rooms, all full of memorabilia, grip you for hours. Outside, further piles of auto-aero-mechanical 'stuff' include tractors and fire engines.

The man who owns all this is a true hero of classic cars and aircraft. That there is a wine museum on the site, only adds to the growing legend of Michel Pont's Château de Savigny. If you know your mustards, or want to learn about real mustard (not the yellow stuff of England) then head down the road to Beaune, where can be found the base of Edmond Fallot – purveyors of what many think are the best exotic and fine mustards in the world, all made locally since 1840. Try the Moutarde Au Basilic (made with basil and white wine). The family also produce mustard with blackberries, nuts, honey and, herbs: other mustards are available, but few are like these.

Head south to get to Mulhouse and the Bugatti Museum gathering of all time. If you tack west across France to the Lot region, you will find the Musée du Machinisme Agricicole et Automobile de Salviac located ten miles or so north of Cahors. There, lies what may be the ultimate 'oily rag' collection of original old cars and many tractors that simply sleep; rust in peace. Turn north for Dordogneshire and head to the Château de Sanxet to see Bertrand de Passemar's evocative collection at his Musée de Sanxet near Pomport – on the D933 road south of Bergerac. Bertrand's place is full of French metal and, a Ghia-bodied Jowett eeks out its forgotten existence too. Monbazillac vines also offer the visitor a refreshing revival from such gems as the 1929 Casimir Ragot Spéciale – which is not a main course, but a car of rarity and significance. And if the French do annoy you, instead of speaking loudly in English, just tell them that you are suffering from a 'griller sauter un joint de culasses' – that you have blown a head gasket. Oh and try to remember that a 'coup du lapin' is a whiplash injury not a rabbit with a fastback body.

The Circuit des Ramparts is a September must at Angoulême if you are into historic classics and their racing – 2016 saw twenty Bugatti type 13 Brescias fighting for tarmac – which was deep joy to see, hear and smell; remaining imprinted in a rash of screaming blue upon my memory.

It was in France, on open sweeping roads under a bright sky, that I had one of my greatest classic car adventures. It involved a Citroën with an Italian engine and a body to die for. The Citroën SM is that car; it has haunted me for decades, an out of focus vignette so often flashing across my subconscious, a ghost tugging at my soul, hinting at a past life. I think it is the car that, today, I still, just simply sit and stare at in schoolboy wonderment at its total accomplishment.

The French threw money at the SM, so much money that the investment, the time and a coincident global economic crisis, played a part in the collapse of the great marque and its falling into Peugeot's hands. But at least Citroën survived. Was SM, the last real French supercar? Was it in fact the *first* hypercar? Was this the last of the spiritual French grand line of all the marques and the grand scale carrossiere that had created the French legend of the motor car? Was the SM the last *true* Citroën on the road to rack and Rouen?

The men who created this car with Robert Opron – outside *and* inside, surely all deserve wider recognition; many of them are invisible footnotes to motoring history. Albert Grosseau led the SM project and Jacques Né sanctioned the building of two DS coupé bodies and even placed an altered Panhard 24 two-door bodyshell over an extended DS base unit as an early experiment; was the moment of the true genesis of the SM? By 1965 the go-ahead for a really big Citroën coupé GT had been given, perhaps as if by corporate and engineering osmosis. Henri Lauve de Segur who had led a design team at Buick joined the SM development team and contributed several ideas. Regis Gromik also drew a stunning ellipsoid rendering of a grant tourer idea for SM. Soon after joining Citroën in 1961, as Flaminio Bertoni was ageing, it was Robert Opron who began sketching and then sculpting small scale models of a sports car that would not be a DS derivative but a truly new car – this was the beginning of what eventually became the SM. Henri Dargent made early sketches for the SM's fascia, and Jean Giret and he worked together to realise the final form with Michel Harmand and Regis Gromik also closely involved.

Opron concentrated on the frontal aspect of the design and how to meet the aerodynamic issues. After weeks of work and wind tunnel research, the SM gained its frontal treatment, an unusual glazed display, a sort of 'showcase' that housed six headlamps, a licence plate, and provided excellent leading edge airflow penetration as well as undercar and under bonnet flow. Key to its form was the ovaloid shaping. So was born the Citroën SM – powered by a Maserati quad-cam V-6 engine not a rattly old Citroën lump.

SM was hailed as a success and adored by many. Famous SM owners included John Barry, Charlie Watts of the Rolling Stones, President Brezhnev, Idi Amin, Mike Hailwood, and Johan Cryuff, to name just a few. David Lillywhite of *Octane* magazine runs a gold SM.

Not too long ago, an SM gave me one of my favourite classic car moments. It came to life one bright clear morning at St Malo. I turned the key, SM sighed, levitated upon its oleo-pneumatic legs, then slipped off Brittany Ferries great big white liner the *Bretagne* and headed down a Route National to Rennes, then to take to the by-ways to Guer through the remains of a great forest of Broceliande that is packed with remnants of Arthurian legend. We stopped briefly at Merlin's grave and wondered if the wizard had cast his spell upon Citroën and the SM. Then, watched by even the French, we left. The SM simply traversed the tarmac, dismissing all behind; I drove further southwards in this shimmering torpedo, cocooned inside its tobacco brown-leathered capsule. I parked the SM in the main square of Redon and sat in a café and watched the French gather to stare at their last grand tourer, a vision of a great past and a forgotten future in a changed world. Was this, Louis – the sun king's car? Did Leonardo da Vinci influence it by remote channelling? How the hell did Citroën get away with it?

Then it was out onto the fast, open, beautifully cambered bends of the road to Malestroit. Driving an SM cross-country on French main roads was beyond comparison: not point and shoot but, point and scythe. Yet we were gliding through the space time continuum – as if being teleported to another dimension. SM simply strode along as if on mythical, seven league boots. In the medieval square of Malestroit, we left the SM settling down on its hydro-pneumatics as the hot engine ticked loudly and a shimmer of heat vented from it: light dancing upon SM's bronzed flanks.

My memories of that SM endure and will always last. There was that quad-cam bark from the Maserati engine, the exquisite sensitivity of the steering and the need to place the car perfectly and concentrate to create the desired effect, was utterly compelling. The manner in which air skipped over the car's fuselage and off its tapered rump; this was a character of a car and an adventure beyond compare.

SM was an amazing amalgamation of intellect and knowledge: a car and yet something else. And it is one that to this day captivates and endures. As Citroën themselves said in their SM advertisements: '*The Citroën SM has four wheels like other cars. That is the only way it is like other cars.*' They also called it: '*Precision Scientifique*', and indeed it was.

SM was unique, utterly intergalactic, a true warp-design and drive. A car to ache for, something beyond rational comprehension from an age we will never see again. No criticism will be tolerated and readers' letters to the contrary will be ignored. SM, rules.

Only an Espada, a Bugatti Type 57 Atalante, or a Portout Talbot 150C SS comes close!

What of recreations and evocations? A new, lightweight E-Type or XKSS built by Jaguar cannot be called a replica, and is of course a 'continuation' built by its originators, yet there are those who would stop such a device appearing at a true classic car event or competing. A 2017 Allard built by the Allard family from original bits is or course a superb 'continuation' that is bound to appreciate. A Lister Knobbly recreation built by Listers must occupy similar ground. Surely a

'Suffolk Jaguar'-built SS100 is a good thing and not a bad' un. But how far do we take purism? Some new 'old' vehicles should of course be burned (not least on grounds of taste and of safety). But when *does* re-creation become replica and when does replica become wretched?

Americarna?

The Americans gave us the likes of the Cord and its front-driven, Gordon Buehrig-designed Model 810. They gave us the Chrysler Airflow and a vast catalogue of designs that captured the public imagination. Cadillac's chief engineer Ernest Seaholm created the world's first production V-16 engine in 1930. In 1928 the Stutz Black Hawk Special came second at Le Mans and also took the world land speed record. Harry Stutz had founded the marque after building his first car in a month and then entering it in the first Indianapolis 500 race. From Buick, Cord to De Soto, Lincoln, Mercury, Pierce-Arrow pre-WWII American cars were a massive statement of intent. This was proven by the 1950s years of GM-led styling and engineering developments. Yet GM and its tribe of sub-brands would, in recent year,s come to an impasse when it copied British Leyland's school of thought into a badge-engineered, accountancy-led landscape of mediocre products and too-clever marketing.

Meanwhile, we revere the 'muscle car' era and rightly so, for who can argue that the original 1960s Dodge Charger, Pontiac GTO and the Firebird, Plymouth Barracuda, Chevrolet Camaro, and early Ford Mustang ranges, were not a classic blend of motoring enthusiasm served up for the average man. Remember, in the 1960s these cars gave easy access to 350bhp power. Could any true petrol head really look the other when faced with a 'Cuda 400 of 7.2litres and orange paint? And simply saying the name, Pontiac or Oldsmobile, evokes a classic car enthusiasm. And there was Preston Tucker's futuristic Tremulis styled Torpedo – all fifty-one of these amazing rear-engined devices of the immediate post-war era that were glorious in their failure. As with other American independents (such as Kaiser Frazer,) the Tucker could grasp unconventional thoughts, yet delivering them as production-reality was to prove difficult.

The Modern Classic

For many people, it is the classic cars from 1960-1980 that remain accessible and drivable. A 1970s-1980s modern classic movement is burgeoning. Some say that these are *lesser* classics, but does it matter? I think not. You can have as much fun in an old Mini, a Capri, a CX, a GT6, an Austin 7 or a Morris Minor, or Corvette or a Mustang, as you can in a Bentley Continental, a Mercedes 'Gull Wing' or a Frazer Nash BMW.

1950-1970s classic cars might not all be high-end, but they represent a world of car enthusiasm to a great many people who cannot afford to spend the cost of a house on a spare car, however classic it might be.

Can Porsche 911s just keep on increasing in value? As this is written, Dick Lovett want £850,000 for a 1973 911 RSL; it is a lot, but they will get it. Will the Lamborghini Espada finally be seen for the hidden gem it is? Morgan remains marvellous – building 'new' eighty year old cars, sadly now with fake 'stick-on' leather bonnet straps of all things... Meanwhile a Triumph TR4 or TR5 has exceeded £20,000 for a good one. MGBs are on the rise and a Lotus Cortina is £50,000! But you can still buy a 1950s-1960s mainstream marque classic car for under £5,000 and drive it regularly without breaking down beside the road, or you doing likewise in the psychiatrist's chair. The average man, while dreaming of his fantasy garage, *can* still go out and buy an American, British, or European classic car for £5,000- £10,000 or the same in Euros or US Dollars. Likely classics to cherish must include the Rover P6 as 2000 or 35000, Triumph Dolomite, GT6, Spitfire, Renault 4, Peugeot 304 coupé, Porsche 924/944/968, the Mercedes-Benz W123, Hillman Minx, Sunbeam Rapier, Saab 96, Lancia Fulvia or any Zagato derivative. What of an Alfa 75 – all these and many others are out there, waiting behind the facade of more expensive fare, waiting to be cherished and fettled by the 'average' classic car enthusiast. MGBs and Triumph Spitfires still seem to be a sub-£5,000 starting point for 1960s classic car ownership, although there are some very interesting alternatives to be had; the excellent Lotus Excel is a forgotten modern classic starting point for similar money. A Morris Minor, random Fiats, Mazda RX7s, Toyota Celicas and MR2s, all beckon. If an Alfa Romeo GTV is already beyond reach, how about Alfa 33, 75, 90, 164, or a Fiat Argenta?

Surely these cars-to-buy-now are all brilliant modern classics with all the fun of the frustration that they will charm you with. £10,000 or its Euro or US$ equivalent will soon be the starting point for a 'normal' life classic car ownership – values of modern classics are going up, as values of elite metal being to plateau and even fall. What of Matra and its wonderful Bagheera, or the Murena? Murenas are also sadly invisible Matra made 48,800, a few dozen remain. The Simca-based Matra Rancho might best side stepped though. What of the Citroën BX (try a GTi!) Talbot Tagora, or the knock-kneed Morris Marina 1.8GT two-door which went well – in a straight line; few remain and some people rejoice in that. What of the BMC Austin Morris 1800 or 18-22 'Landcrab', the Maxi, and the 18-22 Mk2 series renamed as the

Princess and then as the charming Ambassador, a car like so-many BL issuances that was a 'stop-gap' until better times arrived (they did not). Such cars will soon be gone, utterly voided from the classic car consciousness. Yet the old BL cars reeked of character and an amalgam of the bad and the far less bad than claimed, amid the late evening of the life of the British car industry. Opel's lovely little 'mini-Corvette' GT designed by Erhab Schnel must become a classic car icon, so too must the Lancia Beta Montecarlo. But only a Brit might think that Austin Rover Group Montego might achieve classic car cult status. Vauxhall's Firenza and Magnum coupé and 2300 estate with 'droop snoot' must be a certain slow-burning classic car investment and are great examples of GM-era styling when Vauxhalls were desirable and different – even Calibras now seem special rather than simple.

Bargains of the moment and likely to appreciate? Forgotten Alfa Romeos, Lancia Fulvia, NSU Ro80, Rover P6, Triumph GT6, early Mazda rotaries, BMW 5-Series, Citroën CX, Jaguar XJ-S, all seem good candidates, as do Opel Monza or Vauxhall Royale as a coupé. What of other Opels, or the old Holdens of Australia? Also worth considering are 'oily rag' originals of any era – as long as they run and are not about to break in half. Even apparently shiny, six-figure classic cars for sale can hide rust and £50,000 restoration costs. Be very careful: all that glitters might well be camouflaged excreta.

The British and others further afield lapped up the Ford Capri – even a wheezy 1.3 litre-engined version that surely was the epitome of hope over ability. Despite using many propriety Ford parts, Capri in its larger-engined iterations *was* superb, a car of the moment, a car that took design, style, ability, and a distinct character to the mass motoring experience. That stylish fascia, made you feel rich, the styling hinted at St Tropez, not St Neots. You cannot really argue with that, can you? Capri prices – from early models to late 2.8 specials and South African 'Perana' racing variants, are on the up, and Ford's once prosaic car is now on the cusp of classic cultdom. Despite such Capri moments, it seems as if the British motor industry in 1976 was still stuck in the thinking of 1956. Badge engineering ruled the roost and mainstream car makers resisted the shock of the new. It was a world that replaced daring-do with daring-didn't. Leaf springs, vinyl, cast iron, and bi-focal windscreens ruled for far longer than you may care to remember.

Quite how we convinced ourselves that the likes of a Metro with an asthmatic engine, four-speed gearbox and lightweight body, was the future and a 'British car to beat the world' now seems utterly bizarre if not clearly delusional. Memories of Maestros and Montegos and invisible build quality live on; working within Austin Rover Group (ARG!) I recall seeing a new Metro with side stripes of differing colours per side and, a Maestro that came off the production line with L and HL seat trims in the front and rear respectively! The supervisor yawned and said: 'Oh.'

The ultimate antidote to modern life may be to choose a 'Woodie' and join that particular cult. Niches mean much in modern classics – the Nissan Skyline offering the perfect example. Not all Skylines are 'Nineties R34 GT cars with turbos and drifting history. Giovanni Michelotti styled the first big two-door Japanese coupé – the Prince company's Skyline of 1957. Under its skin, the Prince Skyline, soon to be absorbed into Nissan, had shades of Italy as well, with a Lancia level of technicality in its advanced suspension design and drivetrain. The Prince Company's engineers had been a talented and dedicated small team of car enthusiasts who seeded Nissan with its Skyline history. By 1965, Skyline S54s were competing in official class races and on one occasion gave Porsche a run for its money. The GT-R tag emerged as early as 1969 and throughout the 1970s and 1980s, Datsun/Nissan produced a series of boxy and fastbacked Skylines, including the C110 model. Today we have the Nissan GTR and, Toyota are set to revive their Supra.

What of the Z-cars of Nissan (as Datsun)? The man behind their engineering, Yutaka Katayama has recently died aged 105. He was 'father' of the Z-cars (stemming from working in California) and was also Nissan's top rally team manager and was one of Japan's greatest. The value of his cars, even 280 Z instead of 240Z, must be soon ascend.

Honda's lovely little S800 is a certain classic car investment – as are the 'Type R' modern classics and the NSX.

As we wander through the woods of automotive history, there is so much to be seen, so much to learn. I cannot be alone in looking across the old car landscape and wondering what happened and why. For example, how did a great marque like DKW, a company that made front-wheel drive cars of style and ability from as early as the 1930s, die, and be forever gone? The 1960s saw great cars like the Borgward, disappear and by the 1970s so also were sown the seeds of the downfall of the likes of Lancia, Triumph, and Rover amid the rise of Japan's automotive industry. Who could have ever have predicted MG of Abingdon ending up being the builder of Chinese cars. Who would have thought that Detroit would become a derelict wasteland of abandoned factories that once sang with the tune of metal bashing. They call it the 'rust belt' now, and it is a tragedy. There is so much that we have lost, so many marques – from Allard and Alvis, Riley, from Lagonda to Saab, of Horch to Hotchkiss, and of Panhard and to Voisin, to cite just a few evocative examples.

There was also a time when car makers employed journalists and artists in-house too – Rover's Dudley Noble being a key early expert – he thought of the 'Blue

Rust in Peace: old Renault grilles sleep at Loheac Museum's autojumble

Train' race between a Rover Light Six and the express train to the south of France, but Bentley 'stole' the story with its subsequent version of the event! Noble's work was also precursor to the establishment of the Guild of Motoring Writers and he also edited *Mileposts*, a post-war magazine designed to reignite popular motoring enthusiasm in the dark days of the 1940s.

Saab employed Gunnar Sjögren and Rony Lutz as designer-artist-writers and PR men.

The safety factor in old cars should not be ignored. Some classic cars are passive safety, crash-test horrors – cars that split or peel open, especially under offset frontal or side impacts. But not all old cars are unsafe or structurally unsound and some are far stiffer than certain 1960s-1980s cars with very soft torsional rigidity ratings. Best not to name names, as lawyers love a feast. Suffice it to say, that if you are driving an old classic car, especially one with sharp things on the dashboard and a face-shredding early laminated windscreen, I proffer one piece of opinion (with neither warranty implied nor liability accepted) and that is, *never*, ever rely on a retro-fitted modern inertia-reel seatbelt (that will lack pre-tensioners) to arrest your face and torso in time to stop it hitting the car or windscreen. In old cars, we are placed much closer to the body, the glass, the windscreen, and the impact. Inertia-reel belts cannot keep you from hitting them. Why not fit *static* seatbelts or a harness and make sure you wear them very tight and low, with the buckle and lap strap away from your vulnerable stomach. If driving a soft-top, a roll-over bar is advised to accompany belts as decapitation is never pretty. Remember, like everything in life, cars can have adverse side effects and informed decision taking is down to chance.

Design – the Fundamental Thing

Alongside the driving of the classic car, the aspect of the classic that makes it such, has to be its design. Design and engineering lie at the core of the content and the appeal of old cars, be that as stand-alone, or as an act of driving or motor sport. In the old days, the industry was about design and design differences, that's how they made their tribes of customers stay loyal to the tribes of the marques!

Design, styling? What is a debate about a word. The reality is that styling is not just about a matter of taste, it is about a blend of art, sculpture, architecture, science, or it was. These days, the court of public opinion – relying as it does I am afraid, on fashion and 'celeb' obsessed individuals – has made 'style' something else. But in days of old, the days of our classic cars, styling was not dictated by the public.

Styling was about three-dimensional sculpture in steel. Today it is more about two-dimensional lines on a CAD screen and fake light falling upon flat surfaces and the 'fat' cars that result. There is no room for a sculptor or a designer who wants to rush from thought or doodle to hands-on sculpting in clay or similar medium. If this had been the case decades ago, William Lyons, Flaminio Bertoni and many others would never have designed a car! Would Peter Stevens' original 1993 McLaren F1 have been what is was in terms of its wonderful body design, if Stevens had not studied art and sculpture as well as industrial design? Of critical reference, see how the light falls and plays upon the F1 – brilliantly – as it does on other cars touched by sculpture. Today we seem to have lost something in car design when most cars either look similar or lack visual cohesion, are devoid of exquisite detailing and of that quality of light dancing over metal.

Look at Gordon Bashford's and C. Spencer King's 'real' Range Rover Mk1 and compare it with today's Range Rover Evoque. One, the former, is about defining design and intelligence; the latter is a good car, but it is also a troubling embodiment of passing fashion, 'bling' status marketing and the heavy scale that current opinion embraces. Evoque symbolises the triumph of the new society, its 'things', its surface gloss, its weight, its excess, over the old. At least the new Range Rover proper, retains the magic of its genesis. As for that original Range Rover – it remains one of the most influential exponents of industrial design and its affect upon society – timeless beyond fashion or thinking.

Yet new car design is *not* timeless. Even the revered Mercedes have gone 'bling' and grotesque in flanks and details. I blame the fixation with China – a land that has little design history because of politics. Mercs with big lamps, pouting lip-filler proboscis bonnets and grilles, bejewelled trinkets, tinted windows, seem to be popular. Only whitewall tyres are missing from the crop of horrid new cars and their obscene body mass indexes. Hell, am I turning into Brian Sewell? Best not.

Car design as currently prescribed by car makers and marketeers, with a few honourable exceptions, is in a deep rut of repetition and digital regurgitation. A disturbance of design. The borders between engineering design and the designing of style are now more about marketing and focus groups and what non-engineers and non-designers want. Even once-revered Audis now seem to breed like wheeled clones that show no attempt at originality. Fashion has a lot to answer for. Yet there *are* highlights of modern design – various McLarens, Jaguars, Citroëns, Renaults, VWs, Porsches. And Honda, Ford, GM, and Chrysler are all fighting back with *design* and cars that 'drive'. Yet there also far too many new cars that are digitised amalgams of marque motifs that have been blended into cars that resemble several themes meta-morphed into a melange of anti-design. Grafting on an angry front

Porsche 911 (993) Turbo: elegance of a classic function

grille, beady eyed headlamps and the fashionable baboons-bottom red tail lamp clusters, hardly creates *style*, does it? And ride quality has disappeared at the altar of the alloy wheel and its flash fashion. Oh and 'footballers wives' and urban warriors, dictate design!

Meanwhile the odious trend of creating heritage by retro-pastiche design continues.

People with power have created the current situation in car design and people too scared to say things like those written above have gone along with it. Hierarchies steeped in status and arrogance now rule mainstream design. Maybe it is time for a shock to wake such thinkers in the industry from the torpor of the design doldrums. Old cars do not suffer from such unresolved conflicts in their designs, true classic cars are not fashion victims. That is why we have turned to them.

These then are the issues why any classic car conversation needs to discuss the crucial ingredient of design – of style – from an age when design was individual and cars could be identified by their looks, their *characters* and their abilities on the road and on the track. These parameters were set by engineers and designers, *not* by customers, fashion, or customer focus groups telling designers how and what to design. In the old days, design was left to designers not 'marcomms' men or celebs. We should know that in exterior and interior design lies the essential fundamentalism of old cars and classic cars, ingredients *so* diluted in today's new cars. From drawing board to sketch and clay model, to the artisan skills of leather work and metal turning, across the skills of making panels using an English Wheel, to tuning up carburettors or fettling suspension, prior to the mechanical act of driving; *these* are the classic details of the classic car.

The men (and a few women) that did these things were special indeed; they were and remain heroes to many, and so too do their cars. Surely, classic car enthusiasts will always gather and talk of such things, or read about them in magazines, or in a book. The magic of man's motoring *must* be preserved. From pub to club, from auto jumble to the cabinet of easement: from exquisite supercar to delightful old jalopy, this is the classic car conversation – the essence of our automania.

Looking over your shoulder and viewing the past racing towards you in a mirror that distorts the image and the memory of time, seems a good way to drive through the gates of remembrance and smell the reek of wheeled nostalgia. Suddenly, the afterwards and the before have become intertwined, welded into a motoring adventure that knows no bounds.

Notes

Introduction

1. Lantilly, *The Automobile*, Enthusiast Publ Ltd, August 2016 pp, 62-64.

Chapter 1

1. Alpine-Renault Club, North West France, at Malestroit, Bretagne, 2014.

Chapter 2.

1. Bernabo, F., *History of Lancia* From 1906, Drawn from *Lancia Revue*, Stampa Lancia, August 1969.

Chapter 3

1. Rishton, J. Lincoln-Zephyr The Tjaarda-Gregoire-Ford Concept, *The Automobile* 30th Anniversary Edition Enthusiast Publ Ltd pp152-159.
2. Aichele, Y., *Porsche 911 Engine History and Development*, MBI Publ Osceola WI, 1999 p21.
3. Schliperood, P., *The Extraordinary Life of Joseph Ganz*, RVP, New York, 2012.
4. Cole, L.F., (Editor/Contributor) *The New Illustrated Encylopedia of Automobiles* 2nd Ed (after Burgess Wise, D., Ed. 1st Ed), Quantum Books / Greenwich Editions, London 2000.
5. Margolis, I., & Henry, J,G., *Tatra: The Legacy of Hans Ledwinka,* SAF Publ, Harrow, *1990.*
6. Georgano, N., *Beaulieu Encyclopedia of the Automobile*, The Stationary Office, London, 2000.

Chapter 4

1. Personal Communications, Ferguson, A., Historit. Bicester, May 2016.
2. Conway, H.G., *Bugatti,* Octopus Books Ltd, London, 1989.

Chapter 5

1. Glancey, J,. Personal Communications 2013 after; *Spitfire*, Atlantic Books, London, 2011.
2. Whyte, A., *Jaguar:History of a great British car*, Patrick Stephens Ltd, Cambridge 1980, pp
3. Skilleter, P., XJ-S Historical Article, *Jaguar Enthusiast,* October 2015, Vol 31 No.10.
4. Sayer, S., Personal communications, 2014-2016.

Chapter 6

1. Personal Communications A. Allard 2010-2016.
2. Personal Communications M. Knapman 2010-2016.

Chapter 7

1. Robson, G. The Rootes Swallow *Autocar* w/e 8 June 1974, pp. 20-23.
2. Daniels, J., *British Leyland The Truth About the Cars,* Osprey, London, 1980.

Chapter 8

1. Aichele, Y., *Porsche 911 Engine History and Development*, MBI Publ Osceola WI., 1999.

Chapter 9

1. Cole, L. F., *Saab the Complete Story,* The Crowood Press ,2013.
2. Cole. L.F. Elliptical Excellence *The Automobile*, 30th Anniversary Edition, Enthusiast Publ Ltd, 2012.

Chapter 10

1. Norbye. J.P., *The Wankel Engine*, Chilton Books, Radnor, Penn, USA. 1975.
2. Buckley, M., Rearguard Action, *Classic & Sports Car,* August 2014..3. Bayley, S., Brave New Worlds, *Octane,* Issue 158 August 2016.

Chapter 11

1. *Car Styling*, Michelotti Tribute 1982, and of personal communications Michelotti S.p.A.
2. Sparke, P., *A Century of Car Design*, Mitchell Beazley, London 2002. pp.170-171.

Chapter 12

1. Blain. D., Driving the Dino. *Car,* May 1967, pp.19-21.

Chapter 13

1. Cole, L.F., *Citroën the Complete Story,* The Crowood Press, 2014.
2. Personal communications to Wilson, G.H. 2013.

Chapter 14

1. Norbye. J.P., *The Wankel Engine*, Chilton Books, Radnor, Penn, USA 1975 pp.387-406.
2. Charlesworth, S., Get In a Spin, *Classic Cars*, November 2008, pp.62-71.

Chapter 17

1. Cole L.F. Rover SD1: If They had got this right, we would still have Rover. *The Independent* London 10 November, 2006.

Chapter 18

1. Pininfarina S.p.A. *Pininfarina Cinquantanni*, Automobilia / Industrie Pininfarina S.p.A. Torino. 1980.
2. Charlesworth, S. Restrained Elegance, *Classic Cars,* November, 2008.
3. Sparke, P., *A Century of Car Design*, Mitchell Beazley, London 2002,pp.174-175
4. Texas University, Austin. Exhibition: Norman Bel Geddes Designs America, September 2012 – 2013.
5. Sparke, P., *A Century of Car Design*, Mitchell Beazley, London 2002.pp.30-43

Chapter 19

1. 1. Multiply told, cited to the author by Sir Stirling Moss in 2015. Also at: Edwards, R. *Stirling Moss The Authorised Biography*, Cassel & Co, London.

2. Dron, T., The Truth Behind the Lotus LX: This Was No Dud, *Octane,* October 2014*,* Issue 136, p.58.

3. Simanaitis, D., Personal Communications, USA, June, 2016.

4. Cited to the author at Erik Carlsson's memorial service and also at: Henry, A., & Tremayne, D., Hellraisers Incorporated *Classic Cars,* November 2008, p.58.

5. Personal Communications Innes Ireland, Kiln Cottage, Wickham, Berks. 1983-1985.

Bibliography

Books and Articles

AICHELE, Y., Porsche 911 Engine History and Development, MBI Publ Osceola WI. 1999

ANDRADE, J., Wind tunnel tests and body design. *Journal Society Automotive Engineers*. Vol 29 1931.

BARKER, R., **HARDING** ,A., (Editors) *Automobile Design:Twelve Great Designers and Their Works* Penn 1992.

BEL GEDDES, N., Archive at Humanities Research Centre, University of Texas, Austin.

BERK, Gijsbert-Paul., *Andre Lefebvre and the cars he created for Voisin and Citroén,* Veloce

Publishing Ltd 2009.

BERNABO, F., *History of Lancia* From 1906, Drawn from Lancia Revue, Stampa Lancia, August 1969.

BERTONI, Leonardo., *Flaminio Bertoni – la vitta il genio e le opere,* Macchioni. Milan, 2002.

BOSCHEN, L., & Barth. J., *The Porsche Book,* Patrick Stephens Ltd, 1977.

BRIOULT, Roger., *l'Histoire et les Secrets de son Bureau d'Etudes 5/6,* EDI, 1987.

BUCKLEY, M. & Rees, C., *The World Encyclopedia of Cars*, Aness Publ, London 1998.

BUCKLEY, M., Separated at Birth, *Classic & Sports Car,* March 2016.

BUSH, D. J., *The Streamlined Decade*, New York: Braziller, 1975.

Car Styling San'ei Publ, Tokyo 1980-1986.213

CONWAY, H.G., *Bugatti,* Octopus Books Ltd, London 1989.

CULPEPPER, L., *Collectors Cars*, Octopus Books Ltd, 1970.

DANIELS, J., *British Leyland The Truth About the Cars,* Osprey, London 1980.

DE DUBE, B.P.B., Tatra: Constant Czech, *Automobile Quarterly,* Vol 7, No.3.

EDWARDS, R. *Stirling Moss The Authorised Biography*, Cassel & Co, London .

FRERE, P., *Porsche 911 Story* Patrick Stephens Ltd, Cambridge, 1976.

FROEDE. Dr. Ing. W. & **JUNGBLUTH**, Dipl. Ing G., Der Kreiskolbnemotor des NSU Spider. *Automobiltechnische Zeitiung*. May-August 1968.

GEROGANO, N., *Art of the American Automobile – the greatest stylists and their work,* New York, 1995.

GEROGANO, N. *The Beaulieu Encyclopedia of the Automobile*, Stationary Office, London 2000.

GOLDBERG, G., *Lancia and De Virgilio,* David Bull Publ, 2014.

KNIGHT, P., **COLTMAN**, D., **LEVIEUX**, E., *Le Corbusier, The Radiant City,* Trans. Dover Publ, New York 1967

LONG, B. and **CLAVEROL**, P., *SM Citroën's Maserati-engined supercar,* Veloce Publishing, 2006.

LUDVIGSEN, K.: NSU Ro80, *Car Life*, December 1967.

MARGOLIS, I., *Automobiles by Architects,* 2000

MARGOLIS, I., & Henry, J,G., *Tatra: The Legacy of Hans Ledwinka ,*SAFPubl Harrow, 1990.

MEIKLE, J., *Twentieth Century Design Limited: Industrial Design in America 1925-1939.* Penn, USA, 1979.

NOBLET, J de., Dir Centre de Recherche sur le Culture Technnique. Editor *Industrial Design Reflections of a Century,* Flammarion APIE, Paris. 1993.

NORBYE. J.P., *The Wankel Engine*, Chilton Books, Radnor, Penn, USA, 1975.

PININFARINA S.p.A. *Pininfarina Cinquantanni*, Automobilia / Industrie Pininfarina S.p.A. Torino. 1980.

SCIBOR-RYLSKI, A.J., *Road Vehicle Aerodynamics,* Pentech Press, London, 1975.

SPARKE, P., *A Century of Car Design*, Mitchell Beazley, London, 2002.

SHELTON, T., *Automobile Utopias as Traditional Urban Infrastructure Visions of the Coming Conflict* 1925- 1940, TDSR Vol xx 11:No11: 2011.

Texas University, Austin. Exhibition: Norman Bel Geddes Designs America, September 2012 – 2013.

WHYTE, A., *Jaguar: History of a great British car,* Patrick Stephens Ltd, Cambridge, 1980.

WINSTONE, D.R.A., *My 1000 Cars* Gabriel Voisin, English Reference Edition, Faustroll Publishing 2013.

WINSTONE, D.R.A., *Gerin,* Faustroll Publishing.

Journals/Peridocals

Autocar

Bugantics

Car

Car and Driver

Car Styling

Car Design News

Classic Cars

Classic and Sports Car

Jaguar Enthusiast

Motor Sport

Old Motor

Practical Classics

Road and Track

Octane

The Automobile

The Citroënian

The Tailwagger

Photographs and Illustrations

All are by the author unless otherwise stated

Index

A

Adler 45–46, 119
ADO 89–91, 137
    16 137
    17 89–91, 137
    77 137
Alfa Romeo 37, 61, 109, 159,
    195–196
    75 195
    90 195
    164 195
    Alfasud 20
    GTV 195
    Guiletta 185
    Montreal 20
Allard 7, 15, 48, 72–80, 127, 168,
    186, 193, 197
    J2 76–77
    J2X 76–77
    JR 76–77
    K2 76
    K3 76
    Le Mans 72–74, 76
    M 78
Allard, Alan 80
Allard, Sydney 72–73, 75–77, 80
Alpina 183
Alpine 23–30, 123–124
    A110 23–24, 26–29, 124
    A310 25, 28–29
    A610 23, 25, 28–29
Alpine-Renault 23, 25, 27–28
Alvis 197
Amann, Dr 59
Ambramson, Dan 159
Amelia Island Concours 188
Amilcar 17, 20, 186
Anderson, Gillian 15
Andersson, Ove 27
Armstrong Siddeley
    Sapphire 81
Ashton Keynes Vintage Restoration
    187–188
Aston Martin 73–74, 128, 155, 160,
    165, 174–175
    DB4 165, 175

DB6 175
    V8 Vantage 155
Audi 20, 39–40, 94, 116–117, 120,
    131, 146, 157, 160, 200
    Quattro 20, 40, 160
Austin 36, 76, 81, 84–86, 90, 92,
    136, 144, 164, 181–182, 195–196
    18-22 195
    Allegro 16, 87–91, 184
    Ambassador 90, 195
    Landcrab 85, 195
    Maestro 90, 92, 196
    Maxi 115, 136, 195
    Metro 92, 196
    Montego 90, 92, 195
    Princess 90, 195
    Westminster 16
Austin Rover Group 86, 92, 196
Austro-Daimler 46
Autenreith 61
Autocar 7, 18–19, 91, 102, 136, 174,
    176
Autofarm 7, 79, 94, 185
Automotora 100

B

Bache, David 152
Bahnsen, Uwe 91
Bailey, Paul 70
Barker, Ronald 19, 31
Bashford, Gordon 200
Bayley, Stephen 19, 114, 122
Beattie, Kevin 164
Beddoes, Gary 66
Bedelia 17, 186
Bel Geddes, Norman 166–167
Belgrove, Walter 164
Bell, Derek 27
Bell, Phil 19
Bell, Roger 19
Bentley 21, 34, 52, 164, 172, 199
    Bentaga 184
    Continental 195
    Turbo R 160
Bertone 18, 36, 39, 123–124,
    128–130, 158–159, 175

Nuccio 158
Bettega, Attilio 40
Biason, Massimo 40
Bicester Heritage Centre 52
Binder, Robert 97
Bishop, George 19
Bitter 165
Blain, Douglas 19, 79
Blake, Bob 68
Blake, Phil 143
Blakeslee, Art 159
Blatchley, John 164
Blomqvist, Stig 40, 99
BMW 12, 47, 59, 61, 81, 84, 90, 92,
    111, 117–120, 123–125, 132, 142,
    152–153, 157, 161–163, 165, 179,
    183–184, 195–196
    850 183
    Cheetah 165
    Neu Klasse 118
    Touring 39
Bohemia 17, 42, 44–45, 47–49, 106,
    161
Bohlin, Nils 150
Borgward 197
Bott, Helmuth 97
Bracq, Paul 161
Breer, Carl 43, 166
Briggs, Walter 43
Bristol 7, 16, 55, 57–62, 68, 77, 102,
    124, 186–187
    406 60–61, 124, 186–187
Bristow, Chris 169
British Leyland 66, 86–87, 124, 137,
    144, 146, 152, 184, 194
    BL 66, 85–93, 136–137, 144–146,
    152, 155, 160, 164, 181, 184, 196
British Leyland Motor Corporation
    BLMC 86, 144, 164, 184
British Motor Corporation 144
    BMC 81, 84–86, 88–89, 91–92,
    160, 184, 195
Brittany Ferries 20, 190, 192
Bretagne 190, 192
    Pont Aven 190
Brooklands 20, 76, 82, 172–173,
    188–189

Brown, Roy 166
Bugatti 7, 12, 18, 21, 48, 50–54, 62, 75, 119, 182, 193
  Trust, The 189
  Type 57 16, 52–54, 188, 193
Buick 17, 44, 145, 152, 155, 192, 194
Burnett, William 166
Burzi, Riccardo 84, 164

C

California 14, 18, 110, 138, 179, 197
Callum, Ian 69
Callum, Moray 163
Camuffo, Sergio 37
Car 19
Car and Driver 19, 209
Carli, Renzo 158
Carlsson, Erik 18, 23, 27, 99–100, 172, 206
Carlsson, Pat Moss 99
Carmel 187–188
Castagnero, Pierro 37, 161
Castagno., Aldo 37, 161
Chapman, Colin 109, 168, 173
Château de Sanxet 191
Château de Savigny-les-Beaune 190
Chenard et Walcker 21
Chequered Flag 36
Cherry, Wayne 159, 164
Chevrolet Camaro 194
Cholmondley Pageant 20
Chrysler 15, 31, 43, 81, 111, 164, 166, 194, 200
  Airflow 43–44, 166, 194
Circuit des Ramparts 191
Citroën, André 33, 134
  2CV 15, 18, 138, 162
  Ami M35 15, 118
  Birotor 135, 139
  BX 158, 195
  C6 139
  Citroën 7, 31, 33, 43–44, 46–48, 85–91, 116, 118–120, 134–139, 144, 153, 158–159, 162–163, 165, 191–193, 195–196, 200
  CX 138, 153, 195–196
  DS 16, 20, 103, 106–107, 114–116, 134, 139, 185, 192, 209
  GS 16, 101, 134–139, 159, 185–186
  GSA 135–139
  SM 16, 20–21, 31, 185–186, 191–193
  Traction Avant 20, 33, 107, 144

Visa 168
Clark, Jim 169–171, 173
Classic and Sports Car 79, 138, 209
Classic Cars 7, 79, 176, 187, 205–206, 209
Classic Remise 188
Coates, Eric 78
Coker, Gerry 159
Cole, Tom 76
Collins, Peter 79, 173
Cord 136, 194
Corvair 42, 85, 113
Corvette 25, 73, 166, 186, 195–196
Costin, Frank 63
Couch, Cyril 68
Craecker-Valbray, Hedwige de 190
Cresto, Sergio 40
Cropley, Steve 19
Curtiss Wright 140

D

Dacremont, Christine 37
Daniels, Jeff 19
Dargent, Henri 136, 160, 192
Darl' Mat 52
Darrin, Howard 167
Datsun 93, 146, 197
  240Z 197
Delage 21, 43, 52
de Larringa, Rupert 76
Depailler, Patrick 27, 137
De Soto 194
Dewis, Norman 55
Dimbleby, Richard 78
DKW 103–104, 106, 120, 197
Dodge 12, 194
  Charger 12, 194
Donney, Tom 99
Dreyfuss, Henry 166
Dron, Tony 19, 79, 170
Ducassou-Pehau, Rene 160
Duntov, Zora Arkus 73

E

Eagle 64
Earl, Harley 35, 42, 167
Ecurie Ecosse 64, 173
Egan, Sir John 66, 93
Ekkers, Erik 105
Embricos, Andre 52
European Classic Cars 187
Evans, David 138
Exner, Virgil 166

F

Fallot, Edmond 191
Farina, Battista 34, 158, 167
Fedden, Sir Roy 59
Federation of British Historic Vehicle Clubs 10
Ferguson, Andrew 51
Ferrari 18, 27, 32, 34–38, 40–41, 67, 70, 73–74, 79, 124, 128–132, 153–154, 158, 173–175, 178, 182
  275 21, 186
  308 18
  330P 174
  Daytona 153–154
  GTO 27, 174
Ferrari, Enzo 70, 129, 178
Fiat 29, 31–32, 38–39, 41–42, 85–86, 111–112, 128–132, 136, 158, 165, 181–182, 195
  124 129–132, 136
  130 130–132, 182
  132 182
  Dino 16, 36, 128–132
  Samantha 131–132
Figoni et Falaschi 52
Figoni, Joseph 52–53
Fioravanti, Leonardo 158
Fiore, Trevor 88, 162
Fleming, Rex 85, 159
Fogolin, Claudio 32
Ford 11–12, 16, 25, 42–44, 75, 77, 80–81, 86, 88, 90–91, 101, 104, 111–113, 115, 117, 129, 140–141, 160–161, 163–167, 185, 194, 200, 203
  Capri 12, 88, 155, 164, 196
  Cortina 80, 104, 115, 145, 182
  Edsel 42
  Escort 16, 88, 136–137
  Fiesta 11
  Granada 90, 178
  GT70 16, 165
  Major 16
  Model Y 43
  Mustang 163, 166, 185, 194
  Sierra 91, 178
  SVO 11, 164
  Thunderbird 141
Foster, Sir Norman 49
Frankl, Andrew 136
Fraser, Ian 19
Frayling, John 160
Frost, Sam 49
Frua, Pietro 149, 158, 165

G

Gandini, Marcello 158
Gangloff 52–53
Gann, Ernest 19
Ganz, Joseph 45, 119
GAZ 14
General Motors 100–101, 111, 118,
 140, 148, 166
Gerin, Jacques 47, 160
Ghia 161, 165, 167, 191
Giacosa, Dante 158
Giles, Eric 52
Giret, Jean 136, 192
Glancey, Jonathan 61, 71
Gloucestershire Vintage and Country
 Extravaganza 189
Glover, Sam 49
Goddard, Martyn 19
Goodwood 15, 20, 31, 96, 172–174,
 187–188
 Festival of Speed 188
 Members Day 20, 96
 Revival 188
Gordano 60–61
Graham-Paige 166
Greenslade, Rex 19
Gregoire, Eugene 12, 43
Gregory, Ken 173–174
Gresley, Sir Nigel 71
Gromik, Regis 136, 160, 192
Grosvenor, Lady Mary 79
Guild of Motoring Writers 7, 18,
 171, 199
Gunn, Richard 7, 88
Gurney Nutting 52, 164

H

Hailwood, Mike 192
Hallet, Chas 71
Ham, Geo 52
Harmand, Michel 136, 160, 192
Hassan, Walter 55, 66
Hasselblad 107–108
Haynes, Roy 88, 159
Helfet, Keith 66
Heynes, William 55
Hickman, Ron 159–160
Hill, Graham 168, 173–174, 177
Hillman Imp 42, 85, 89, 113
Hispano Suiza 188
Historit 51
Holden 145–147, 196
FX 145–147
Holland, Cyril 55
Holloway, Hilton 19

Holm, Svante 105
Honda 12, 17, 42, 84, 86, 93, 101,
 139–140, 147, 152, 154–155,
 181–184, 200
 NSX 12, 181–182, 197
 S800 21, 197
 Type R 182, 197
Honick, Hans 97
Hooper, David 77
Hopkirk, Paddy 18
Horbury, Peter 151
Horch 197
Hotchkiss 197
Hutton, Ray 18–19

I

I.D.E.A. 165
International Automotive Design 160
Ireland, Innes 19, 84, 168–170, 173,
 179–180, 206
Itier, Anne-Cecile 50–54

J

Jabouille, Jean-Pierre 27
Jackson, Alan 159–160
Jaguar 16, 18, 20, 55–71, 73–74,
 76–77, 93, 132, 136, 141, 160,
 163, 165, 182, 184–186, 190,
 193–194
 D-Type 55, 59, 62–64, 185
 E-Type 55–56, 59, 61–68, 70–71,
  126–129, 141, 174, 193
 XJ6 65–66
 XJ13 16, 55, 62, 66–67, 182, 186
 XJ-S 18, 55, 60, 65, 67–70, 196
 XKSS 62, 64, 193
Jano, Vittorio 34, 129
Jaray, Paul 45–46
Jensen 12, 14, 67, 77, 109, 164–165
Interceptor 12, 67, 164–165
Jonckheere 52
Jones, Mike 164
Jowett 84, 183, 185, 191
 Javelin 84, 183, 185
 Jupiter 183
Joyce, Jeff 68

K

Kaiser Frazer 194
Kamm, Wunibald 46, 120
Karen, Tom 39, 159–160
Katayama,Yutaka 197
King, C. Spencer 200
Kippax, David 160

Knight, Bob 56, 65–66
Kadoorie, Hon. Sir Michael 20, 188
Koot, Paul 40
Korner, Reg 183
Kremer, Simon 121
KWE 70

L

Lada 17
Lai, Pinky 95
Lamborghini 66–67, 128, 132,
 158–159, 165, 188, 195
 Espada 158, 195
 Muira 67, 128, 132, 158, 188
Lancia 17, 21, 24, 29–41, 46, 73, 84,
 99–101, 116, 123–124, 128–129,
 142, 153, 159, 164–165, 167, 174,
 182, 186–187, 195–197, 203,
 207–208
 Appia 34, 36
 Aprilia 33
 Ardea 34
 Astura 31, 33
 Augusta 33, 203, 207
 Aurelia GT 31, 34, 36
 Beta 32, 37, 40, 116, 182, 196
 Dedra 32
 Delta 31–32, 37, 39–40
 Eta 32
 Flaminia 31, 36
 Florida III 36, 167
 Fulvia 32, 37–38, 195–196
 Gamma 32, 37, 39, 153, 182, 186
 HPE 37
 Kappa 32
 Lambda 31–32
 Montecarlo 37, 196
 Sibilo 39
 Stratos 36, 39, 129
 Thema 32, 40
 Theta 32
 Trevi 39
 Zagato 31, 36, 38, 187, 195
Lancia, Vincenzo 32–33, 41
Land Rover 16
Lane, James 61, 187
Laugier, Pierre-Yves 50–51
Lawson, Geoff 69
Le Courbusier 103
Ledwinka, Hans 43–46
Lexus 142, 157
Leyat 14
 Helica 14
Lillywhite, David 7, 192
Lincoln-Ford Zephyr 42
Lindgren, Olle 105

Lister Knobbly 193
Ljungström, Gunnar 103
Lotus 23, 25, 29, 66, 159–160,
  168–174, 177–178
  11 172–174
  21 177
  Cortina 25, 185, 195
  Elite 25, 109, 160, 164, 169
  Excel 195
Lovett, Dick 7, 186, 195
Lovett, Edward 187
Lovett, Peter 154
Lush, Tom 73
Luthe, Claus 116, 119
Lutz, Bob 84, 91, 111
Lutz, Rony 199
Lynx 64, 82, 92
Lyons, Sir William 7, 18, 55, 69,
  171, 176, 182

M

Mackerel, Julius 47
Mallet, Delwyn 49
Mann, Harris 86–89, 91–92,
  159–160
Marriott, Bill 79
Martin, Paulo 158
Maserati 17, 21, 31, 35–36, 123–124,
  165, 175, 185, 188, 192–193, 208
  Ghibli 21, 188
  Mistral 165
Matra 21, 161, 190, 195
  Bagheera 21, 195
  Murena 21, 195
  Rancho 195
Matra-BRM 190
Matsuda, Jujiro 140
Matthews, Geoff 159
Mazda 17, 117–118, 121, 140–143,
  195–196
  Cosmo 17, 121, 140–142
  MX-5 31
  RX3 14
  RX7 142–143, 195
  RX8 121, 140, 143
McCarthy, Mike 19
McCourt, Mark 7, 19
McLaren, Bruce 170, 173
McLaren F1 200
Mellde, Rolf 103, 108–109
Mercedes Benz 161
Mezger, Hans 45, 94, 97
MG
  1300 182
  Metro 18, 92
  MGB 93, 160, 195

Mille Miglia 26, 35
Molander, Greta 99
Monte Carlo Rally 27, 72, 82
Monteverdi 21, 165
  375L 21
Morgan 75, 124, 190, 195
Morris 15–16, 81
  Marina 16, 91, 144, 182, 195
  Mini 15, 83, 91, 101, 195
  Minor 15, 91, 101, 185, 188, 195
Morris, William 83
Moskvitch 14
Motor 19
Motor Sport 19, 72, 209
Mullin, Peter 18
Musée de Sanxet 191

N

Najjar, John 166
Nesselsdorfer Wagenbau-
  Fabriksgesellschaft 45
Nichols, Mel 19
Nissan GTR 197
Noble, Dudley 197
Noble M15 98
NSU 15–16, 85, 112–113, 115–122,
  135, 138, 140–141, 143, 208
  KKM 113, 141
  Prinz 113, 119
  Ro80 15, 115–121, 138, 143, 186,
    196
  Rotary 112
NSU-Fiat Automobili AG 112
Nystrom, Elizabeth 99

O

Octane 49, 79, 100, 170, 192
Opel 196
  GT 196
  Monza 196
Opron, Robert 134, 136, 160, 192

P

Palmer, Gerald 84, 159, 183
Palm, Gunnar 18, 99
Panhard 21, 64, 73, 141, 159, 192,
  197
Partington, Chris 105
Paulin, Georges 52, 54
Pebble Beach 187
Petersen Museum 18
Peugeot 15, 23, 28, 36, 40, 52, 87,
  92, 161, 186, 192, 195
  304 28, 186, 195

Pfaender 112
Philpott, Frank 66
Piech, Ferdinand 97, 160
Pierce Arrow 20
Pininfarina, Sergio 36, 158
Pironi, Didier 27
Pontiac 15, 17, 166, 194
  GTO 15, 194
Pont, Michel 190–191
Porsche 15–16, 18, 20, 23, 34, 42,
  44–46, 48, 73–74, 79, 94–99, 103,
  113, 115, 119, 132, 137, 141, 143,
  161–163, 173, 179, 184–187, 197
  356 26, 48, 115, 161, 185, 195
  550 45, 185
  911 15, 26–29, 94–95, 97–98,
    132, 141, 161, 185–186, 195
  914 94–95
  928 18
  944 94, 143, 195
  959 18
  964 94, 113, 186
  993 95
  997 186
  Cayman 95–96
  GT4 95–96
  Macan 184
  Panamera 20, 45
Porsche, Butzi 161–191
Porsche, Ferdinand 44–46, 119
Port, Martin 189
Pourtout, Marcel 52
Practical Classics 49, 89, 100
Praxl, Ewald 116
Prescott 17, 20, 188–189
Prince Skyline 123–124, 197
Prunneau, Leo 164

R

RAC Club 171
Randle, Jim 66
Range Rover 16, 200
  Evoque 200
Rankin, William 55
Rédelé 26, 29
  Emile 26
Renault
  4 21, 23, 25–30, 42, 73, 85–87,
    89–90, 93, 115, 123–124, 134,
    146, 159, 165, 182, 189, 195,
    198, 200, 203
  5 29
  14 21, 23, 25–29, 42, 73, 85, 87,
    89, 115, 123–124, 134, 146,
    159, 165, 182, 189, 195, 203
  16 27, 115, 134

Alpine 23, 25–30, 123–124
  GTA 25, 27–29, 189, 195
  Megane 275 RS 29
  Twingo 42
Riley 81–85, 87, 144, 146, 172, 197
Riley, Percy 82
Riley, Stanley 82
  Kestrel 82–83, 146
  Lynx 82
    Nine 82, 84, 172
    Pathfinder 81, 84–85
    RM 5, 81–85, 87, 172
    Transformable 84
Rindt, Jochen 170
Road and Track 19, 79, 171, 176, 179, 209
Röhrl, Walter 40
Rolls-Royce 12, 52, 65, 68, 97, 136, 164–165, 172, 182, 188
Rootes 5, 26, 42, 81, 85, 164, 204
  Swallow 42, 85
Rover 41, 81, 84, 86–87, 90, 92–93, 113, 115, 145, 147, 152–156, 184, 186, 195–197
  100 92
  800 154
  P5 152, 184, 186, 195–197
  P6 113, 115, 145, 147, 152, 154–156, 184, 186, 195–197
  SD1 90, 93, 152–156, 186
  Sterling 155
Rozenblat Foundation 100
Rozenblat, Krystof 100
Rumpler, Edmund 45
Rybick, Irv 159
Rydberg, Erik 106

S

Schou-Neilsen, Henrick 50–54
Saab 11–12, 18, 20, 23, 31, 41, 43–45, 63, 88, 91, 99–111, 115, 137, 184, 187, 195, 197, 199
  92 99, 102–110
  96 16, 195
  99 99–111
  900 99–102, 111, 148–149, 179, 195
Sonett 99, 104–105, 109–110
Sadler, Josh 79
Saoutchik, Iakov 52
Sason, Sixten 43, 103, 107–108, 162
Sayer, Ceol 66
Sayer, Malcolm 57–60, 67, 69–71, 160, 173, 182
Sayer, Sam 66
Scaglione, Franco 158, 161

Scarlett, Michael 18–19
Schloss Dyck 188
Seaholm, Ernest 194
Setright, Leonard 19, 31, 172
Shelby, Carol 72, 76
Shenstone, Beverley 58–59, 68
Shute, John 160
Silverstone Classic 189
Simanaitis, Dennis 19, 179
Singer 911/964 94
Sked, Gordon 160
Sloniger, Jerry 19
Smith, Martin 159–160
Sodomka 52
Sopwith, Tommy 79, 173, 175
South China Morning Post, The 7
Spada, Ercole 16, 37, 158, 161
Sparre, Claes 106
Sports and Exotic Car 7, 100, 184
Stablimenti Farina 124, 165
Standard Triumph 25, 123–124, 127
Stephens, Paul 94
Stevens, Brook 167
Stevens, Peter 159, 163, 200
Steyr 44, 46
Stutz Black Hawk Special 194
Suchstala, Ignác 45
Sunbeam 73, 89, 92, 164, 195
  Rapier 164, 195
  Stiletto 89
Suzuki 21, 42, 118
  Whizzkid 21, 42
Swedish Day 100

T

Talbot 23, 52–53, 73, 92, 188, 193, 195
  Sunbeam 92
  Tagora 195
Talbot Lago 52–53
Targa Floria, 35, 186
Tatra 17, 21, 42, 44–49, 85, 97, 103, 119, 186–187
  617 47, 49
  T77 46–48, 186
  T80 47, 49
  T97 47
Thatcham Classic 20, 138
The Automobile 7, 14, 17, 79
Thorpe, Douglas 69
Tjaarda, John 12, 43
Tjaarda, Tom 161
Todt, Jean 40
Toivonen, Henri 40
Toyota 16–17, 88, 93, 124, 141, 147, 182, 195, 197

Celica 195
Trintignant, Maurice 173
Triumph 12, 15, 25, 86–87, 91–93, 123–127, 136–137, 152, 155, 160, 164, 195–197
  1500 86
  2000 123, 125, 152, 195
  2500 125
  Dolomite 86, 123, 125, 136–137, 155, 195
  Ginevra 125
  GT6 15, 123, 125–127, 195–196
  Herald 25, 123, 125–126, 144
  SD2 86, 91–92, 152, 155
  Spitfire 125–126, 195
  Stag 123–125, 164
  Straight Six 15
  TR7 92, 123, 125, 164, 195
  Vitesse 125–126, 155
Tucker, Preston 194

V

Van den Plas 52
Van Vooren 52
Vauxhall 84, 115, 136, 164, 196
  Equs 164
  Firenza 164, 196
  Magnum 196
  Royale 196
  Viva 136
Villa d'Este 187
Villain, Antony 29
Virgilio, Francesco de 33–34
Voisin 16–18, 20–21, 43–44, 62, 186, 197, 207, 209
  C25 16–17, 186
  C27 16–17, 186
Volkswagen 42, 45, 85, 119, 136
  Beetle 136
  Corrado 17
  Golf 136
  Sirocco 17
Volvo 5, 28, 89–90, 99, 114, 124, 130, 148–151, 153–154, 160, 165
  120 148–149, 151
  140 148–151
  240 28, 148–151, 182
  850 151
  C70 148, 151
  V70 148, 151
VSCC 52, 188

W

Waldegaard, Bjorn 36
Wallis, Ken 17

Walshe, James 7, 89
Wankel 15, 17, 113, 115, 117–121,
    134–135, 140–143
Warburton, Guy 73
Warner, Bill 188
Warner, Graham 36
Warren Classic 189
Weaver, Phil 68
Webster, Harry 86, 126, 145
Wenderoth, Georg 118

Wheels 19, 187
White, Derrick 67
White, Sir George 59
Wilding, Richard 79
Wilkie, Ian 161
Wilson, Peter 66
Wilson, Quentin 19
Winstone, Reg 19
Winterbottom, Oliver 70, 160
Wirth, Ursula 99

Wolseley 84–85, 87, 90, 144
    6/80 84

Z

Zagato 32, 36–38, 40, 165, 187, 195
Zastava 181
Ziebart 182